The Mobility of Memory

Worlds of Memory

Editors:
Jeffrey Olick, University of Virginia
Aline Sierp, Maastricht University
Jenny Wüstenberg, Nottingham Trent University

Published in collaboration with the Memory Studies Association

This book series publishes innovative and rigorous scholarship in the interdisciplinary and global field of memory studies. Memory studies includes all inquiries into the ways we—both individually and collectively—are shaped by the past. How do we represent the past to ourselves and to others? How do those representations shape our actions and understandings, whether explicitly or unconsciously? The "memory" we study encompasses the near-infinitude of practices and processes humans use to engage with the past, the incredible variety of representations they produce, and the range of individuals and institutions involved in doing so.

Guided by the mandate of the Memory Studies Association to provide a forum for conversations among subfields, regions and research traditions, *Worlds of Memory* focuses on cutting-edge research that pushes the boundaries of the field and can provide insights for memory scholars outside of a particular specialization. In the process, it seeks to make memory studies more accessible, diverse, and open to novel approaches.

Volume 5
The Mobility of Memory
Migrations and Diasporas across European Borders
Edited by Luisa Passerini, Milica Trakilović, and Gabriele Proglio

Volume 4
Agency in Transnational Memory Politics
Edited by Jenny Wüstenberg and Aline Sierp

Volume 3
Resettlers and Survivors
Bukovina and the Politics of Belonging in West Germany and Israel, 1945–1989
Gaëlle Fisher

Volume 2
Velvet Retro
Postsocialist Nostalgia and the Politics of Heroism in Czech Popular Culture
Veronika Pehe

Volume 1
When Will We Talk about Hitler?
German Students and the Nazi Past
Alexandra Oeser

THE MOBILITY OF MEMORY

Migrations and Diasporas across European Borders

Edited by Luisa Passerini,
Milica Trakilović, and Gabriele Proglio

berghahn
NEW YORK • OXFORD
www.berghahnbooks.com

First published in 2021 by
Berghahn Books
www.berghahnbooks.com

© 2021, 2024 Luisa Passerini, Milica Trakilović, and Gabriele Proglio
First paperback edition published 2024

All rights reserved. Except for the quotation of short passages
for the purposes of criticism and review, no part of this book
may be reproduced in any form or by any means, electronic or
mechanical, including photocopying, recording, or any information
storage and retrieval system now known or to be invented,
without written permission of the publisher.

Library of Congress Cataloging-in-Publication Data
Names: Passerini, Luisa, editor. | Trakilović, Milica, editor. | Proglio, Gabriele, editor.
Title: The mobility of memory : migrations and diasporas across european borders /
  edited by Luisa Passerini, Milica Trakilović, and Gabriele Proglio.
Description: First Edition. | New York : Berghahn Books, 2020. | Series: Worlds of
  memory; vol 5 | Includes bibliographical references and index.
Identifiers: LCCN 2020018349 (print) | LCCN 2020018350 (ebook) |
  ISBN 9781789202335 (hardback) | ISBN 9781789202342 (ebook)
Subjects: LCSH: Collective memory—Social aspects—Europe. | Human geography—
  Europe. | Europe—Emigration and immigration.
Classification: LCC HM1027.E85 M64 2020 (print) | LCC HM1027.E85 (ebook) |
  DDC 909/.094—dc23
LC record available at https://lccn.loc.gov/2020018349
LC ebook record available at https://lccn.loc.gov/2020018350

British Library Cataloguing in Publication Data
A catalogue record for this book is available from the British Library

ISBN 978-1-78920-233-5 hardback
ISBN 978-1-80539-323-8 paperback
ISBN 978-1-80539-437-2 epub
ISBN 978-1-78920-234-2 web pdf

https://doi.org/10.3167/9781789202335

Contents

List of Illustrations   vii

Acknowledgments   ix

Preamble. The Mobility of Memory in the Context of Intersubjectivity   1
Luisa Passerini

Introduction. Europe and Beyond   9
Milica Trakilović and Gabriele Proglio

Part I. Mobility Framed by Language: Constraints and Possibilities

Chapter 1. Between "Fleeing" and "Taking Flight":
Negotiating the Refugee Label   29
Milica Trakilović

Chapter 2. "Languages of Mobility/Mobility of Languages":
Between Words and Imagery   49
Giada Giustetto

Part II. Subjectivities in Educational Settings

Chapter 3. Represented Bodies, Broken Bodies: Visions of
Transnational Subjectivities and Memories among Italian Students   79
Graziella Bonansea

Chapter 4. Transcultural Itineraries and New Literacies:
How Memories Could Reshape School Systems   104
Emmanuelle Le Pichon-Vorstman, Sergio Baauw, Debbie Cole, Suzanne Dekker, and Marie Steffens

Part III. Diasporic Memories and Archival Trajectories

Chapter 5. Conceptualizing Diasporic Memory: Temporalities and the Geography of Emotions in Eritreans' Oral Tales   131
Gabriele Proglio

Chapter 6. *Eva Nera* Reloaded: An Archive in the Making   152
Liliana Ellena

Part IV. Visualizing Memory and Resistance

Chapter 7. Counter-Images of Migration: (Visual) Memories of Refugee Migration That Resist an Anti-Immigrant Discourse   183
Iris van Huis

Chapter 8. Visualizing Violence: Political Imaginations from the Syrian Diaspora in the Netherlands   207
Sara Verderi

Epilogue. Bodies Crossing Borders   229
Rosemarie Buikema

Index   233

Illustrations

Figure 1.1. The respondent's drawing of his migration trajectory. Photograph by the author. Published with permission.   37

Figure 1.2. Olga Grigorjeva's painting *Niemandsland* (No Man's Land) featuring refugees' multiple mobilities. Published with permission.   43

Figure 2.1. Ana Rosa's Map: *The Situatedness of Memory between the Spoken and the Written, Emotion and Reason, and the Body and Identity*. Published with permission.   54

Figure 2.2. Hakima's Map: *Visual Memory, the Geography of Emotions, and the Mother Tongue*. Published with permission.   61

Figure 2.3. Moulay's Map: *Universal and Biographic Language; Words Said and Denied*. Published with Permission.   67

Figure 3.1. "*Ragazzo ombra*" – "Shadow Boy." By Giovanni P., Ginevra C., Gaia D. F., Leonardo B., Maria Laura T., and Rebecca A. Palermo, 2016.   87

Figure 3.2. The imprisoned body and exit strategies: photograph (Figure 3.2a, by Selene M., Pinerolo, 2014) and drawing (Figure 3.2b, Chaima C., Pinerolo, 2014).   89

Figure 3.3. A series of pictures depicting hands and feet. Creators from left to right: Rebecca A. (Palermo 2016), Alessandra M. (Pinerolo 2014), Maria A., Rebecca A., Ginevra C., Isabella L., Katia M., Federica Z. (Palermo 2016); Asia H. I, Veronica R., Massimo M., Denisa B. (Pinerolo 2014).   96

Figure 3.4. From the body perimeter to the shadow body. Creators from top to bottom, then left to right: Massimo M., Pinerolo, 2014; Madalina M., Pinerolo, 2014; Marco G., Pinerolo, 2014; Photo y Chaima C., Pinerolo, 2014.   98

Figure 4.1. Two representations of the same activity conducted with students in the Dutch project component. Photograph by the authors. Published with permission. 120

Figure 6.1. Pia Cemulini with her father, Asmara 1954. Courtesy of Pia Cemulini Sieber. 156

Figure 6.2. *Eva Nera*'s advertising published on the weekly magazine *Epoca* 1954. 162

Figure 6.3. First Festival Internazionale della Cinematografia Africana, Mogadishu, 1955. Advertising poster signed by Furlani. Museo Nazionale Collezione Salce, Treviso. Courtesy of MiBACT—Direzione Regionale Musei Veneto. 167

Figure 7.1. A painting by Yara Said (untitled). Published with permission. 191

Figure 7.2. Marahi's drawing produced during his interview. Photograph by the author. Published with permission. 193

Figure 7.3. Photographs by Marahi, taken during the journey. Published with permission. 194

Figure 7.4. Images of refugee centers in the Netherlands. Published with permission. 198

Figure 7.5. Resistance in art. Top-left: a collage by Hala Namer; top-right: *Refugee Nation Flag* by Yara Said; bottom-left: the Refugee Company logo with "Refugee" crossed out; bottom right: paintings by Yara Said (untitled). All published with permission. 199

Figure 8.1. *Human Rights*. Photograph taken by the author on 9 August 2016. Published with permission. 216

Figure 8.2. *Je Mag Je Gelukkig Prijzen Aylan!!* Photograph taken by the author on 9 August 2016. Published with permission. 217

Figure 8.3. *Zo Is het Begonnen*. Photograph taken by the author on 9 August 2016. Published with permission. 219

Figure 8.4. Amer Al-Wahibi, acrylic and gold leaf painting on canvas, courtesy of the author. 222

Figure 8.5. Amer Al-Wahibi, direct etching on metal, courtesy of the author. 223

Acknowledgments

The process of coediting this book has been an adventurous experience—at times challenging, but always interesting. It entailed some difficult moments, but there was also the satisfaction of seeing the volume coming together and observing the appearance of unexpected links between the various chapters, including those by contributors other than BABE (Bodies Across Borders: Oral and Visual Memory in Europe and Beyond) members. It is our common regret that not all of the research trends that emerged within our project could be represented in this book. However, *The Mobility of Memory* is just one of the many BABE products, which include several other books,[1] three exhibitions, two documentaries,[2] and the entire body of audiovisual and written material deposited in the Historical Archives of the European Union at the European University Institute (EUI), Florence.

Our thanks go first of all to the interviewees who shared their manifold stories and trajectories with us during our encounters. This experience was enriching and humbling. In the course of our fieldwork, individuals who played a critical role in the conceptualization, planning, and conduct of our research shared many life stories with us. These individuals include cultural mediators and teachers at participating high schools, universities, Centri Territoriali Permanenti (CTP)—now termed Centri per l'Istruzione degli Adulti (CPIA, or Centers for Adult Education in Italy)—and in migrant language centers in the Netherlands. We are deeply grateful to all of these individuals who were involved in the preparatory process and in the collection of our sources for their help, kindness, and cooperation. We appreciate very much the exchanges that we had with Rosemarie Buikema in the course of our research and the Epilogue she wrote for this book. We would like to thank the EDINA research team (Emmanuelle Le Pichon-Vorstman, Sergio Baauw, Debbie Cole, Suzanne Dekker, and Marie Steffens) and Sara Verderi for accepting our invitation to contribute to this book; our perspective was enriched through our exchanges with all of these individuals. We would also like to thank our colleagues in the BABE team (Graziella Bonansea, Liliana

Ellena, Giada Giustetto, Leslie Hernández Nova, and Iris van Huis) for their collaboration in this joint effort. In particular, we would like to acknowledge the contribution of Liliana Ellena, who originally suggested the title *The Mobility of Memory*, thus drawing attention to the connection between memory and mobility that anchored this project.

All the material collected for the project has been deposited at the Historical Archives of the European Union, at the EUI, Florence, and will, in compliance with the privacy regulations, be made publicly accessible. We are grateful to Dieter Schlenker, the Director of the Archives, for his acceptance of this fund. All documents are accompanied by authorizations signed by the interviewees, some of which requested the use of a pseudonym. In other cases, either only the first names are used or the documents are completely anonymous.

We would like to acknowledge that the BABE Project received funding from the European Research Council under the European Union's Seventh Framework Programme (FP/2007–2013)/ERC Grant Agreement no. 29585. In the years 2013–2018, the Project was based at the EUI's Department of History and Civilisation. We would like to thank all colleagues at the Department, especially the two directors who headed the Department during the period 2013–2018: Federico Romero and Pieter Judson, for their hospitality. We would also like to extend our thanks to Anna Triandafyllidou of the Schuman Centre for her participation in exchanges and in joint initiatives. We owe much to the departmental assistants, in particular Laura Borgese, whose help was indispensable for carrying out and completing the project. We are grateful to Maddalena Tirabassi of the Centro AltreItalie, Turin, for having hosted the meetings of the BABE Project that took place in Turin between 2013 and 2018.

We are very grateful to Radhika Johari, whose invaluable contribution to this book was not limited to language editing but included extensive exchanges with the authors and editors in a spirit of collaboration.

—The Editors

Notes

1. These publications are as follows: Luisa Passerini, *Conversations on Visual Memory*, http://hdl.handle.net/1814/60164 2018; Graziella Bonansea, ed., *Quaderni della memoria e dell'oblio, Memorie migranti: Visualità, sentimenti e generazioni in una prospettiva transnazionale* (Perugia: Morlacchi, 2018); Gabriele Proglio, *The Horn of Africa Diaspora in Italy: An Oral History* (London: Palgrave, forthcoming 2020); and contributions by Liliana Ellena, Iris van Huis, Luisa Passerini, Gabriele Proglio, and Milica Trakilović in *Dissonant Heritages and Memories in Contemporary Europe*, ed. Tuuli Lähdesmäki, Luisa Passerini, Sigrid Kaasik-Krogerus, and Iris van Huis (London: Palgrave, 2019).
2. The first exhibition, titled "Corpi attraverso i confini: immaginari soggettivi e integrazione europea" [Bodies Across Borders: Subjective Imaginaries and Integration in Europe], was held at the Palazzo delle Aquile in Palermo from 28 May–29 June 2016 and was supported by the Municipality of Palermo and by Leoluca Orlando, the mayor of Palermo. This exhibition, which was conceptualized by Graziella Bonansea of the BABE team, presented the results of research conducted by teachers and students at the Vittorio Emanuele II High School, who worked with the audio-visual materials collected by the BABE researchers. The second exhibition was part of the "Biennale Democrazia 2017" program organized at the Fondazione Merz in Turin (29 March–5 April 2017). A documentary, *In Viaggio per Torino*, on BABE's fieldwork in schools was produced for this exhibition by Giulia Ciniselli. The third exhibition, held at the State Archive in Florence, was the outcome of a collaborative initiative between BABE, the Historical Archives of the European Union, and the European University Institute, Florence. BABE commissioned Valerio Finessi to produce a documentary, *MemoriaImmagine* (https://youtu.be/98Rnim9gjCw), placing the exhibition in the context of the BABE research.

Preamble

THE MOBILITY OF MEMORY IN THE CONTEXT OF INTERSUBJECTIVITY

Luisa Passerini

"Mobility of memory" is a general term that can take on multiple meanings in specific contexts. The specific terms used in our subtitle, "Migrations and Diasporas across European Borders," elucidate the origin of our usage of the term within research conducted on mobility toward and across Europe. In fact, the title of this book emerged as a central keyword in the research implemented for the "Bodies Across Borders: Oral and Visual Memory in Europe and Beyond" (BABE) Project funded by the European Research Council, of which this book is one outcome. The expression "mobility of memory" punctuated our exploration of a cluster of processes centering on visuality, mobility, and corporeality while conducting this research. In the course of our work, it became clear to us that memory was inseparable from such processes; it not only accompanied them but also made their continuity possible through subjective and intersubjective exchanges. While visuality, mobility, and memory constitute a cluster of notions and practices that assumes its full import when considered as an intrinsic and indivisible whole, the central role of visuality cannot be underestimated. It is visuality that embodies the corporeal dimension within oral forms of intersubjective memory, serving as a foundation for the development of audiovisual archiving methods. In doing so, it connects the acts of researching and producing memories, anchoring them within mobile bodies.

Our intention in situating the mobility of memory in the context of intersubjectivity was, first of all, to draw out the implications of the movements of memory between subjects engaged in the process of remembering—memory is mobile in the sense that it is created through exchanges between different subjectivities. This realization is indicative of how far we have come from oral historians' original claim of discovering and documenting reminiscences of the past. When historians first conceived of memory as a form of subjectivity in the late 1970s, their initial concern remained with the introduction of the subjects, that is, the historian as well as the individual and collective subjects of history. Given social historians' application of concepts such as working class or gendered subjectivities in relation to collective subjects at the time, special attention was accorded to individuals. A plurality of subjectivities—those of interviewers and interviewees as well as transcribers and translators—is at play within the practice of oral history. Attempts to situate oral and other sources within a temporal context illuminate a multitude of other subjects who actively participated in the construction of the sources and in their propagation throughout the ages. The application of a lens of subjectivity, understood as historical agency, renders visible a myriad of subjects who have played formative but behind-the-scenes roles in the production of historiography.

During the late 1970s and early 1980s, I used the term "accumulated subjectivity" in my own research practice to convey the transactions between individuals and social and age groups presiding over the construction of memory. This usage of the term entailed connecting it with narrativity and especially with *shareable narratives* (Passerini 2002) that have been constructed and reconstructed by successive generations in the process of building traditions. The term was intended to convey the temporal depth of subjectivity, but the emphasis was still on the mentalistic and linguistic aspects of subjectivity. With the expansion of oral history, encompassing visuality and therefore multiple media, "accumulated subjectivity" began to appear as a rather static concept. Concomitantly, a wider conceptual shift based on the recognition of the "primacy of intersubjectivity" (Passerini 2007) evolved in the late 1990s and early 2000s. While the notion of shareable narratives remained the *topos* of this type of intersubjectivity, the BABE research, which took cognizance of these developments, later introduced the more complex notion of an "active repository of intersubjective practices."

This conceptual shift took place within a context in which "intersubjectivity" was assigned increasing importance as a research tool in fields related to social and cultural research. In recent decades, intersubjectivity has emerged as a notion with considerable potential for forging connections among people as well as among different methodological approaches and fields of knowledge. As a powerful promoter of multidisciplinary connections, the concept has proved seminal within the disciplines of philosophy, sociology, psychology, psychiatry, neuroscience, the philosophy of language, and political thought as well as, critically, in the relationships forged between these and other disciplines (Crossley 1996; Davidson 2001; Zahavi 2012). Consequently, the meaning of intersubjectivity has broadened from an initial focus on mentalistic and linguistic dimensions of subjectivity to semantic and affective ones (Kirshner 2017; Passerini 2018; Silva Filho 2015).

The main novelty introduced by the BABE Project has entailed applying the lens of visual intersubjectivity to the collection of testimonies by recording visual memories of subjects moving toward and across Europe. In turn, this meant prioritizing moving bodies conceived as embodied subjects (Passerini, Gabaccia, and Iacovetta 2018). The BABE research attempted to combine two lines of inquiry on memory: an exploration of the construction of visual memory through art, notably video art, photography, and cinema, focusing on migration to and across Europe, and the collection of visual memories through interviews.

Our research endeavors confirmed that intersubjectivity can be effectively employed as an observatory for identifying and elucidating the intellectual and practical bridges connecting different fields of knowledge, including art and the humanities, which were of focal interest to us, being the original source of inspiration for the BABE Project (Passerini 2018). In our fieldwork, we applied an approach of "induced reception" that began with the display of artworks to mobile interviewees or "migrants" in Italy and the Netherlands. This approach generated a practice of indirect or mediated intersubjectivity, entailing an exchange between the subjectivity expressed in a work of art on the one hand and its reception during our fieldwork by interviewees on the other hand. Only after completing this first phase of our research did we ask our subjects to share their stories of mobility. Various subjectivities were evidently at play: those of the artists, the interviewees, and our own, beginning with our choices of certain art works as forms of visual memory capable of stimulating new intersubjective reactions.

Posing the question of the mobility of memory in the context of intersubjectivity within the BABE Project led to this conceptual tool's transformation into a methodological tool that could be applied within research practice. The researchers were prompted by their interactions with the interviewees to reflect on experiences of mobility that had affected them and their families, thus disrupting the assumed division between sedentary interviewers and mobile interviewees. Our historical awareness of the circulation of peoples across the world (Bhambra and Narayan 2016) became experiential as a result of our interviewing strategy, considered both as a place of conversation (Grele 2019) and as an encounter. This interaction entailed a perception of intercorporeality in face-to-face relationships, mediated by a focus on visuality.

The movement of memory in the process of its construction within a visual and corporeal environment is not considered novel within the disciplines of psychology and neurology. Over a period of decades, these disciplines have demonstrated how, in early infancy, an interaction or "solidarity" is forged between a child, another person, and an object, whereby the child easily and naturally creates intersubjective references that constitute the basis of the dialogical experience of knowing (Trevarthen 1979; Bruner 1986). Specifically, in the 1990s, a broad concept of intersubjectivity was developed by the neuroscientists of the Parma School in Italy, who discovered that "mirror neurons" are activated not only when an animal makes a movement but also when the animal observes the same movement made by another animal. Beginning in 2010, these findings were extended to humans after studies showed that intersubjectivity is not merely grounded in the similarities between individual bodies; rather, human sensory motor systems are wired to achieve similar basic goals and to experience similar emotions and sensations. The neuroscientific perspective has particular relevance for the domain of art: artwork becomes the mediator of motor and emotional resonance arising between the artist and the observer, enabling the beholder to feel art in an embodied manner (Ammaniti and Gallese 2014; Gallese 2007; Gallese and Cuccio 2016; Rizzolatti and Sinigaglia 2008).

Our own research practice resonated with all of these findings, as evidenced in the connections that were established between the BABE research and the arts, both visual and corporeal. Our research strategy in pursuit of our objectives included a conceptual and practical orientation that brought our attention to the links forged between various types of mobility—collective as well as individual. These movements included those executed within contemporary dance forms, which can be considered as bodily forms of communicative action (Franco and Nordera 2005, 2008; Hernández Nova 2017). This methodological approach, and its underlying premises, led to the creation of a series of multimedia products within the BABE Project, comprising two exhibitions, two documentary films, one performance inspired by the material that we collected during our fieldwork, and an e-book largely based on visual images (Passerini 2018). The present volume is situated within this context while simultaneously illuminating those achievements (see https://babe.eu for more details on the project outcomes).

Against a theoretical background entailing cognizance of the symbolic and intellectual implications of the notion of "mobility of memory," the BABE Project assumed a fan-shaped trajectory, spreading out in different directions, some of which are reflected in the various sections of this book. At the same time, the organization of these sections illustrates different ways of relating the two countries—Italy and the Netherlands—that were the study locations. For instance (and in brief, because the introductory chapter covers the content of the sections), our aim in the first section was to delineate some of our concerns relating to language. This focus on language stems from our awareness—emerging from the practice of interviewing—of the restrictions imposed on oral expression by the predominant colonial languages in the countries of origin and by the new languages in the countries of arrival, specifically Italian and Dutch. It also stems from our grasp of the problematic relationships existing between the oral, the written, and the graphic. Part I simultaneously illustrates two different approaches pursued by BABE researchers in the two countries where we worked. Thus, researchers in the Netherlands engaged in cultural-historical reflections centering on the public terminology applied to "migrants" and "refugees." By contrast, researchers in Italy analyzed classroom experiences wherein the subjects engaged in oral and visual experimentation to convey the stories of their mobility.

Part II offers a similar methodological contrast, revisiting the duality of an autobiographical approach and a social-historical approach, including a quantitative perspective. While the Dutch essay in this section provides a context for the Italian essay, both insist on didactic research that responds to a primary concern with communication and the transfer of knowledge relating to mobility across Europe (Bonansea 2018). These two sections are intended to illustrate an area of tension by pointing indirectly to a European dimension, explored in BABE and other intellectually aligned projects. Experimental initiatives aimed at connecting European projects have already been attempted in relation to a specific theme, namely that of European cultural heritage (Lähdesmäki, Passerini, Kaasik-Krogerus, and van Huis 2019). However, the present volume extends the field of inquiry to encompass a wider cluster of notions and practices. Furthermore, while the two first sections of the volume focus alternately on Italy and the Netherlands, the third focuses on research conducted in Italy and the fourth focuses on the Netherlands. The relationship between the two essays in Part III is a dialogical one, entailing confrontations with oral and visual traces of the colonial past and between two approaches respectively referring to art and the collection of oral/visual forms of memory. Lastly, Part IV focuses on forms of visual expression and political imagination that further enlighten the relationship between visual art and collected visual memories.

This organizational structure also has a functional purpose of supporting wider collaboration for this volume, covering a range of contributors and topics that extended beyond the scope of the Project. Grouping themes and approaches into different sections enabled us to present diverse, qualitative ways of lunging and foraying into various fields of study relating to mobility and memory within a European space. This was a collateral choice associated with the decision not to engage in a direct comparative historical approach regarding the coupling of Italy and the Netherlands. There are historical reasons (see the Introduction) for choosing these two countries differentially positioned along a spectrum that allowed us to introduce a European perspective while avoiding the deceptive assumption of a "Europe" considered as the sum of constituent countries. A common aim of the BABE Project and of this volume has been to explore salient questions pertaining to contemporary Europe rather than to enter the debate on comparative history that has been particularly compelling in the fields of modern history and historical sociology. One of our assumptions was that an experimental approach such as ours that seeks to innovate the study of memory and expand it to incorporate the visual would benefit from another methodological approach, namely establishing a field of tension between the two countries rather than following a strictly comparative approach. An example of this approach can be found in the case study of the film *Eva Nera* in Part III, which presents an analysis of convergences between two different colonial histories within an actress's biography. Thus, Italy and the Netherlands are coupled within an exploration of colonial amnesia and aphasia, creating a tension between the two countries rather than attempting to compare them historically.

The lines of inquiry described thus far, while integral to the BABE Project in quantitative terms covering much of our work, only cover some of the several investigative directions that we pursued. Another direction—equally important in qualitative terms—was "archival memory," entailing an understanding of the archive as a set of intersubjective practices aimed at creating and transmitting memory and making it accessible. This definition encompasses both theoretical and practical considerations, such as acquiring an understanding of the complex and far-reaching nature of the repertoire of memory along with recognition of bridges or new links forged between memories. In a wider historical sense, this line of research implies exploring and enriching the theory and practice of the cultural archive—an endeavor that encompassed a perception of bodies as living archives (https://babe.eui.eu/activities/workshops/15-1-2014/programme/). In a practical sense, this approach was implemented through the construction of an audiovisual archive at the Historical Archives of the European Union housed at the European University Institute in Florence. The enterprise of constructing this archive resonates with an observation made by Rosemarie Buikema, one of the BABE Project's scholarly interlocutors, cited in the epilogue of this book: an archive on movement and memory based on a dialogical response to oral histories and artworks can engender new conceptualizations not only of displacement but also of time, space, and citizenship.

Luisa Passerini is professor emerita at the European University Institute, Florence, and was principal investigator of the European Research Council project Bodies Across Borders: Oral and Visual Memory in Europe and Beyond (BABE) from 2013 to 2018. Her work has focused on actors of social and cultural change: from twentieth-century African liberation struggles to worker, student, and women's rights movements to migration in Europe in recent decades. At the core of her research is the theme of memory in its oral, written, and visual forms. Among her books are *Conversations on Visual Memory* (2018); *Women and Men in Love: European Identities in the Twentieth Century* (2012); *Memory and Utopia: The Primacy of Intersubjectivity* (2007); *Europe in Love, Love in Europe* (1999); *Autobiography of a Generation: Italy 1968* (1996); and *Fascism in Popular Memory* (1987).

Note

1. Here, I would like to provide a brief explanation of the three frames developed in relation to the main text of this book. This Preamble serves to clarify some preliminary points that have been seminal in relation to both the present volume and the research on which it is largely based, and the connections between the two. Its underlying objectives are to situate our efforts within the history of oral history, to acknowledge some of our intellectual debts to other disciplines, and to elucidate the methodological and conceptual choices that have structurally framed the book. The Introduction presents the volume, focusing on the relationship between mobility and memory in postcolonial Europe. It highlights convergences and divergences between Italy and the Netherlands against the background of changing configurations of the bordering process in Europe. The Epilogue casts a final evaluative glance at the work accomplished, taking the place of a conclusion that would have been inappropriate for a volume covering multiple research directions.

References

Ammaniti, Massimo, and Vittorio Gallese. 2014. *The Birth of Intersubjectivity: Psychodynamics, Neurobiology, and the Self.* New York: W. W. Norton & Company.

Bhambra, Gurminder K., and John Narayan, eds. 2016. *European Cosmopolitanism: Colonial Histories and Postcolonial Societies*. London: Routledge.

Bonansea, Graziella, ed. 2018. *Quaderni della memoria e dell'oblio, Memorie migranti: Visualità, sentimenti e generazioni in una prospettiva transnazionale*. Perugia: Morlacchi Editore.

Bruner, Jerome S. 1986. *Actual Minds, Possible Worlds*. Cambridge, MA: Harvard University Press.

Crossley, Nick. 1996. *Intersubjectivity: The Fabric of Social Becoming*. London: Sage Publications.

Davidson, Donald. 2001. *Subjective, Intersubjective, Objective*. Oxford: Oxford University Press.

Franco, Susanne, and Marina Nordera, eds. 2005. *I discorsi della danza: Parole chiave per una metodologia della ricerca*. Torino: Unione Tipografico-Editrice Torinese.

———. 2008. *Ricordanze: Memoria in movimento e coreografie della storia*. Torino: Unione Tipografico-Editrice Torinese.

Gallese, Vittorio. 2007. "Before and Below 'Theory of Mind': Embodied Simulation and the Neural Correlates of Social Cognition." *Philosophical Transactions of the Royal Society B* 362: 659–69.

Gallese, Vittorio, and Valentina Cuccio. 2016. *The Paradigmatic Body: Embodied Simulation, Intersubjectivity, The Bodily Self and Language*. Mainz: Johannes Gutenberg-Universität.

Grele, Ronald. 2019. "Comment." *The Oral History Review* 46, no. 1 (Winter/Spring): 183–90.

Hernández Nova, Leslie N. 2017. "En face de toi, en face de moi: pour une archive corporelle de la mémoire culturelle péruvienne et mexicaine." ("In front of You, in front of Me: For a Corporeal Archive of Peruvian and Mexican Cultural Memory). Conference-performance presented at the *Ateliers de la Danse*, Cannes, 8–10 December 2017. Cannes: Centre Transdisciplinaire d'Epistémologie de la Littérature et des Arts Vivants (Université Nice Sophia Antipolis) and the Festival de danse de Cannes.

Kirshner, Lewis. 2017. *Intersubjectivity in Psychoanalysis: A Model for Theory and Practice*. London: Routledge.

Lähdesmäki, Tuuli, Luisa Passerini, Sigrid Kaasik-Krogerus, Iris van Huis, eds. 2019. *Dissonant Heritages and Memories in Contemporary Europe*. London: Palgrave Macmillan.

Passerini, Luisa. 2002. *Shareable Narratives? Intersubjectivity, Life Stories and Reinterpreting the Past*. Accessed 16 August 2002. www.bancroft.berkeley.edu/ROHO/education/docs/shareablenarratives.doc.

———. 2007. *Memory and Utopia: The Primacy of Intersubjectivity*. London: Routledge.

———. 2018. *Conversations on Visual Memory*. http://hdl.handle.net/1814/60164_(ISBN 979-12-200-3693).

Passerini, Luisa, Donna R. Gabaccia, and Franca Iacovetta. 2018. "Bodies Across Borders: Oral and Visual Memory in Europe and Beyond (BABE): A Conversation with Luisa Passerini, Donna Gabaccia, and Franca Iacovetta." In *Borders, Conflict Zones, and Memory: Scholarly Engagements with Luisa Passerini*, edited by Donna R. Gabaccia and Franca Iacovetta, 114–25. New York: Routledge.

Rizzolatti, Giacomo, and Corrado Sinigaglia. 2008. *Mirrors in the Brain: How Our Minds Share Actions and Emotions*. Oxford: Oxford University Press.

Silva Filho, Waldomiro J. 2015. "Intersubjectivity: Commentary on Intersubjectivity." In *Jerome S. Bruner beyond 100: Cultivating Possibilities*, edited by Giuseppina Marsico, 65–72. Basel: Springer International Publishing AG Switzerland.

Trevarthen, C. 1979. "Instincts for Human Understanding and for Cultural Cooperation." In *Human Ethology: Claims and Limits of a New Discipline*, edited by M. von Cranach, K. Foppa, W. Lepenies, and D. Ploog, 530–71. Cambridge, UK: Cambridge University Press.

Zahavi, Dan. 2012. "*Intersubjectivity*." In *The Routledge Companion to Phenomenology*, edited by Sebastian Luft and Søren Overgaard, 180–89. London: Routledge.

Introduction

EUROPE AND BEYOND

Milica Trakilović and Gabriele Proglio

This edited volume engages with the "question of Europe," which relates to the discursive meaning and function of the term, using a combined lens of postcoloniality, mobility, and memory that highlights the need to foreground noncanonized cartographies of Europe in the current political context. Cartography, as interpreted by the contributors to this volume, does not merely refer to the practice of mapmaking, although this endeavor has always entailed an ideological function of centralizing, universalizing, and personifying Europe (Dainotto 2007: 38). Rather, we conceive of the project of mapping from a broader and more politically informed perspective as an intervention and active engagement with the symbolic chain of meaning, representation, and narration of Europe. The symbolic conceptualization of Europe—that is, the way Europe is and was imagined—is part of the process of border building that informs the framing of all aspects of Europeanness. As Dainotto observes, this "rhetorical unconscious" of Europe "still determines what we think and do about it; what our dailies report; and what our policy makers decide" (2007: 8). Thus, initiatives that challenge discursive hegemonic and representational politics constitute interventions relating to an ongoing reconfiguration of Europe, looking beyond the centrality of the notion of Europe and opening it up to a consideration of multiple significations and associated assemblages.

The task of "looking beyond" also applies to the organization of this volume and permeates its content. While the chapters constituting this collective volume are the cumulative outcome of the "Bodies Across Borders in Europe: Oral and Visual Memory in Europe and Beyond" (BABE) Project funded by the European Research Council, we also invited external collaborators to contribute to the book to foster a dynamic and ongoing investigation into debates surrounding contemporary Europe. Specifically, this book was thematically and theoretically configured by our investigation of the relationship between mobility and memory, considered as a key discursive and conceptual cluster within postcolonial Europe. In the following sections, we expand on each of these notions by highlighting relevant scholarly debates and theoretical insights that have informed our understanding of postcolonial Europe, mobility, and memory. We subsequently describe the organizational rationale and structure of the book.

Postcolonial Europe

At this critical juncture, life in Europe assumes a particular meaning of an enduring peace that is unmarked by the chronological timeline of wars occurring outside of its borders. The idea of Europe as an island of peace and freedom brings to mind the centrality of the colonial conception of modernity that equated Europe with progress and civilization. There is a clear connection between the mid-eighteenth-century imaginary and the contemporary social perception of Europe as a place devoid of conflict under the white man's law. One of the main reasons for the endurance of this collective memory, which, according to Halbwachs (1950), is associated with being European, is the reproduction of a hegemonic cultural heritage through the device of the European border system. Merely reversing the model by refuting the centrality of Europe is not sufficient. What is required is an inquiry into how colonialities have been problematized and deployed within personal and shared memory that necessitates a reconsideration of the positionalities of non-white and non-hegemonic subjects within Europe. Applying multiple research pathways, we sought to do this within the BABE Project.

Two moments are critical to our exploration of Europe, mobility, and memory: the post-9/11 moment and the European migration "crisis." Both of these moments have reverberated in the West, reflected in the rise of an anxiety-ridden politics that has not only led to the framing of migrants as cultural outsiders but has also entailed their subjection to processes of pathologization and racialization that are intended to legitimize their expulsion from, or differential inclusion within the national-cultural frameworks of each of the countries within Europe. A consideration of these processes solely from a presentist framework obscures the ways in which they have been informed by much longer historical legacies of multiple imperialisms and colonialisms that reverberate with Europe's prevailing understanding of itself. This historical dimension is crucial for apprehending the rise of right-wing politics and the forms that it has assumed in different European contexts to oppose this charged figure of cultural otherness. The ways in which the Other is invoked again and again—within the media, popular discourse, and in politics and policies—is indicative of a "neo" hidden within the postcolonial, which, as Gilroy argues, "will have to be ruthlessly and repeatedly uncovered and interrogated" (2016: xvi). Therefore, an understanding of Europe's postcolonial characteristics enabled the contributors to this volume to reflect on how their sources—ethnographic and archival data and visual and discursive material—relating to colonial and imperial historical processes could be critically assessed and connected to the present moment.

While we do not consider the notion of Europe to be singular, we do acknowledge that an idea of Europe as a clearly delineated and exceptional place is a potent one that has been mobilized within contemporary popular and political discourses. As Derrida (1992: 60) famously argued, the discursive construction of Europe as a "heading" or privileged place has always been predicated on its self-propagation according to an image of Western progress through the production of difference and otherness. Moreover, Stuart Hall pointed out that Europe is perennially caught up in a search for its identity, its place in the chain of possible representations, noting that this quest is predicated on the invocation of that which is outside of it (Hall 2002: 60). The contributors to this volume query how notions of the outside (that which is "beyond" Europe) and the Other are mobilized within anxiety-ridden political responses to migrants and refugees in Europe. At the same time, they critique these exclusionary processes, recognizing their long-enduring historical roots in bodies of otherness within colonial discourses. This critique interrogates the meaning of contemporary Europe, which, as Sandra Ponzanesi argues, exists as "a paradox that undermines the idea of Europe as a historical project based on singularity and exceptionalism while subscribing to the future of Europe as a location for hope and cosmopolitan solidarity" (2016: 160). It is precisely this double gesture of producing a critique on the one hand while introducing alternative registers of meaning on the other hand that characterizes our efforts to go "beyond" and "map" Europe differently.

Even though we acknowledge that Europe has been shaped by ideas of difference wherein that which is outside of Europe is othered, we also want to highlight some of the ways in which the idea of Europe is sustained through internal divisions and hierarchies. For instance, we consider how the idea of Europe has been constructed on the basis of a dichotomy that separates centers and peripheries as well as immediate border zones and more "inward" destinations. Étienne Balibar proposed an imaginary of Europe conceived as a composite of concentric circles comprising one central core and several outer areas, the relevance of which progressively diminishes as their distance from the nucleus increases (Balibar 2004: 169). Prevailing anxieties around migration further complicate and augment this construction. Considered from this perspective, Italy as well as countries like Greece, Turkey, and some of the Balkan countries can be considered as places of immediate arrival, whereas countries such as the Netherlands and other more "inward" destinations like Austria, Germany, and Scandinavia can be considered as places that mark the continuation of those journeys, thus revealing a significant geopolitical tension that requires further investigation. In this volume, we specifically consider what the differential placement of Italy and the Netherlands within the political framework and imaginary of Europe reveals about changing configurations of Europe in light of the phenomena of migration and mobility in the early twenty-first century. Italy and the Netherlands are differentially positioned in terms of their colonial histories and legacies and within discourses on European migration. Whereas Italy is metaphorically viewed as one of the "doors" to Europe, the Netherlands is conceived as part of the centers of Europe. Consequently, the picture that emerges from a joint examination of the statuses of migration, mobility, and memory in contemporary Europe, wherein they are brought into dialogue with each other, while not purporting to be a comprehensive one, is nevertheless timely and urgent.

In recent decades, both countries have witnessed significant cultural shifts in public and critical responses to their respective colonial legacies. The public cultural sphere in Italy has been innovated as a result of what can be termed a postcolonial turn effected by scholars, writers, and artists who have drawn attention to the historical responsibilities of the country—continuing to the present—in terms of its relationships with former colonized countries and populations. Of particular interest to the BABE Project has been the demonstration and denouncement of the involution and rigidification of "Fortress Europe" and the role of Italy in this process that have been clearly evident within the postcolonial literature and the visual arts. The Netherlands is undergoing a related process in which various individuals and groups (including scholars, critical thinkers, writers, activists, and artists) are assuming a more prominent role in addressing the country's colonial legacies that are still largely underaddressed or denied. Projects such as *Zwarte Piet is Racisme* ("Black Pete is Racism"), the Amsterdam Black Heritage Tours, and debates emphasizing the need to decolonize institutions, such as the well-known Tropenmuseum (Tropics Museum), are all examples of initiatives taken in the last decade that have sought to highlight, problematize, and dismantle colonial practices that constitute part of the Netherland's cultural capital.

The contributions in this volume consider how both Italy and the Netherlands have been shaped by historically and regionally specific discourses that nonetheless contribute to the symbolic delineation of Europe and to the actual fortification of European borders. According to David Theo Goldberg, Europe is ultimately a raced phenomenon; but within Europe, different racial histories and narratives can be distinguished. These racial regionalizations should be understood as "regional models or mappings, rather than ideal types, broad generalizations as contours of racist configuration, each one with its own material and intellectual history, its prior conditions and typical modes of articulation" (Goldberg 2006: 333). Moreover, these regional models correspond to various national formations and to the tendency to "erase" race from conscious reflection while retaining it as a central pillar of identity that corresponds to the overarching racialized framework of Europeanization, providing a sense of coherence and contributing to the idea of Europe as an exceptional place.

The production of racisms and cultural Otherness both in Italy and the Netherlands can be examined from the perspectives of their particular regionalisms as well as from a broader European perspective. Convergences can be seen in terms of the mounting fear, xenophobia, various forms of racism, as well the explicit efforts of some political parties to exploit these public feelings. In the Netherlands, much of the public response to the current refugee crisis, but also to other cultural phenomena such as the hotly debated Sinterklaas celebrations, has revolved around anxieties that stem from the desire to safeguard some kind of assumed "authentic" Dutch national identity through a disavowal of how colonialism has shaped and continues to inform the Dutch cultural sphere. Growing skepticism and fear regarding the influx of cultural Others have given rise to ever stricter policies and procedures relating to immigration, integration, and the granting of asylum. Whereas previous policies (notably those implemented in the 1960s and 1970s) emphasized cultivating newcomers' languages and cultural practices, the new laws on integration foreground cultural homogeneity, mandating familiarization with the Dutch language and customs. Since the turn of the twenty-first century, Italy, which has long been a country of immigrants, has undergone a process of sensitization—both in a negative and a positive sense—toward the reception and acceptance of new waves of immigration. This shift can be partly attributed to the country's postcolonial geopolitical location extending across the Mediterranean in a way that has been formative of its pivotal role as a "door to Europe." The development of xenophobic and racist attitudes in a country that formerly boasted about "not being racist" is striking when compared with a history of labor emigration from Italy, especially to the Americas but also, to a lesser extent, to Australia and other parts of the world. A postcolonial feature of the Italian situation with negative reverberations is apparent in the enduring perception of past colonial engagements as insignificant and even appeals to this colonizing past as justification for interventions aimed at curbing migration from African countries, as in the cases of Libya or Niger. While memories of Italian colonialism have faded within the public sphere, the language that has evolved within this domain—forged through representations, images, imaginaries, and practices inscribed on black bodies—is being deployed to impose new forms of difference, exploitation, and segregation that are positioned between exclusion and differential inclusion.

Italy and the Netherlands can be understood as sites of potent discursive clusters relating to the configuration of contemporary Europe. In the context of this volume, their positioning is not intended to be comparative; rather, they represent productive analytical starting points because of their convergences and divergences in relation to colonialism and imperialism. It is their contributions to "Europe's undigested colonial history" (Gilroy 2016: xi), viewed through a critical postcolonial lens, that the authors of this volume seek to elucidate.

Mobility

In this volume, we consider the faculty of mobility to be intimately intertwined with literal and symbolic as well as tangible and discursive border-making processes that determine, direct, and are challenged by present-day movements of bodies across European borders. The approach to mobility applied in this volume is theoretically informed by critical border studies, an interdisciplinary field of research on contemporary borders conceived not as fixed phenomena (according to the "line in the sand" metaphor) but rather as a dispersed set of practices. This conceptualization of the border as a set of practices fosters an understanding of the performative dimension of borders that "injects movement, dynamism, and fluidity into the study of what are otherwise often taken to be static entities" (Parker and Vaughan-Williams 2012: 729). These insights are linked to a multiperspectival approach to borders, as proposed by Chris Rumford (2012), which is particularly useful because this kind of study does not focus on a single site or experience of borders. Instead, bordering practices are understood to be dispersed, multiple, and entangled, and the aim is to formulate an account of contemporary bordering practices that acknowledges this complexity while avoiding claims to exclusivity or finality. While the account of Europe that emerges within this volume echoes these principles, the analytical breadth of the contributions is indicative of the need for hybrid conceptualizations of Europe that encompass multiple levels of analysis.

Furthermore, studying mobility through the notion of the border is not a singular enterprise. Given the equivocal quality of borders (Balibar 2002: 78), it is not productive to ask what the border is. A more appropriate inquiry is to examine how it comes into being; how it is constituted and enacted—institutionally and symbolically—in the name of Europe; and how it impacts migrating subjects. Accordingly, Leila Whitley suggests that the border should be conceptualized as a verb, that is, "something that must be done in order to come into being, and that does not exist as a noun without this active, processual, doing of the border" (Whitley 2015: 14). An emphasis on the processual nature of the border within critical border studies also reflects this principle and is indicative of the ways in which borders (and thus mobility) are "intimately bound up with the identity-making activities of the nation-state and other forms of political community" (Parker and Vaughan-Williams 2012: 730). Thus, the studies of the mobility of individual migrants and groups of migrants presented in this volume are always situated within a broader framework of institutionalized border regimes within Europe.

More concretely, and from a geopolitical perspective, Europe has multiplied its boundaries (Mezzadra and Neilson 2013), externalizing its borders to Frontex—the EU agency responsible for border controls—and simultaneously restricting the movements of non-EU subjects toward and within Europe. "Fortress Europe"—a term used during World War II and subsequently reintroduced in recent years by journalists—is riddled with checkpoints, walls, barbed wire, military posts, and border fortifications, such as those constructed in the Spanish North African enclaves of Ceuta and Melilla. The Mediterranean Sea has become an "open-air cemetery," with more than thirty thousand dead since 2000 (Del Grande 2007). The management of the "migration crisis" by Italy, given its location within the central Mediterranean area, has been criticized. Several policies that were planned and implemented by governments of different political orientations in Italy demonstrate continuity in terms of their focus on securing national territories. Moreover, with the shift from Turco-Napolitano Law, enacted in 1998, to the Minniti-Orlando Act of 2017, conditions have worsened for non-EU people attempting to cross borders and apply for national citizenship. The colonial experience and its periodization for each national case can be understood as a common and diversified strategy for controlling mobility within a global and interconnected space. Colonies were practically managed through the creation of a system of routes used to move people and goods that took into account the roles and claims of other nations that were actors performing on the same military and political stage. In this sense, colonialism can be interpreted as a complex system of intertwined and overlapping devices for organizing space and producing, through a process of subjectivation, genealogies and positionalities that continue to endure in contemporary Europe.

During the course of the five-year BABE research project (2013–2018), the researchers who contributed to this volume encountered some of the recent changes in the configuration of Europe's borders. More generally, given the growing dangers entailed in pursuing migration paths or crossing borders for non-European people, it has become progressively more difficult to stay in contact with individuals who have just arrived in Europe. There has been a sudden increase in deportations from the North to the South, both within individual European countries and within a wider geopolitical context. Additionally, as a consequence of the spread of xenophobia across Europe, societies have been resegmented and new liminal positionalities have been defined and assigned to new Europeans. Borders restructure the social hierarchies within each European nation and have been operative in the imposition of a subjectivity of otherness on the bodies of non-Europeans, calling into question the cluster of imaginaries, representations, and practices of domain that have been formative of the colonial archive (Stoler 2008). Consequently, these subjects have been assigned a positionality within Europe that is framed in terms of labor, citizenship, and status.

The arrival in Europe of tens of thousands of people attempting to escape from social, economic, and ecological emergencies has provoked different perceptions of "migrant" mobility. Through the mobilization of the European colonial archive (Said 1978; Stoler 2008; Wekker 2016), images of non-white subjects as enemies preparing to invade and conquer the land, to undermine the health of societies, and to compromise their economic and social equilibria have been evoked within the public imaginary. Populisms promoted by xenophobic parties in Europe have prompted the mobilization of racial hierarchies, some of which originate in the colonial era (Muddle and Rovira Kaltwasser 2017). Within the Dutch public sphere, the onset of the twenty-first century has been marked by debates surrounding the perception of a threatening or unmanageable number of migrants entering the country, resulting in a tightening of the country's immigration and integration policies. Populist sentiments have gained traction through discourses of xenophobia and homonationalism in which the cultural Other, often conflated with the image of the Muslim/refugee, is seen to pose a threat to Dutch traditions and values.

This fear of the Other has generated a genealogy of subjects who are considered "non-something": non-European, non-white, non-French, and so on. At the same time, a vocabulary has been mobilized and deployed for nominating and assigning a positionality to the subject, who is described using a "declaration of negation." Individuals are ranked according to their condition of mobility (migrants), citizen status (refugee, asylum seeker, etc.), place of origin (Morocco, Africa, Maghreb, etc.), and skin color (black or ways of being non-white). Thus, for the most part, descriptions of new Europeans have been and continue to be framed in terms of a "denial of being us" that refers to a national community and as a "denial of self" through a process of subjectivation imposed on their bodies. This process starts with the recognition of bodies in movement at the border, their categorization, and the subsequent attribution of positionalities within or outside of the destination society.

The limited possibility of bestowing a meaning encompassing both "us" and "self" as a metaphor of the physical and social mobility of new Europeans across Europe's borders is being questioned and sometimes subverted. In fact, diasporic networks and black communities within Europe have been introducing other languages along with new meanings, social practices, and cultures. To talk about decolonization from below is not appropriate, as this entails once again assigning positionalities to processes, bodies, and subjectivities. Although diasporic cultural narratives have foregrounded a critique of Fortress Europe, their underlying intent of opposing hegemonic thinking is not always actualized. This does not mean that there is no resistance in place. On the contrary, the daily erosion of the centrality of white privilege within Europe and in its discourse is clearly evident (Mbembe 2013). Diasporic communities have had and continue to have a relevant role in directing individuals during the migratory journey, supporting and helping them to reach Europe. These communities were and are a symbolic refuge from the subjectivation process forged at Europe's internal and external borders through biopolitical practices. They enable new Europeans to stay connected with their loved ones who are thousands of kilometers away and to plan a kind of social redemption in response to their perception of being betrayed upon their arrival in Europe. For all of these reasons, and for many others that cannot be addressed here, diasporic communities are changing the public sphere and face of Europe, which, in the coming decades, will remain white only in the public imaginary.

The above reflections on the notion of mobility reveal the relevance of considering mobility in relation to a multiperspectival understanding of borders. It is important to note that the aim of a multiperspectival-border-studies approach is not to occupy the "standpoint of the subjugated," which is but one perspective. Multiperspectivalism in this case is not synonymous with "bottom up," although it may incorporate this view. Moreover, the borders in question are by no means always at the periphery. A multiperspectival approach to border studies is concerned with borders that are diffused throughout society as well as with those at the edges (Rumford 2012: 899). Adopting this approach allows us to consider how mobility and migration are mobilized and constrained in contemporary Europe by institutions and discourses that produce a "permanent condition of crisis" to legitimize wars, land-grabbing, and xenophobia and racisms in the name of Europe. At the same time, mobility is also a faculty that belongs to migrating subjects, diasporic communities, and "new" Europeans who are constantly crossing borders, challenging and redefining the meaning of Europeanness. It is this multiperspectival approach to mobility and borders that frames the chapters comprising this volume.

Memory

In this volume, we examine the role of memory in fostering as well as contesting wider cultural repertoires and imaginaries of and within Europe, considering its individual and collective dimensions as well as its historical and contemporary ones. Our choice of an elastic conceptualization of memory is a deliberate one, as narrow definitions and "attempts to separate" certain aspects and faculties of memory (whether individual or collective, canonized or unofficial, inside or outside of history, fiction or nonfiction) "prevent us from seeing the threads that connect such phenomena" (Errl 2011: 7). Moreover, "the individual person always remembers within sociocultural contexts," and "cultural formations are based on a 'collective memory'" (Errl 2011: 9). These principles have framed our use of the notion of memory throughout this volume. Along with the notions of postcolonial Europe and borders/mobility, memory served as an analytical tool that enabled us to navigate and study the manner in which Europe has been constructed as a constellation of diverse individual and collective imaginaries. Our inquiry seeks to identify memory discourses that have constituted a dominant conceptualization of Europe and to elucidate how alternative and critical memory practices can open up the question of Europe beyond an insular view.

We also seek to understand how memory politics in Europe have engendered colonial durabilities and forms of aphasia that exist in the present and that inform our understanding of Europe as a postcolonial space. In doing so, we are informed by Ann Stoler's conceptualization of colonial "duress" that demonstrates three key features: namely, "the hardened, tenacious qualities of colonial effects; their extended protracted temporalities; and, not least, their durable, if sometimes intangible constraints and confinements" (Stoler 2016: 7). Such a conceptualization of memory politics extends beyond a simplistic notion of memory as the recalling of events and asks how legacies from the past live on in occluded forms in present-day cultural and institutional practices, recognizing how "[c]olonial entailments endure in more palpably complicated ways" (Stoler 2016: 35). Our inquiry further seeks to elucidate how processes of racial denial and disavowal (Goldberg 2006; Wekker 2016) convey a denial of coloniality, constituting an ideology that severs the link between Europe's colonial history and the management of migration and mobility in contemporary Europe. The fact that migration to Europe in the past decade has been popularly and officially deemed a "crisis" accords with the repression of colonial memory and history, as both migration and colonialism represent forces that are seen as disruptive and alien to the European space and imaginary. Understood as such, their removal and containment is justified. Gurminder Bhambra makes the following observation: "The failure to address their own colonial history is part of the explanation for why

Europe and European politicians and intellectuals are seemingly unable to address their postcolonial present, or even recognize it as something other than an external intrusion disrupting an otherwise ordered European polity" (Bhambra 2016: 188). The denial of coloniality is a selective memory practice that is part of Europe's dominant memory politics and that perpetuates neocolonial practices in the present (Bhambra 2016: 189; Gilroy 2016: xvi). Consequently, the response to the migration "crisis" as well as the management of mobile populations is informed by older discourses of racialization, xenophobia, and European exceptionalism. A further implication of this memory practice is that multiple and oftentimes competing sets of memories exist between "new" Europeans and marginalized and racialized groups of Europeans on the one hand, and those "native" Europeans who experience migration as a crisis on the other. Accordingly, "the victims (and their descendants) of Europe's colonial crimes often know that bloody history [Europe's imperial and colonial past] far more intimately than the Europeans who appear to be doomed to reenact it" (Gilroy 2016: xiv).

This insight has two important implications for how we understand memory practices in relation to Europe in this volume. The first relates to the need to displace the notion of singularity and to think of Europe in pluriform, encompassing many different memory practices that shape it as both a real and imagined space. The question of Europe may thereby be opened up to alternative significations and cartographies, including the memory practices and mobile modalities of "new" Europeans and minorities. Second, dominant memory practices do not cancel out those that are more alternative, marginalized, or even silenced, even when they seem to stand in stark opposition to each other. Following Michael Rothberg's theory of multidirectionality, we consider memory as expansive and expanding, "working productively through negotiation, cross-referencing, and borrowing; the result of memory conflict is not less memory, but more—even of subordinated memory traditions" (Rothberg 2014: 176). Thus, there is a difference between memory as politics (ideological and institutional) and memory as practice (cultural, collective, and individual), although each of these modalities impact each other. Understanding memory as a practice attunes us to the ways in which memory is alive and continually negotiated. We understand memory practices to appear in many forms as plurimedia constellations (Errl 2011: 147) that may be oral, visual, textual, or archival, all of which feature in this volume. Our conceptualization of memory as both politics and practice and our emphasis on alternative and mobile memory challenges a singular narrative of Europe and asks how Europe may be reconfigured according to voices and narratives hitherto considered to be "in, but not of Europe" (Hall 2002: 57).

Mobility assumes a multiform meaning when other possible cultural geographies of Europe that stem from the memories of new Europeans and non-Europeans are considered. It becomes an ongoing, perpetual, and collective process of rethinking memories of migration and colonialisms, entailing the production of informal knowledge. This knowledge, which emerges from the condition of being out of place in Europe and in diaspora within an ongoing dialogue between those people who are not considered European within Europe, is not immediately or necessarily in opposition to the idea of Europe grounded in border practices. Evidently, thousands of people have crossed and continue to cross frontiers illegally and to deploy methods of regularly bypassing and eluding border devices within Europe. Thus, the public and private spaces in which they live are shaped by the mobility of people and ideas produced within diasporic and migrant networks. To affirm the presence of multiple geographies of Europe that coexist with the official ones means to complexify the relationship between the roles of institutions and migrant flows that have no determinate ending. From another perspective, this affirmation suggests that those who are not considered European can resignify places within Europe through a combination of their mobility and memory.

As some prominent scholars have pointed out (e.g., Stoler 2008; Wekker 2016), the colonial archive is an organized system of knowledge constructed from representations, practices, and imaginaries that is primarily responsible for the creation of a past and present geography based on Eurocentrism and whiteness. The border is a device deployed in the production of space that has inherited the legacy of European colonial powers, namely the creation of forms of dominion over other lands and bodies. From this perspective, an analysis of migration paths can focus on the condition of migrant people in relation to both colonial cultures and postcolonial conditions. We adopted this approach to investigate the connection between Italy and the Netherlands, attending to the question of how people coming from former colonies experience multiple forms of violence as material and immaterial heritages of colonialisms along their migratory paths and subsequently in the act of remembering their condition upon their arrival in Europe. Racial minorities within Europe also deploy and reelaborate their memory of colonialisms and slavery to problematize inequality as the outcome of a tension that relates to their status as the descendants of those subjected to colonial violence and also as a consequence of discrimination experienced in postcolonial contexts. A postcolonial Europe can be conceptualized in terms of the assembling of many colonial archives and narratives through the device of the border while applying an interpretative gaze that extends across many countries and frontiers. Accordingly, the connection between Italy and the Netherlands can be viewed as one of many possible assemblages of migrant trajectories that postcolonial Europe imposes on migrants, those coming from multiple counties, and with many positionalities, who are obliged to move across Italy in order to reach the Netherlands. Starting from a conception of this assemblage, which simultaneously encompasses colonialities and postcolonial conditions, all of the contributions in this volume have sought to foreground and analyze the role of memory and mobility in the emergence of multiple cultural geographies within Europe.

Organization of the Book

While *The Mobility of Memory* elaborates on some of the results of the BABE Project, its scope extends beyond these outcomes through the inclusion of two contributions by external collaborators. These analyses complement those of the BABE researchers, as they also grapple with questions of European identity, memory, and mobility. The nature of the topic of our inquiry—namely, the ways in which mobilities and memories currently shape and interrogate the "question of Europe"—necessitated this wider analytical framework. We were guided by the approach taken by Mezzadra and Neilson, who "question the limiting perspective imposed by the view that the breadth of research compromises its depth and rigor [and] proceed with the commitment that breadth can produce depth, or better, produce a new kind of conceptual depth, 'new ideas'" (2013: 10). Similarly, the contributions to this volume demonstrate an expansive analytical configuration aimed at mapping constraints and possibilities relating to the mobilities and memories of migrants as they negotiate the meanings of Europe.

The chapters in this volume deploy diverse datasets—ethnographic and archival data as well as discursive/textual and visual materials (drawings, art, and photographs). Interviews held with individual migrants or with groups of migrants conducted in educational settings, public spaces, and private residences in Italy and the Netherlands are key sources of data collected for the majority of the contributions. While a focus on the subjectivities, memories, and mobilities of migrants and minorities is essential for addressing our question on how Europe could be configured otherwise, our aim was not to produce an essentialized portrayal of the "mobile minority/migrant subject." Nor did we want to restrict our focus to "studying down" without also "studying up." The term "studying up" originates in Laura Nader's influential essay in which she urged anthropologists to turn their attention from the study of disenfranchised groups to dominant and powerful elites who are responsible for the conditions endured by the disempowered. Specifically, she advocated the "study of the colonizers rather than the colonized, the culture of power rather than the culture of the powerless, the culture of affluence rather than the culture of poverty" (Nader 1972: 289). However, Nader's proposition does not simply entail a reversal of focus; as she noted, exclusively studying up would eventually require the investigator to study down again. Therefore, she called for a simultaneity of "up, down or sideways" approaches within anthropological research (1972: 292). We believe that it would be pertinent to revisit this call in the current political climate, which is characterized by heightened attention to migration in Europe, particularly in light of a substantial body of research conducted on (im)migration that could run the risk of "fetishizing the immigrant as an anthropological object of study" (Coleman 2012: 161), thereby not sufficiently accounting for the structures and institutions that create and maintain the category of migrant/refugee. Therefore, the analytical framework developed in this volume should be considered as an "up, down [and] sideways" approach that simultaneously foregrounds migrant trajectories, experiences, and mobilities while offering a critique of the mechanisms of governmentality that generate the conditions under which borders are institutionalized and migrant and minority subjects are produced and regulated.

This book is structured around four sections, each of which engages with the notion of the mobility of memory in Europe from specific thematic positions that have informed the BABE Project. Each of these sections comprises two contributions that provide a focused entry point into the debate in question.

The first section of the book, titled "Mobility Framed by Language: Constraints and Possibilities," is aimed at problematizing and investigating the possibilities that are inherent in subjectivities framed by migration. In the first chapter, Milica Trakilović draws on her fieldwork conducted in the Netherlands to interrogate the constraints imposed on individuals who are made to identify with the "refugee" or "migrant" label while also revealing the potential for negotiating what is often perceived as a confining category. The second contribution in this section by Giada Giustetto explores narrative models communicated through words and images within the works produced by secondary school students in Italy with whom she engaged in the context of the BABE Project. The outcomes of her investigation are what she describes as different "languages of mobility" that are potential building blocks for a "pluricultural European identity."

A central emphasis in the contributions in the second section of the book, titled "Transcultural Subjectivities in Educational Settings," is on didactic practices that encourage the acknowledgment, safeguarding, and nurturing of different cultural backgrounds within the classroom. Graziella Bonansea's chapter is based on her work with secondary school students in Italy in the context of the BABE Project. The chapter explores how the participating students engaged with and responded to questions of cultural difference through their own visual depictions of embodied subjectivity, suggesting the possibility and desire to move from a national to a transnational belonging.

The second chapter in this section is a joint contribution by Emmanuelle Le Pichon-Vorstman, Sergio Baauw, Debbie Cole, Suzanne Dekker, and Marie Steffens, all researchers in the Education of International Newly Arrived Migrant Pupils (EDINA) Project. Drawing on data collected in the course of this project, these authors argue that the incorporation of migrant students' mother tongues within the (Dutch) school curriculum is not only advantageous for the students in question but it also benefits the classroom dynamic and enriches the overall learning process.

The third section of this volume, which is titled "Diasporic Memories and Archival Trajectories," is concerned with the question of how cultural memory is shaped and mediated by embodied subjects and specific cultural narratives. In the opening chapter, Gabriele Proglio conceptualizes the memories of Italy's Eritrean diaspora in terms of a "geography of emotion." The second chapter in this section by Liliana Ellena investigates the colonial archive that underlies two Italian films, both titled *Eva Nera*, which were respectively released in 1954 and 1976. She does so through an examination of the intertwined processes of production, distribution, and representation relating to these films. Both of these contributions are based on data collected during the BABE Project. In Proglio's case, the data were ethnographic, whereas Ellena used archival data.

The fourth and final section, titled "Visualizing Memory and Resistance," proposes a visually oriented conceptualization of resistance to oppressive nationalist and cultural frameworks. In her contribution, Iris van Huis presents an array of visual accounts, ranging from photographs to paintings and plays produced by individual migrants or collectives based on data she collected during her ethnographic fieldwork conducted in the Netherlands. These accounts entail a critique of xenophobic attitudes and discourses concerning migration to the Netherlands. In the second chapter in this section, Sara Verderi specifically analyzes the ways in which the Syrian diaspora in the Netherlands critically engage with violence and militarism through nonviolent visual and artistic means.

The four thematic sections of this volume each approach the topic of mobility, memory, and migration in Europe from distinct but interconnected entry points, thereby expanding the debate on symbolic as well as material European borders. The book not only conveys the reflections of the BABE researchers relating to different facets of their fieldwork experiences but it also includes the perspectives of two external collaborators from the Netherlands who were invited to share their research paths. These contributions have consequently challenged and complexified our own epistemological and methodological standpoints. The volume attempts to elucidate changing configurations of mobility and memory in Europe. At the same time, the individual contributions reflect our restitutive goals as a research group and as individual scholars and trace research paths that illuminate topics, questions, and sociocultural transformations that will likely face Europe in the near future.

Milica Trakilović, PhD, teaches Gender and Postcolonial Studies in the Graduate Gender Programme at the Department of Media and Culture Studies, Utrecht University. As a research associate on the ERC project Bodies Across Borders: Oral and Visual Memory in Europe and Beyond, she conducted ethnographic research on groups and individuals with a migration background, focusing on migration trajectories. She also researched popular and political discourses that produce the categories of "migrant" and "refugee." Her PhD project focuses on border figurations in Europe, specifically the figure of the migrant and the geopolitical space of the Balkans.

Gabriele Proglio is an FCT researcher in the Centre for Social Studies at the University of Coimbra. He earned his PhD at the University of Turin, Department of History, with a research project on colonial imaginaries. He was a visiting scholar at the University of California, Berkeley, and assistant professor in History of the Mediterranean at the University of Tunis El Manar. As a research associate on the ERC project BABE, he conducted oral history research on migrants from the Horn of Africa. His research interests focus on colonial legacies in Europe, postcolonial societies, borders, frontiers, mobilities, and memories of migration across the Mediterranean. His recent publications include *Border Lampedusa: Subjectivity, Visibility and Memory in Stories of Sea and Land* (Palgrave, 2018) and *Decolonizing the Mediterranean: European Colonial Heritages in North Africa and the Middle East* (Cambridge Scholars, 2016).

References

Ambrosini, Maurizio. 2018. *Irregular Immigration in Southern Europe: Actors, Dynamics and Governance.* London: Palgrave Macmillan.

Balibar, Étienne. 2002. *Politics and the Other Scene.* New York: Verso Books.

———. 2004. *We, The People of Europe? Reflections on Transnational Citizenship.* Princeton: Princeton University Press.

———. 2009. "Europe as Borderland." *Environment and Planning D: Society and Space* 27: 190–215.

Bhambra, Gurminder K. 2016. "Whither Europe?" *Interventions* 18, no. 2: 187–202.

Campesi, Giuseppe. 2015. *Polizia della frontiera: Frontex e la produzione dello spazio europeo.* Rome: Derive Approdi.

Coleman, Matthew. 2012. "The 'Local' Migration State: The Site-Specific Devolution of Immigration Enforcement in the U.S. South." *Law & Policy* 34, no. 2: 159–90.

Dainotto, Roberto M. 2007. *Europe (In Theory).* Durham, NC: Duke University Press.

Del Grande, Gabriele. 2007. *Mamadu va a morire: la strage dei clandestini nel Mediterraneo*. Rome: Infinito.
Derrida, Jacques. 1992. *The Other Heading*. Bloomington: Indiana University Press.
Donnan, Hastings, Madeleine Hurd, and Carolin Leutloff-Grandits, eds. 2017. *Migrating Borders and Moving Times: Temporality and the Crossing of Borders in Europe*. Manchester: Manchester University Press.
Errl, Astrid. 2011. *Memory in Culture*. London: Palgrave Macmillan.
Gilroy, Paul. 2016. "Foreword: Europe Otherwise." In *Postcolonial Transitions in Europe: Frontiers of the Political*, edited by Sandra Ponzanesi and GianMaria Colpani, xi–xxv. London: Rowman & Littlefield International.
Goldberg, David Theo. 2006. "Racial Europeanization." *Ethnic and Racial Studies* 29, no. 2: 331–64.
Halbwachs, Maurice. 1950. *La mémoire collective*. Paris: Presses Universitaires de France.
Hall, Stuart. 1992. "The West and the Rest: Discourse and Power." In *Formations of Modernity*, edited by Hall and Gieben, 185–227. Cambridge, UK: Polity Press in Association with the Open University.
———. 2002. "'In, but Not of Europe': Europe and Its Myths." *Soundings* 22: 57–69.
Margulis, Matias, Nora McKeon, and Saturnino M. Borras, eds. 2014. *Land Grabbing and Global Governance*. London: Palgrave Macmillan.
Mbembe, Achille. 2013. *Critique de la Raison Nègre*. Paris: La Découverte.
Mezzadra, Sandro, and Brett Neilson. 2013. *Border as Method, or, the Multiplication of Labor*. Durham, NC: Duke University Press.
Muddle, Cas, and Cristobal Rovira Kaltwasser. 2017. *Populism: A Very Short Introduction*. New York: Oxford University Press.
Nader, Laura. 1972. "Up the Anthropologist: Perspectives Gained from Studying Up." In *Reinventing Anthropology*, edited by Dell Hymes, 284–311. New York: Pantheon Books.
Passerini, Luisa, Dawn Lyon, Enrica Capussotti, and Ioanna Laliotou, eds. 2007. *Women Migrants from East to West: Gender, Mobility, and Belonging in Contemporary Europe*. New York: Berghahn Books.
Parker, Noel, and Nick Vaughan-Williams. 2012. "Critical Border Studies: Broadening and Deepening the 'Lines in the Sand' Agenda." *Geopolitics* 17, no. 4: 727–33.
Ponzanesi, Sandra. 2016. "The Point of Europe: Postcolonial Entanglements." *Interventions* 18, no. 2: 159–64.
Rothberg, Michael. 2014. "Multidirectional Memory." *Auschwitz Foundation International Quarterly: Témoigner. Entre histoire et mémoire [Testimony between History and Memory]* 119: 176.
Rumford, Chris. 2012. "Towards a Multiperspectival Study of Borders." *Geopolitics* 17, no. 4: 887–902.
Said, Edward W. 1978. *Orientalism*. New York: Pantheon Books.
Stoler, Ann Laura. 2008. *Along the Archival Grain: Epistemic Anxieties and Colonial Common Sense*. Princeton: Princeton University Press.
———. 2016. *Duress: Imperial Durabilities in Our Times*. Durham: Duke University Press.
Tazzioli, Martina. 2016. "Border Displacements: Challenging the Politics of Rescue between Mare Nostrum and Triton." *Migration Studies* 4, no. 1: 1–19.
Wekker, Gloria. 2016. *White Innocence: Paradoxes of Colonialism and Race*. Durham: Duke University Press.
Whitley, Leila Maire. 2015. "More than a Line: Borders as Embodied States." PhD dissertation, London, Goldsmiths, University of London.

Part I
MOBILITY FRAMED BY LANGUAGE

Constraints and Possibilities

Chapter 1

BETWEEN "FLEEING" AND "TAKING FLIGHT"

Negotiating the Refugee Label

Milica Trakilović

Whereas in recent years there has been a widespread tendency to represent migration to Europe as a relatively new and exceptional phenomenon, mass movements and relocations have occurred throughout human history. However, as Nicola Magnusson argues, the use of categories such as (economic) migrant, refugee, asylum seeker, and illegal immigrant to classify and label different mobilities and mobile subjects is a prominent characteristic of our times. Magnusson (2011: 15) further points out that these labels are not arbitrary; they are linked concretely to systems of control that direct the social and spatial movements of migrating subjects. Therefore, the categories of migrant and refugee carry particular meanings that may impact strongly on societal perceptions as well as on self-perceptions. These themes featured significantly in the interviews I conducted with individuals in the Netherlands, focusing on their migratory trajectories to and through Europe in the context of the *Bodies Across Borders in Europe: Oral and Visual Memory in Europe and Beyond* (hereafter BABE) Project. Respondents expressed their feelings of being constrained by the labels "migrant," "refugee," "asylum seeker," and others, and they frequently articulated their desire to "lose" these markers so that their "true" identities (e.g., an artist or student) would become apparent. All of the respondents were particularly uncomfortable being perceived as migrants or refugees and professed a desire to shed or overcome this label, deploying various discursive and representational tactics to accomplish this.

Rather than opting to conduct an inventory of the varying responses to the "refugee label" (Zetter 1991, 2007) that entailed a "studying down" perspective, my aim was to "study up" (Coleman 2012; Gusterson 1997; Nader

1972) and also to present the commentaries of my respondents on how they personally negotiated the migrant/refugee label as points of elaboration on the modes of discourse and governance that produce these very same labels. To accomplish these objectives, I studied several critical conceptualizations of the figure of the refugee/migrant that emphasize both the reductive character of this category as well as the possibilities of its modification at an individual level, and then I read my respondents' views in dialogue with these theoretical framings. In doing so, I critically examined the possibility of— and potential problems associated with—"recovering" the notion of the refugee/migrant from its current marginal position and according it a more central position within the discourse. Accordingly, I examined Dutch responses to the recent migration crisis that have been widely manifested in polarized and sensationalist public opinion. One of the aims of this chapter is to instill a more nuanced understanding of the migrant/refugee label into this discussion. The need for this nuanced understanding has become particularly urgent in light of the fact that borders in contemporary times have undergone a shift from the "physical (the gate to European territories and citizenship) and [the] symbolic (the myth of Europe and its idea of superiority) to material borders (the marked body of foreigners, immigrants and asylums seekers) which become 'border' figurations (through constructions of otherness, foreignness, and alienness)" (Ponzanesi and Blaagaard 2011: 3). In the above quote, Ponzanesi and Blagaard are referring to the phenomenon of an "embodied border" in which certain groups of people come to stand for larger societal forces. Accordingly, the migrant *becomes* migration. At times, migration even becomes a natural force, thereby losing all of its societal, historical, and political connotations. Conceived in this way, it may be framed as a natural disaster, as seen, for example, in references to "waves" or "streams" of migrants, or of migrants "flooding" European shores. Such framings indicate that the discourses surrounding migration not only render people as other but also dehumanize them.[1]

Both "migrant" and "refugee" could be relatively loaded terms during my interviews, which centered on migratory trajectories and implicitly or explicitly addressed the interview subjects as migrants and/or refugees. There are, I believe, two factors that can help explain the apprehension toward these terms. First of all, the act of addressing someone can be understood as an interpellative[2] gesture that produces, in a sense, the addressee. Secondly, however, as Ramaswami Harindranath points out, the "politics of naming the Other," conceived here as the refugee, migrant, and/or asylum seeker, is predicated on "residual aspects of the colonial era" that "continue to colour perceptions of the non-Western world through the politics of naming, thus establishing the ideological difference from the West" (Harindranath 2007: 3). Together, these two factors work according to a mechanism of interpellative Othering that results in further alienation, rather than subjectification, as migrants and refugees are already made to occupy a liminal role in culture and society and not infrequently experience a "linguistic and cultural void" (Longinović 2018: 892) in the spaces they come to inhabit. In this chapter, I consider how my respondents *navigated* the restrictions they experienced as a result of being labeled (as migrants and/or refugees) and examine to what extent the strategies they employed reproduced or contested existing discourses.

Analytical and Methodological Framework

The central preoccupation of this chapter is to understand how the notion of the refugee/migrant operates at individual (personal), symbolic, and structural levels and according to which (dominant) discourses. I take my respondents' views on their own experiences with labeling as my analytical starting point, subsequently expanding the focus of the analysis to include a reflection on the migration discourse that produces the refugee/migrant through using the "up, down and sideways" (Nader 1972) approach whereby individuals' responses to the migrant/refugee label are studied in tandem with and as a response to the discursive and institutional frameworks that produce and uphold these categories.

In the course of my fieldwork undertaken for the BABE Project, I carried out semistructured interviews with approximately thirty people with a migration background[3] covering fourteen countries of origin. Most of these interviews were conducted with individuals, but several were also conducted in group settings, and they typically lasted from forty minutes to an hour. During these interviews, the emphasis was on how the respondents perceived their journey to the Netherlands, focusing on and how they described, remembered, and visualized this trajectory. Aside from differences of gender, age, and educational level, and the amount of time they had spent in the Netherlands up to the time of the interviews, the respondents differed markedly in terms of their backgrounds.[4]

Respondents' accounts of their journeys to and through Europe also tended to differ greatly, varying from a few days to several months. Although this group of respondents was highly heterogeneous in many ways, almost all of them expressed their dissatisfaction at being perceived exclusively as migrants or refugees. Many professed a desire to somehow escape or at least transform this category, which in their experience was confining. These responses not only reveal something about individuals' self-perception, but they also form a critique of the discursive and institutional mechanisms that produce these categories. My aim is to understand these individual responses within a wider political discourse on migrants and refugees, while attending to how individuals negotiate their relationships to these labels. Nevertheless, my selection and highlighting of the views of the small number of respondents in this chapter does not imply that these views straightforwardly echo sentiments shared by other respondents in the study, who are not featured here. Nor should they be considered representative of other individuals not included in this study who are labeled as migrants/refugees. These responses should be understood as individual accounts that nevertheless communicate something about the larger political moment currently unfolding in Europe that is characterized by a charged and not infrequently hostile social and bureaucratic climate with regard to migration. The individuals whose narratives are presented here all expressed how they have been personally impacted by the constraints placed upon them through the ascription of a migrant/refugee label. Accordingly, it was possible to contextualize the ways in which dominant discourses surrounding migration take shape.

While these individual responses cannot simply be viewed as disruptions or displacements of the larger structural frameworks in which they operate, there should be room in the analysis for agential possibilities of individuals to resist, subvert, or negotiate the migrant/refugee label in their own lives. A nuanced approach that can account for both personal, lived experiences as well as the confining structures that contain them without collapsing one into the other is therefore required. Alice Szczepaniková points to the dualism inherent in refugee studies, which tend to emphasize structures of control on the one hand, and strategies of resistance on the other hand (2008: 35). In other words, within the literature on refugees, there is a tendency to produce a separation between studies focusing on the *concept* of the refugee (deployed in policies and debates, and within institutional frameworks) as a mechanism of control, and studies highlighting the refugee *experience*. The latter works emphasize the agency of the research subjects in question, but do not necessarily complexify this agency by embedding it within a broader structural framework (2008: 35). Szczepaniková addresses these issues as follows:

> What seems to be missing is a perspective or a framework which would allow us to see displaced people as embodied and diverse actors who continuously strive to adopt the rules of the game to their own goals, yet are always already constrained by these rules. That is, to see them not only as objects of political violence back home and restrictive policies in their destinations but to take account of their strategic actions and decisions in the sense that they continuously challenge and transform the content of the refugee category. (2008: 36–37)

Thus, Szczepaniková advocates for research that can accomplish both actions, that is, provide an account of the ways in which the label of the refugee is produced as a normative category operative in policies and politics, while also allowing for experiential accounts of the label bearers who challenge this category in their day-to-day lives. She therefore introduces a "strategic-relational approach" to the notion of the refugee. Accordingly, from the start, the domains of "structure" and "agency" are conceptualized not as separate entities but as categories that operate together and coconstitute each other (2008: 38). I find this approach productive and have attempted to use it in this chapter to produce an account of the dominant discourses and institutional constraints that characterize the migrant/refugee experience, as well as the ways in which these constraints are managed and negotiated by those subjects who live these realities.

The Netherlands was selected as the site of analysis because all of my fieldwork, and hence all of the interviews I have conducted in the context of the BABE Project, took place there. Many respondents, notably those featured in this chapter, referred specifically to the Dutch cultural and political context when speaking about integration procedures and their experiences of social inclusion and exclusion. Yet, the Dutch response to migration in the twenty-first century, and especially following the 2015 "migration crisis"—which has entailed increased securitization, fortification of borders, and the rise of xenophobic political sentiments—is part of wider European and even global tendencies. Accordingly, the chapter's analytical focus extends beyond the national, but without losing sight of the specificities of the Dutch situation. In the following section, I examine how the migrant/refugee category is rejected, questioned, and reappropriated, as reflected in some of my respondents' views, and how these experiences reflect larger societal and institutional constraints and existing ideologies of citizenship, nationhood, and belonging.

Negotiating Belonging through the Refugee Label

In the interviews I conducted in the context of my fieldwork for the BABE Project, my respondents would largely express dissatisfaction with identity categories that marked a certain kind of distance (from an assumed "authentic" national subject), which then subsequently "stuck" to them. Some of these categories were "migrant," "foreigner," "refugee," and the specifically Dutch *allochtoon*, which is explicitly connected to land or soil.[5] In *The Cultural Politics of Emotion* (2004), Sara Ahmed introduces the notion of the sticky sign, viewed as an interpellation that is intended to keep subjects in place by defining and drawing a border around their identity. These signs truly "stick" as they carry with them additional meanings that mark bodies and keep them from moving in other (possible) directions. Ahmed provides the example of the racist proclamation *Paki*, with its underlying meaning of immigrant and outsider. One of my respondents[6] reflected on the impossibility of being "unmarked," especially when it comes to the "refugee" label:

I did not know that I would be labeled, although I'm open-minded if you know me, and I speak English, but I did not know that I would not be welcome, or [that] I'd be treated based on my race or such things. I'm not a religious guy, my family are Muslims—I'm not—but I am treated as such because I'm from Syria. I'm labeled, I mean, as a refugee. I thought, "If you don't consider yourself a refugee, you would live as an expat." But I figured out it's not like [that]. Even people who are being good to you—they're good to you because you're a refugee. So, you will be labeled anyway, even if you never have any bad experience with racism or discrimination—you will be labeled as a refugee. So that was . . . unexpected.

Here, the respondent uses the word "label" himself (instead of using "word" or "term," for instance), thereby invoking the ideological dimension of this conceptual category, which can function as a mechanism of control. Scholars have engaged with the problem of signification that inheres in the term "refugee." Notable among such works is Roger Zetter's 1991 analysis on the practice of "labelling" refugees in bureaucratic and humanitarian aid contexts that sought to reveal how these mechanisms frequently produce narrow, constraining definitions of refugees according to the interests and internal workings of the concerned organizations (Zetter 2007: 193).

In the contemporary era, which is characterized by intricate migratory trajectories associated with a "process of bureaucratic fractioning" (Zetter 2007: 174), the complexity of this practice has increased. Bureaucratic fractioning entails the invention of ever-proliferating labels in a (failed) attempt to accommodate a multiplicity of new situations of persecution and statelessness. According to Zetter, faced with mass migration, national governments in the Global North (notably Europe at present) are transforming the refugee label—a process that was previously "monopolized" by NGOs. Moreover, this label (and those connected to it) has become politicized and has been consequently deployed actively in populist, antimigration, national agendas, becoming part of a wider political discourse (Zetter 2007: 174).

This process has been clearly apparent within Europe since the 2015 "migration crisis." Further on in this chapter, I will elaborate on the current political climate prevailing in the Netherlands, specifically in relation to the migration debate. Zetter (2007: 187) argues that the label "refugee," which was previously relatively homogeneous, has been transmuted in the current era into a plethora of other labels (e.g., illegal/economic/bogus asylum seeker), signifying marginality, a threat, and otherness. He points out that whereas previously, the refugee label was equated mainly with "rights and entitlements," in the current political situation, it operates within a discourse of "identity and belonging embedded in debates about citizenship and the 'other' in an era of global migration" (2007: 190). This holds true for the above testimony, in which the respondent reflected on the constraints placed upon his identity as a result of being "pushed" into the refugee category by prevailing social and political discourses in the Netherlands.

Zetter's analysis highlights the role of language/discourse as an apparatus of meaning as well as of control. He explains his choice of the word label in connection with refugees as follows: "As opposed to other terms, for example, 'category,' 'designation,' or 'case,' the word 'label' better nuances an understanding which: recognizes both a process of identification and a mark of identity; implies something independently applied, but also something which can be chosen and amended; has a tangible and real world meaning, but is also metaphorical and symbolic" (Zetter 2007, 173).

In other words, the term "label" is useful because it signifies the governmental and bureaucratic structures that impose it on (or deny it to) individuals, while also signifying an agential dimension through a process of individual appropriation or rejection. My approach to the migrant/refugee discussion is very similar. Recognizing that labeling is frequently a top-down action that imposes on or withholds from individuals certain (institutional) categories, I all the more want to acknowledge and leave space for exploring the ways in which these categories are managed, contested, and possibly reworked by individuals according to a bottom-up logic. The respondent cited above described the refugee label as a social and discursive constraint, impacting his self-perception and how others perceived him. However, as I show later, other respondents appropriated and reworked this label, according to their personal situations, into a less constraining category.

Furthermore, this testimony reveals that the "reading" of an individual as a refugee is directly linked to their place of origin (Syria in this case), even though the respondent perceived himself as an "expat," implying a choice over his mobility rather than the compulsion to flee. The term refugee, in particular, conveys a strong connotation of helplessness, prompting host societies to offer their services to this disadvantaged group and creating the perception of a burden. In this respondent's view, being an "expat" gives him considerably more agential status because the presumed relationship between the "native" subject and the expat can be one of exchange, whereas the refugee is relegated to a position of passivity and dependence; a position that is expected to result in an attitude of gratitude toward the host country (Ghorashi 2014: 111). For the respondent in question, "expat," is a term and a condition that he has chosen intentionally, whereas "refugee" is a label that was imposed on him. However, "expat" refers to a "different category of foreigner" (Smith 2014) and is frequently applied to someone from the West. Because this individual is from Syria, others perceive him as a migrant or a refugee. Consequently, while he could easily claim to be an expat at a personal level, this is not possible at a social/structural level. The expectations he had of the circumstances that would await him in the Netherlands did not coincide with the reality of the situation, which is also apparent in the diagram he drew (see Figure 1.1), depicting his life trajectory, including his migration experience. In this diagram, the red line represents his life trajectory up to the time of the interview; the black line represents the reality of his overall life satisfaction; and the green line represents his expectations for his unfolding life. It is evident from the diagram that his expectations and the reality he experienced differ markedly. Of note are his expectations, envisioned as a steadily rising line throughout the course of his life, whereas the reality is in striking contrast. There is considerable divergence in his expectations and the reality he encountered after his arrival in the Netherlands. The process of categorization, entailing the assignment of the refugee label and the social constraints accompanying it seem to have directly impacted this situation.

Another respondent[7] spoke of the distancing gesture and categorical thinking entailed in the term refugee in relation to his own experiences:

> [When I] first I came here, I didn't realize that when I started to talk with people and meet people . . . [that they] have ideas about refugees [as if they] are other creatures coming from other lands, maybe from Mars, and they [think they] don't know anything about us, and we don't know anything about them. But actually, we know about them—we know almost like everything, and it's just normal. I had this conversation with a Dutch friend, and we're talking about refugees and how people look at refugees, and one of my friends, she told me, "When I'm talking with my friends about [how] I have you and other Syrian friends, they say, 'What's it like to have a refugee as a friend?'" So, she invited us to her house to cook and make dinner there, and she invited her friends also. And we went there, and after we finished talking, they told her, "Yeah, they are almost like us."

The expression "almost like us" is simultaneously placating and distancing, seemingly allowing entry into the realm of Dutchness and/or Europeanness, while serving as a reminder that this transition will never be complete. Thus, refugees are positioned outside of the imagined community[8] of a nation-state, even when they physically inhabit it. The term "refugee" signifies a sudden arrival, whereas "authentic" national subjects are not burdened by this signification. Sara Ahmed observes, "We only notice the arrival of those who appear 'out of place.' Those who are 'in place' also must arrive; they must get 'here,' but their arrival is more easily forgotten, or not even noticed" (2004: 9–10). Specifically, Ahmed talks about (national) belonging actualized through the inclusion and exclusion of racialized bodies. In the above testimony, the respondent describes the refugee as a cultural other, which reflects his experience of interacting with Dutch people.

As my fieldwork was conducted in the Netherlands, I am situating this analysis in the specificity of the Dutch context regarding the discourse on the

Between "Fleeing" and "Taking Flight" • 37

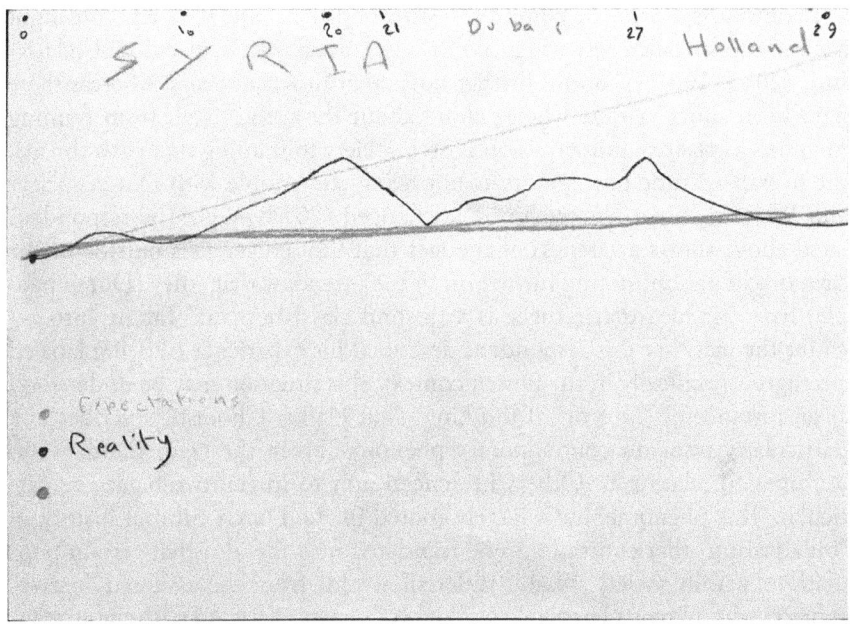

FIGURE 1.1. The respondent's drawing of his migration trajectory. Photograph by the author. Published with permission.

cultural Other, particularly in light of Europe's migration "crisis." First, it is necessary to foreground an understanding of the way in which the language of Dutch racism has changed over time. As Philomena Essed points out, racism in the Netherlands became less overt during the second half of the twentieth century, which, of course, does not mean that it was absent. Following 9/11, the language of racism in the Dutch context was most notably directed at the imagined threat embodied by the Muslim Other, which is reflective of a wider European tendency. However, Dutch racism is also very specific because there is no established discourse for addressing its "layered nature" (Essed and Hoving 2014: 10). In the post-9/11 period, the voicing of negative opinions toward Muslim minorities and immigrants (often collapsed into one category) became more acceptable in the Netherlands. Moreover, with the prompting of a "new realism" discourse (a term coined by Baukje Prins) in the Netherlands, which legitimized explicitly xenophobic and racist stances against the cultural Other, the propagation of antiracist and multiculturalist values for which the Netherlands had been renowned in the past came to be perceived as not being in touch with reality (Essed and Hoving 2014: 15).

Critically reflecting on the backlash against the "ungrateful Other in the Netherlands," Halleh Ghorashi notes that "the new realist is someone with guts; someone who dares to call a spade a spade; someone who sets himself up as the mouthpiece of the common people and then puts up a vigorous fight against the so-called left-wing, 'politically correct' views of cultural relativism" (2014: 108). Ghorashi further notes that in recent years, whereas there have been shifts in tone when talking about the Other (e.g., from framing migrants as positive influences on Dutch society to framing them as a threat), the overall attitude to migrants as not being compatible with Dutch society and Western values has remained unchanged (2014: 111). The respondent cited above shows awareness of the fact that the refugee falls outside of the category of nation, stating further on in the interview that "they [Dutch people] have the idea that refugee is a [second class] human." Taking into account the fact that this respondent described his experience of being labeled a refugee, specifically in the Dutch context, this situation may be understood as an instance of "categorical thinking" that Halleh Ghorashi describes as a particularly resonant contemporary phenomenon in the Netherlands when it comes to relating to Others in general and to migrants/refugees in particular. This phenomenon is largely rooted in the Dutch cultural history of "pillarization" that continues to be translated into the idea that certain populations within society inhabit different worlds from the assumed "native" subject, who remains largely unmarked (Ghorashi 2014: 11). The sentiment expressed in this respondent's testimony ("they are almost like us") attests to the notion that refugees are perceived as cultural others, and that their practices are incompatible with Dutch cultural practices, or at the very least that the Dutch are completely foreign and unknowable to them.

The new realism discourse makes it possible to use discriminatory language explicitly in the name of "honesty," while the pointing out of racism becomes forbidden (Ghorashi 2014: 113). According to Gloria Wekker, racism in the Netherlands is operative because of its deniability and the overwhelming disconnect that still exists with regard to the dominant Dutch self-conceptualization and the four-hundred-year-old Dutch colonial history (2016: 1). Additionally, Wekker argues that in general, there is no identification with migrants (and, by extension, refugees) in the Netherlands, even though every sixth person in the country has migrant ancestry (2016: 6). The dominant conception of Dutchness is still equated with whiteness and Christianity, and anyone who carries outward signs of otherness (reflected in language, skin color, and/or cultural belonging) is encouraged to shed these markers (either symbolically or literally) through acceptance of "the assimilation model of monoethnicism and monoculturalism" (Wekker 2016: 7). Therefore, the above respondent's assessment of the refugee being a "second class human being" falls within the discourse of the cultural other in the Netherlands, which has always been racialized, even if this has not always been overt.

Responses like these enabled me to reflect on language constraints within the scope of my research and to explore the possibility of reconfiguring static identity markers according to a more deconstructive and subversive logic. Although it may be very difficult to intervene in the discourse on refugees at a structural level, respondents constantly applied strategies of rejection, appropriation, and even subversion of the refugee label at an individual level. For instance, the second respondent's wish to unmark himself as a "refugee" would appear not to entail a desire to become Dutch per se:

> For me, personally, I don't want anyone anymore to treat me as refugee. That's why I tried as soon as possible to start with my studies and my university. If someone asks me, I don't have to say, "Yeah, I am refugee," but I can say, "Yeah, I am student." Student is really a better word than refugee, because when you say refugee, they say, "Okay, I see, [I'm] sorry for you."

The self-definition as a student rather than as a national subject appears to circumvent notions of national belonging altogether by stepping outside of the bounds of (non)Europeanness and claiming a space for alternative self-conceptions. A student, belonging to no nation in particular, is presumably a cosmopolitan subject whose movement is not restricted. However, the categories of refugee and student are also considered incompatible, implying that a refugee cannot be a student and vice versa. Whereas the refugee is bureaucratically, discursively, and socially positioned outside of the nation, the student is much more structurally embedded within society as a member. Therefore, although this respondent did not directly refer to national and cultural belonging, his rejection of the refugee label in favor of the student label should be understood as an attempt to achieve integration in terms of the Dutch model of citizenship. In the Dutch citizenship test, which is a popular European model, newcomers are urged to integrate within Dutch society by adopting markers of Dutchness that are configured according to liberal and secular values (de Leeuw and van Wichelen 2012). Against this background, the label "student" should be understood as a "safe" category in the sense that it does not convey overt markers of cultural and racial difference, or possibly of historical and imperial violence, unlike the label "refugee," which serves as a reminder of such difference and violence, therefore representing a threat to cultural and national autonomy.

According to de Leeuw and van Wichelen, for migrant/refugee/non-Western newcomers, the pressure and need to integrate into Dutch society are associated with "civilizational pathos" that results from "the erasure of violence in the past" (2012: 202). This view echoes Wekker's argument that the suppression of colonial history and memory within the national consciousness contributes to and actively produces a racialized image of the Other. Based on a study of postcolonial migrants in the Netherlands, Ulbe Bosma concludes that a postcolonial discourse is absent and that integration policies are predominantly assimilationist, thereby foreclosing the possibility of cultural diversity in the country (2012: 210). Associated with this civilizational logic are secular and liberal conceptions of the self, emphasizing self-realization, productivity, and individualism. The responsibility for turning the refugee label into a label such as that of student, which is more acceptable and useful, falls on the individuals themselves. This is apparent in the following testimony of a third respondent:[9]

> I tried to get out of these clothes—the "refugee clothes"—and I thought that after taking the permit, I was no longer a refugee. I am not [an] *asielzoeker* [asylum seeker]; I am [a] *statushouder* [in possession of a residence permit]. So, I thought that I was not a refugee anymore. But then I met a lawyer who told me that I am a *statushouder* with the status of refugee. So, I am a refugee, still. I cannot fight against being a refugee anymore. But, I always fight against using that name "refugee." Because, the image of a refugee is that of a person who has nothing to provide; who doesn't know anything about the civilized nature of the country; who doesn't know about mobiles or laptops; who rides donkeys or camels and goes to work, which is farming. But, I have had a laptop since 2007, and I have used Internet since the day I got the laptop as a kid and a mobile a long time ago. I know the Internet; I had three emails and I had a Facebook account, which is amazing [laughs], and I had Twitter, I had LinkedIn, and I am educated. I speak several languages. So, it's not like I'm the empty person who is known as a refugee—that type of image. And that's why the Prime Minister of Hungary [Orban] was angry with people who came in with the iPhone 6 because it doesn't fit with the image [of the refugee]. But the refugees are not people who came for commercial and economical reasons, they also came from a war, and Syria was really modern and civilized before the war; we had everything. I had fast Internet in my house. That was the actual situation.
>
> People approach me because I have a huge number of connections in Amsterdam now, and in the Netherlands in general—I am able to reach political people and normal people and many organizations in the Netherlands. I am creating my own business and my own organization, so with all of these things, people approach me as someone who is, let's say, the "good newcomer." And I am trying to change the name "refugee" to "newcomer" or "global citizen." People know that that I am a refugee, but I am not a refugee [associated] with this type of image. And people know me as a person who is a good talker and who is convincing. . . . People know that I am a matchmaker, a storyteller; they know me as an ambassador. . . . They know me as an entrepreneur, a student at the hotel school. They never describe me as a refugee. They can say, "Oh, he's from Syria"; but they never say, "He's a refugee from Syria," because that's so annoying. That's somehow insulting.

The third respondent describes his initially false and somewhat naive assumption that he would be able to fairly easily shed the refugee label. When this did not turn out to be the case, he opted for resignification of the label into something that he considered more positive. He opposes the popular conception of the refugee as a person who is completely destitute, helpless, and disconnected from the world—a "speechless emissary" (Malkki 1996). Against this image, he has fashioned an alternative understanding of the refugee as someone who is capable, connected, modern, educated, and entrepreneurial. However, this more positive notion also fits neatly into the secular and liberal model of the Dutch citizen that de Leeuw and van Wichelen critique. In describing his self-conception, the respondent emphasizes self-realization, self-presentation, personal and professional connections, and ultimately the ability to be a productive member of society, implicitly implying that these are *not* the characteristics of a refugee. His desire to change the refugee label into "newcomer or global citizen" is grounded in the idea of a cosmopolitanism that entails discursively erasing specificities of cultural and historical contexts and processes of political violence. Although this may appear as a circumvention of national categories and norms, cosmopolitanism is actually better understood as an ideal that supports a particular kind of Western-coded nationalism (Derrida 1992). Moreover, cosmopolitanism as an ideology is operationalized through institutions like the European Union, promoting a shallow idea of national diversity that erases historical and cultural specificities. It also negates Europe's historical involvement in colonialism and imperialism and the reproduction of these structures in current neocolonial capitalist frameworks. Cosmopolitanism therefore exists due to the historical disavowal of old and new colonialisms (Bhambra 2016). Therefore, apart from contributing to a liberal, secular notion of personhood that is based on ideas of self-actualization, productivity, and participation in the (host) society, and to class identities, the cosmopolitanization of the refugee label implies a coerced loss of historicity and political context. While this strategy may be questionable at the structural and symbolic levels, at a personal level, it appears to be a beneficial one for individuals, as it can improve their self-image and confer on them a sense of agency with regard to a social category that they experience as highly coercive and constraining. Cosmopolitanization of the refugee label, then, is one way for an individual labeled as a refugee/migrant to diminish the associated experience of distancing at a personal level. This desire to universalize the "cosmopolitan refugee" label may be expressed more strongly by individuals who arrived in Europe/the Netherlands more recently—notably post-2015, when the migration phenomenon was constructed as a "crisis," as in the above three cases.

However, cosmopolitanization of the refugee label should not be understood solely as a reiteration of established identity norms; it can also serve as a possible ideological critique. One of my respondents,[10] a visual artist, aims to convey a less static idea of the migrant/refuge in her work. For instance, one of her paintings (see figure 1.2) features a transformation of the trope of "fleeing" refugees to one of refugees "taking flight," which suggests multiple modes of mobility. In this depiction, the refugees cease to be constrained by a static marker and take on the possibility of being multiply mobile on account of previously having been forcibly mobile. In this painting, figures are shown flying over a distinctly Dutch landscape (indicated by scattered windmills), suggesting that this mode of mobility allows for a dissolving of the structures of national territory occurring on the ground. The painting's allusion to a (European) space existing beyond the nation–state suggests a possible nomadic mode (Braidotti 2011) that enables the recovery of the figure of the marginalized refugee.

It is worth considering whether, and to what extent, the nomadic figuration of the refugee differs from the previously discussed cosmopolitan conceptualization. According to Genevieve Lloyd, Rosi Braidotti's notion of the nomadic subject is based on the notion of nomadism as an ontological reconceptualization of "the human," which is realized through an "enlarged cosmopolitan subjectivity" (Lloyd 2014: 188). The key point here is that the refugee/asylum seeker/migrant should not be thought of *as* a nomad, which might lead to yet another process of categorization. Instead, the challenge is to think "nomadically" *through* these conditions so as to possibly bring to light "assumptions implicit in prevailing ways of thinking, assumptions that can be shaken to make space for imagining alternative approaches to 'problems' which have otherwise proved intractable" (Lloyd 2014: 187). For Braidotti, the nomad represents a figuration; a conceptual entity that can shed light on existing conditions and could potentially offer alternatives to existing institutional and discursive constraints. The nomad represents a mobility that the traditional notion of the refugee lacks, given that it is usually "fixed" in and by a particular definition, resulting in the overdetermination of its meaning. Conceptualizing the refugee "nomadically" implies the ability to dislodge this term from these static contexts. This does not mean that the nomad stands for nothing; rather, as Braidotti herself points out: "The nomad does not stand for homelessness, or compulsive displacement: it is rather a figuration for the kind of subject who has relinquished all idea, desire or nostalgia for fixity. It expresses the desire for an identity made of transitions, successive shifts and coordinated changes, without an essential unity" (2011: 39).

Braidotti's conceptualization of nomadic subjectivity, described above, does not stand in contrast to the refugee experience, which, in reality, is frequently characterized by homelessness, displacement, and rhythmical movements.

Between "Fleeing" and "Taking Flight" • 43

Figure 1.2. Olga Grigorjeva's painting *Niemandsland* (No Man's Land) featuring refugees' multiple mobilities. Published with permission.

Nomadic subjectivity is not an identity category so much as a modality that favors change over fixity. In that sense, this configuration echoes the desires of my respondents, who did not so much reject the word "refugee/migrant," as they rejected the stagnant and reductive conceptualization of identity for which it stands. In this way, the artist attempts to reimagine the refugee at a representational (visual) level, but also at a semantic one. Her reconceptualization of the refugee as someone who takes flight is all the more compelling in the Dutch context because of the strikingly close semantic resemblances of the two concepts of fleeing and flight: whereas the Dutch word for "refugee" is *vluchteling*, *vlucht* connotes "fleeing," but it can also mean "flight" in general, or "airborne movement." Grigorjeva's representational reconfiguration also signifies a semantic shift entailed in attempts to dislodge the refugee label from its overdetermined and static context. It should be noted that working through a visual artistic medium enables her to approach the topic of labeling from a level that is abstract and discursive, which allows a certain creative and conceptual distance that is not immediately available to the other respondents, whose negotiations of the refugee label occur at a more immediate, personal level. Nevertheless, all the respondents' views represent a negotiation of ideologically charged terminology.

Concluding Remarks

Drawing on the political moments of 9/11 and those that followed it, Jacques Derrida[11] advocates the destabilization of static and violent ideological terminology as an act of political resistance:

> Semantic instability, irreducible trouble spots on the borders between concepts, indecision in the very concept of the border: all this must not only be analyzed as a speculative disorder, a conceptual chaos or zone of passing turbulence in public or political language. We must also recognize here strategies and relations of force. The dominant power is the one that manages to impose and, thus, to legitimate, indeed to legalize (for it is always a question of law) on a national or world stage, the terminology and thus the interpretation that best suits it in a given situation. (Derrida 2004: 105)

Language can become a border apparatus that must be challenged through interventions in the discursive logic of certain practices that simultaneously bear knowledge of the institutional power underlying the dominant terminology. As revealed by the case studies in this chapter, the endeavor by individuals to destabilize the conceptual cluster of the refugee/migrant/asylum seeker is difficult to accomplish in practice because the rejection of one ideological category not infrequently means replacing it with another. Thus, for instance, the refugee label may be shed in favor of a cosmopolitan notion of the refugee. However, these personal strategies and modes of self-definition also point to the inherent need of those labeled as refugees to construct overdetermined categories of their own; and in doing so, these individuals seek to shift the category of refugee from a marginal to a more central position within discourse and society. The cosmopolitanization of the refugee label therefore emerges as an ambivalent phenomenon, signifying both the reiteration of a relatively closed conceptual category as well as the possibility for producing a more expansive notion of subjectivity. But beyond this, the responses analyzed also point to social and political processes through which migration is being framed as a threat, invasion, or simply Other in the contemporary European context.

In conclusion, I want to point to the original conflict that spurred me to write this chapter. This chapter represents my aspiration, fueled by the sentiments expressed by the majority of my respondents, to do justice to the specificities and complexities of migratory experiences that oftentimes are lost when the above labels are invoked. The issue here is not simply that the "migrant" and "refugee" labels are reductive signifiers, although this chapter focuses on representation and discourse in particular. Luhman and Vuoristo (2015) make the connection between (public, popular) discourses, policies, and rising support for anti-immigration parties across Europe in light of the ongoing "migration crisis." Pointing to research that links negative public opinion to increased securitization of borders and a growing affiliation with right-wing politics, these authors illustrate how the framing of migration hinges on different contexts (popular, political, legal, and cultural) that reinforce and coconstitute each other. In other words, there is a feedback loop between the way we conceptualize and talk about migration and how governments deal with migrants. Moreover, as Hovil (2016) points out, the practice of labeling migration frequently overlooks "the multiple ways in which refugees forge spaces of belonging in ways that often contradict—or even subvert—national and international policies." That is to say, the lived realities of migration are far more complex and contradictory than the popular/legal/political terms "migrant" or "refugee" suggest. Therefore, nuancing and destabilizing these meanings is a pressing political question.

Milica Trakilović, PhD, teaches Gender and Postcolonial Studies in the Graduate Gender Programme at the Department of Media and Culture Studies, Utrecht University. As a research associate on the ERC project Bodies Across Borders: Oral and Visual Memory in Europe and Beyond, she conducted ethnographic research on groups and individuals with a migration background, focusing on migration trajectories. She also researched popular and political discourses that produce the categories of "migrant" and "refugee." Her PhD project focuses on border figurations in Europe, specifically the figure of the migrant and the geopolitical space of the Balkans.

Notes

1. Geert Wilders, the Dutch far right politician, used the term "asylum tsunami" to connote the need to "waterproof" Dutch borders.
2. Louis Althusser argued that subjects come into being through a process of "interpellation" or "hailing," that is, speech acts directed at a person and which, through their pronouncement, serve to define the person to whom they are directed. The addressee recognizes that he or she is being addressed and thereby enters into a state of subjectivity, implicitly recognizing that the interpellation in question is being directed at him or her. Althusser argued that identification through interpellation is indicative of the working of ideology: "Ideology 'acts' or 'functions' in such a way that it 'recruits' subjects among the individuals (it recruits them all), or 'transforms' the individuals into subjects (it transforms them all) by that very operation I have called interpellation or hailing, and which can be imagined along the lines of the most commonplace everyday police (or other) hailing: 'Hey, you there!'" (Althusser 1971: 162–63).
3. In the Dutch context, "person with a migration background" carries a loaded meaning, since it is also the term that is since 2016 officially in use by the Central Bureau for Statistics (CBS), replacing the previously criticized and polemical term *allochtoon* (*allochtone*) to denote a person of whom at least one parent was not born in the Netherlands. The new terminology appears more descriptive but ultimately performs the same ideological function as its precursor, namely to distinguish between "native" and "nonnative" Dutch as a way to establish degrees of national belonging. Thus, I am aware that "person with a migration background" is an ideologically inflected term; my use of it here is part of my aim to problematize the meaning of such labels. In the context of my research, the term had a more specific meaning as well, as all of the individuals I interviewed (save one) had themselves migrated to the Netherlands at some point in the last twenty to twenty-five years and thus were "first generation migrants."
4. Interviews were also influenced by the different backgrounds of the respondents. For example, when interviewing a visual artist, I focused on the respondent's migration trajectory as well as on his or her artistic outputs.
5. The Dutch terms *allochtoon* and *autochtoon* describe a difference in origin or descent, serving to keep a considerable part of the Dutch population symbolically outside of the nation (Jones 2014: 69). An individual is considered *allochtoon* if he or she, or even if one or both of this individual's parents, was born outside of the Netherlands. By contrast, an *autochtoon* is a person who was born on Dutch soil. In popular and political Dutch discourses, *allochtoon* has become synonymous with non-Dutchness, regardless of birth status, meaning that both terms operate in a social/cultural dimension. Paul Mepschen writes that "ethnicized and racialized groups are now construed and defined as cultural Others and as such are asked to integrate into the fiction we call Dutch 'culture'" (Mepschen 2016: 23). This means that the term *allochtoon* can "stick" to somebody who falls outside of its definition if this individual is racially and/or ethnically marked as "Other."
6. A twenty-nine-year-old man from Syria whom I interviewed in Amsterdam in January 2017. At the time of the interview, he had spent approximately one year in the Netherlands.
7. A twenty-two-year-old man from Syria whom I interviewed in Utrecht on 17 December 2015.
8. In *Imagined Communities*, Benedict Anderson writes of the imagined or constructed nature of nations and national belonging. He posits that nations are imagined because

most members of a nation will never meet the majority of their compatriots. Nevertheless, the imagery of joint belonging is instilled into every subject (Anderson 1991: 6).
9. This interview was conducted in Amsterdam in January 2017.
10. This interview was conducted in October 2015 in Den Haag with Russian-Dutch visual artist Olga Grigorjeva.
11. Derrida (2004: 93) attends to how discourse, viewed as an apparatus, operates through "a combination of public opinion, the media, the rhetoric of politicians and the presumed authority of all those who, through various mechanisms, speak or are allowed to speak in the public space," thus instilling a certain norm that becomes naturalized and, in this case, operates according to a lexicon of violence.

References

Ahmed, Sara. 2004. *The Cultural Politics of Emotion*. London: Routledge.
Althusser, Louis. 1971. "Ideology and Ideological State Apparatuses." In *Lenin and Philosophy and other Essays*, edited by Louis Althusser, 127–86. New York: Monthly Review Press.
Anderson, Benedict. 1991. *Imagined Communities: Reflections on the Origin and Spread of Nationalism*. London: Verso.
Bhambra, Gurminder K. 2016. "Whither Europe?" *Interventions* 18, no. 2: 187–202.
Bosma, Ulbe. 2012. *Post-Colonial Immigrants and Identity Formations in the Netherlands*. Amsterdam: Amsterdam University Press.
Braidotti, Rosi. 2011. *Nomadic Subjects: Embodiment and Sexual Difference in Contemporary Feminist Theory*. 2nd ed. New York: Columbia University Press.
Coleman, Matthew. 2012. "The 'Local' Migration State: The Site-Specific Devolution of Immigration Enforcement in the U.S. South." *Law & Policy* 34, no. 2: 159–90.
de Leeuw, Marc, and Sonia van Wichelen. 2012. "Civilizing Migrants: Integration, Culture and Citizenship." *European Journal of Cultural Studies* 15, no. 2: 195–210.
Derrida, Jacques. 1992. *The Other Heading*. Bloomington: Indiana University Press.
———. 2004 [2001]. "Autoimmunity: Real and Symbolic Suicides." In *Philosophy in a Time of Terror: Dialogues with Jürgen Habermas and Jacques Derrida*, edited by Giovanni Boradori, 85–136. Chicago: University of Chicago Press.
Essed, Philomena, and Isabel Hoving. 2014. "Innocence, Smug Ignorance, Resentment: An Introduction to Dutch Racism." In *Dutch Racism*, edited by Philomena Essed and Isabel Hoving, 9–30. Amsterdam: Rodopi B. V.
Ghorashi, Halleh. 2014. "Racism and 'the Ungrateful Other' in the Netherlands." *Thamyris/Intersecting* 27: 101–16.
Gusterson, Hugh. 1997. "Studying Up Revisited." *PoLAR* 20, no. 1: 114–19.
Harindranath, Ramaswami. 2007. "Refugee Experience, Subalternity, and the Politics of Representation." Presented at *Communications, Civics, Industry* at the Australia New Zealand Communications Association Conference, edited by J. Tebbutt, 1–8.
Hovil, Lucy. 2016. "Refugees, Conflict and the Search for Belonging." Accessed 6 March 2018. http://citizenshiprightsafrica.org/refugees-conflict-and-the-search-for-belonging-2/.
Jones, Guno. 2014. "Just Causes, Unruly Social Relations: Universalist-Inclusive Ideals and Dutch Political Realities." In *Revisiting Iris Marion Young on Normalisation, Inclusion and Democracy*, edited by Ulrike M. Vieten, 67–86. London: Palgrave MacMillan.

Lloyd, Genevieve. 2014. "Nomadic Subjects and Asylum Seekers." In *The Subject of Rosi Braidotti: Politics and Concepts*, edited by Bolette Blaagaard and Iris van der Tuin, 185–189. London, New York: Bloomsbury.

Longinović, Tomislav. 2018. "The Migrant Crypt: Cultural Translation Across the Balkans," *Interventions* 20, no. 6: 890–905.

Luhman, Meghan, and Kaisa Vuoristo. 2015. "Framing Migration: Rhetoric and Reality in Europe—An Introduction." Accessed 12 January 2018. http://critcom.councilforeuropeanstudies.org/framing-migration-rhetoric-and-reality-in-europe-an-introduction/.

Magnusson, Nicola. 2011. "Refugeeship—A Project of Justification: Claiming Asylum in England and Sweden." PhD Dissertation, Stockholm, Stockholm University.

Malkki, Liisa H. 1996. "Speechless Emissaries: Refugees, Humanitarianism, and Dehistroicization." *Cultural Anthropology* 1, no. 3: 377–404.

Mepschen, Paul. 2016 "Everyday Autochthony: Difference, Discontent and the Politics of Home in Amsterdam." PhD Dissertation, Amsterdam, Amsterdam University.

Nader, Laura. 1972. "Up the Anthropologist: Perspectives Gained from Studying Up." In *Reinventing Anthropology*, edited by Dell Hymes, 284–311. New York: Pantheon Books.

Ponzanesi, Sandra, and Bolette B. Blaagaard. 2011. "In the Name of Europe." *Social Identities: Journal for the Study of Race, Nation and Culture* 17, no. 1: 1–10.

Szczepaniková, Alice. 2008. *Constructing a Refugee: The State, NGOs and Gendered Experiences of Asylum in the Czech Republic*. PhD thesis, Coventry, University of Warwick.

Smith, Justin E. H. 2014. "Does Immigration Mean 'France is over'?" *New York Times*. 5 January.

Wekker, Gloria. 2016. *White Innocence: Paradoxes of Colonialism and Race*. Durham: Duke University Press.

Zetter, Roger. 1991. "Labelling Refugees: Forming and Transforming a Bureaucratic Identity." *Journal of Refugee* Studies 4, no. 1: 39–62.

———. 2007. "More Labels, Fewer Refugees: Remaking the Refugee Label in an Era of Globalization." *Journal of Refugee Studies* 20, no. 2: 172–92.

Chapter 2

"LANGUAGES OF MOBILITY/ MOBILITY OF LANGUAGES"

Between Words and Imagery

Giada Giustetto

In this chapter, I examine diverse narrative models conveyed in images, and in spoken or written words, tracing the modalities of the transmission of memories and their content, and their reciprocal influences, across different routes entailed in the "journey maps" that I collected during my field research within the "Bodies Across Borders" research project. In the course of my fieldwork, I traveled to various Italian cities, such as Turin, Florence, Mestre, and Marghera. Some of these places were chosen because of the large numbers of migrants living in them while others, such as Venice, constituted strategic "border zones," marking exits from and entry points to Europe. I encountered migrant students within the school context, basically at centers for adult education, that is, Centri Territoriali Permanenti (permanent territorial centers) and Centri Provinciali Istruzione Adulti (provincial centers for adult education) as well as in various libraries and associations. The data collection period, during which interviews were held with migrant people and asylum seekers, extended from 2013 to 2016. Professor Passerini, the Project's principal investigator, and I met 198 people aged between 16 and 65 years, whose education levels in their countries of origin and knowledge of the Italian language varied significantly. Thus, they exhibited highly diverse cultural, social, and geographical origins.

We met each student two or three times during our field research. The procedure that we generally followed on meeting a group of migrants for the first time was as follows: During the first meeting, we presented the project to the group. Subsequently, we showed the students some artistic works that focused thematically on migration. Sometimes a brief debate took place, especially with classes or groups in class with higher levels of proficiency in the Italian language. Almost all of the communication of students who were less proficient in Italian was conveyed via visual inputs and outputs, and in some cases, we used vehicular languages[1] (mostly French and English).

In this chapter, I particularly focus on problematizing different "languages" and the connections or dissonances between images and words. Memories acquired along "routes of mobility" are transmitted through pictorial representations and oral narratives. In some cases, stories constitute a third level of memory transmission entailing the combined weight and meaning of the written word and images. This study was integrated with a second educational inquiry concerning students' choices of whether to use a language other than their mother tongue. Thus, it considered the relationship between "represented" or "narrated" records, the role of the first or second languages, and collective and private memories and their relationship with identities. In sum, it was aimed at mapping "languages of mobility," comparing the particular components of memory that the students chose to record using one modality in preference to any other. "Mobility," which is an integral aspect of identity, can be understood here to refer to similar and diverse expressions of memory.

Several forms of expression of the students' memories, notably images and "white space," as well as words and silence, were identified from their numerous and diverse creations. Figurative images connected to an itinerary were abstract and symbolic or photographic. They conveyed, supported, emphasized, or contradicted words, and vice versa. A second form comprised mentally spoken or unspoken words that were translated, written, or erased. A third form comprised "other" languages and techniques of memory transmission, or the use of combined techniques such as patchwork or sticky notes.

Because the range of studies on language is very broad, encompassing widely differing disciplines, I prefer to rely on my own experiences as a researcher and teacher of Italian L2[2] while conducting this research. Professional experience has taught me the importance of taking into account and somehow trying to overcome the "structural monolingualism" that continues to plague the scholastic world. For instance, giving students the option to express themselves in whichever language they preferred was critical. Moreover, the presence of a cultural mediator during the Italian course attended by one of the students, Hakima, fostered an ambience of trust and freedom of expression that was made possible primarily by a practice of "freedom of language" and "self-expression."

The goal of this study was not only to study connections whereby specific "areas" of memory are conveyed within a specific language but also to reflect on the necessity and usefulness of expressing memory through different channels and to explore these outcomes. Out of numerous case studies conducted for this research project, three have been selected that are specifically on and about languages. As this chapter will show, these interconnected case studies open up a debate on important issues relating to memory and languages.

The conceptual framework of this study centers on the interpretation of memory as a subjectification process of language, supporting the interpretation of the three case studies presented in this chapter and initiating a dialogue between them. As Lacan (1971) has shown, in general, "parole" (the word) is the main starting point of subjectification. Moreover, Lacan's notion of the "full word" imbues life with "historical meaning," "humanizing" it through its symbolic power. Accordingly, Lacan frames an existentialist assimilation process of subjectification and historicization whereby individuals "subjectivize themselves" simply by expressing themselves.

In the context of this work, our interviewed subjects' subjectivization of themselves entailed conscious or unconscious choices, whether deliberate or not, of the languages they used to express their memories. Moreover, in line with Lacanian thought, we posited that the unconscious is "structured as a language" and its elaboration leads to different ways of expressing memories. During the process of memory sharing of the interviewed subjects, the subjectification process whereby language served as a "memory conduit" did not follow a chronological order. Instead, a certain degree of language mobility was apparent, entailing several switches, steep turns, and reversions from one language to another. Such a process comprises several moments and stages, entailing similarities and differences, harmonies and dissonances between the three examined case studies that usefully highlight different kinds of subjectivity and intersubjectivity.

The first noteworthy point relating to a comparison of the three subjects is that each of them first chose a visual language, which offers an immediate language code, from the perspectives of both the witnesses of memory and the receivers. The first thing that the students did was to draw, indicating that figurative language served as the primary channel for the release of memory. A second commonality was that each of the three case studies revealed a second stage involving the written word that appeared to be more rational and less "immediate." I would suggest that this second stage represents the desire to be understood to allow for a true transmission of the memory. Our subjects wished to reach out to their audiences and to convey meaning through their interpretations of their own "memory maps."

It is noteworthy that all three subjects shared the need to support their visual representations with words (written and/or spoken). This need may have arisen because of differences relating to production and reception between artistic expression and information/reportage/autobiography. This proved a thorny problem that was frequently discussed within the BABE Project. Our subjects either did not grasp the fact of memory maps belonging to the domain of art, or if they did, they expressed doubt and hesitation, saying, for example, "I cannot draw," or, "I am not able to create aesthetically valuable work." However, the researchers always sought to reassure them, explaining that the project had a different goal, thereby enabling them to correctly perceive this exercise as an opportunity to share their memory. Sometimes, that opportunity was perceived as personal, and sometimes, it had an informative purpose (this was significant in the third case study) that concerned a collective condition. If an image does not include written text, it can convey ambiguity, which is evidently advantageous for artistic images. This is because images that can be interpreted in multiple and contrasting ways are correspondingly considered more effective, although this does not apply to the same extent to modes of communication such as photo reportage, which only attains its goal of being informative if it demonstrates the right balance between images and words.

The first case study included a key map that served as an "interpretative table," whereas the second one included text in Arabic, resembling a caption. It is noteworthy that the English word "caption" is a translation of the Italian term *didascalia*, which, in turn, stems from the Greek word διδασκαλία ("education"), which ultimately originates from the source word διδάσκω ("to teach"). In contemporary usage, "caption" means any kind of informative sentence attached to an illustration.[3] The relationship between an image and its caption has always been extremely complex. Keim (1963) suggested that captions are universal, while Barthes (1982), in his writings on photography, posited that each photographic structure has a specific language structure attached to it. Consequently, the two elements can be seen to be inseparable, and the resulting unity ensures that the meaning is grasped in greater depth as opposed to one that is derived from simple aesthetic enjoyment or a "diffused impression" originating from observation of an image that lacks text.

The various stages typically entailed in the above described subjectification process accommodate the need to belong as well as to stand out, thus creating two opposite yet complementary aspects of human life and feelings. Accordingly, in this chapter, I examine how the interviewed subjects expressed their need to stand out, to become, or to remain, themselves in manifold ways. For instance, some chose silence, allowing their drawings to "speak" while others felt the need to engage in a monologue "on stage." At the same time, however, the students not only demonstrated their need to be easily understandable but they sometimes also wished to speak about something universal, affecting the self as well as "us." The latter term denoted "us migrants," "us learning a second language," "us seeking asylum," and so on. At times, political connotations emerged in a telling, becoming choral, collective, and asserted as a right to feel outrage and as a resolution to protest.

The choice and use of different languages as part of the subjectivization process was a notable comparative feature of all three studies, but this choice could not always be interpreted as a deliberate one. Several questions arise from observing the use of different languages and speeches. For instance, in what languages do we remember? What linguistic forms do such memories take? To what extent does the language in which we remember affect the memory itself, or the way it is expressed? Last, does sharing memories in different languages originate in different memories? The three case studies of memory maps are presented below.

The study was designed as a qualitative experience and not as a quantitative, statistical analysis. The case studies presented here have been selected because some of the transmitted memories that we collected revealed the importance of a plurality of expression and the use of different languages as memory channels. Had we only considered oral, written, or visual languages in our study of these testimonies, we would have accessed fragmented and partial memories. It is only through the richness and complexity of "multifactorial-multilanguage memory" that the subtleties of memory can be grasped. Even though gender, geographical origin, and social class were considered in the selection, we did not presume that we were presenting cases that were generally representative of the experience of migrants.

The first map is that of Ana Rosa, a journalist from Venezuela who was interviewed in Mestre in October 2014. Ana Rosa was born in 1972 in Caracas and was in the last year of her university course in journalism at the time of her arrival. Her map conveys migratory trajectories that bring together and intertwine several generations. All of Ana Rosa's pain was expressed through symbols and colors as well as through oral telling. The second map was drawn by Hakima from Morocco, who was born in Settat in 1986 and had completed middle school. She was interviewed in Turin in December 2015. Her map conveys a visual explosion of pain that appears to be strengthened by the written word, which expresses it more logically and rationally. However, the oral word does not play a significant role in this map. The third map was produced by Moulay, also from Morocco, who was born in Casablanca in 1970 and had completed his primary education. He was interviewed in Turin in December 2013. Moulay's map embeds an autobiographical memory that is inclined toward the community. Visually symbolic, it features written counterpoints. Moulay wrote and erased his story, then rewrote it in a private notebook, and ultimately chose to share it only orally.

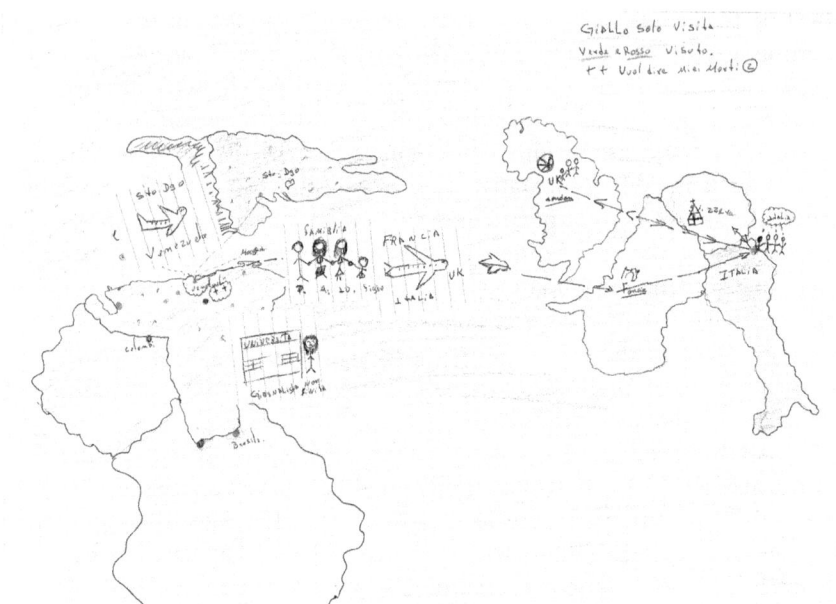

FIGURE 2.1. Ana Rosa's Map: *The Situatedness of Memory between the Spoken and the Written, Emotion and Reason, and the Body and Identity*. Published with permission.

An Emotional Key Map

Ana Rosa's memory map notably shows a wide variety of elements (both visual and written), as well as a "key map" that "organizes" her emotional self in a distinctive and conflicting manner that is almost dichotomous. She directly and unhesitatingly identifies people she has portrayed as "my dead ones." To contextualize and clarify why Ana Rosa chose to express her memory not only visually but also verbally, I will make a small detour with the aim of illuminating key differences between written and oral language that pertain to this case. Liu (1996: 21) elucidates these differences with reference to the literature, noting that writing has been treated as a visual symbol system (Sapir 1921), visible marks (Bloomfield 1933), derivative of the face-to-face conversational norm (Fillmore 1981), or simply as an artifact (Aronoff 1985). Moreover, Liu notes that while written language cannot compare with speech in terms of historical depth or in daily communication, it nevertheless has a crucial role to play. The relative stability of the written makes possible the transmission of knowledge of human civilization. In other words, speech is generally temporary whereas writing is permanent. This consideration has a direct bearing on what Ana Rosa's map was intended to convey; she felt the need to share the most significant periods in her life by means of the written word, which stems directly from and relates explicitly to memory. Thus, she wished to leave a trace through writing. Evidently, for her, drawing and oral narration were inadequate for portraying the most important "things," such as her "dead ones," places, and the forced displacements to which she and her family were often subjected. This becomes even clearer in view of the fact that interviewed subjects knew that they would be invited to share their completed maps with us (the researchers) and subsequently with their peers. Their oral memory would be recorded and their longing for a "double permanence" and a "double transmission" would be received and acknowledged. Ana Rosa felt the need to write to leave a trace and to offer the "viewer of memories" a clear and implicit intersubjective logic that would serve as a precise guide.

"Legend" is a Latin word meaning "things that shall be read; what is to be read."[4] A legend textually defines symbols, enabling a map to be interpreted. However, unlike maps with universal and objectively codifiable legends, this Venezuelan woman's map provides an "emotional legend" that on the one hand conveys her desire to reach the audience unequivocally and on the other hand reflects her somewhat oxymoronic personal need to rationalize her emotions. Contrasting with legends used in conventional maps, which are considered rational communicative devices with fixed and objective features, Ana Rosa created her own "floating" language in which elements of memory that are difficult to reconcile were merged.

The creation of this "key map" entailed a new method of transmitting autobiographical memory through attempts to "snapshot" certain keywords within the memory flow, recording them beside their visual representations (crosses, a plane, her family, and university). In addition to the legend, Ana Rosa's memory map features an interesting third element creating variation: the use of small "patches" of memory that reflect diversified application of images and writing compared with their classic deployment. Within such memory patches, words and drawings become stills; frozen images in anticipation of the racing flow of Ana Rosa's words, emerging as a stream of consciousness. Over the course of her long and complete narrative, Ana Rosa spoke of and clarified the details, engaging emotionally with the patches and keywords of her legend. Therefore, these different forms of memories, though appearing almost frozen here, were expressed and transmitted through their telling, visual portrayal, and text.

I now turn to an analysis of some of the characteristics of the written language that are directly connected to the way in which Ana Rosa chose to use it. The first is that written language—generally as well as Ana Rosa's specific application of it—entails logical relations encoded in text. In this case study, many connections with the visual representation were apparent. Second, written language is more decontextualized and autonomous than speech and is consequently less dependent on shared situations or contextual knowledge. In fact, any viewer of this writing can understand instinctively what happened, even if the details and information provided in Ana Rosa's oral expression are removed. Third, written language is more abstract and detached than speech, entailing a lower degree of personal involvement. Here, it is noteworthy that sketching people (which is discussed further on) serves as a means of almost transforming them into symbols—as typically illustrated by key maps—that migrants and others can potentially identify with, even though this memory is highly autobiographical.

Last, written language is more deliberately organized and planned than speech. Ana Rosa's legend, and the traces and arrows depicting different itineraries provide an overview not only of her travels and her family but also of her relationship with space and with other individuals who feature in her story.

Body Language and Memory

Among the many compiled memories, a third form of expression and transmission of memory was evident, namely nonverbal language, comprising expressions, gestures, pauses, silences, and eye movements. Such methods of communication, entailing an absence of words, may either complement words or else be entirely dissonant with them. In most of the oral narratives, the interviewed students used many indicative gestures, specifying their maps, their countries of departure and arrival, and the various stages of their migration itinerary. Ana Rosa used a great variety of nonverbal language (gestures) with different communicative goals. She did so primarily when talking about the situation in Venezuela, using some intentional gestures to emphasize the state of her country's economic collapse that she described and her consequent decision to leave. When she entered a more autobiographic territory (such as the forced closure of her family's two restaurants), she used some involuntary emotional indicators (gestures linked to an emotional state, such as repeatedly running her fingers through her hair). Her body language disclosed an area of her experience that is strongly associated with painful emotions of anger, denunciation, and indignation. This area is directly connected to her visual memory and remained hidden when she expressed herself orally.

Such forms of nonverbal, body-based communication of emotions are foregrounded within a theoretical perspective that focuses on affect. Affect theory offers an approach for examining nonlinguistic forces, or affects, in relation to culture, history, and politics. Affects are constitutive of individuals, but they are neither under their conscious control nor even necessarily within their awareness, and affects can be captured in language only in some cases. Affect theory can be integrated with other conceptual lenses applied within the humanities, including Michel Foucault's "analytics of power," a renewed attention to the study of animals, the study of secularism, and my own discipline of religious studies. Affect theory helps us to understand power by encouraging us to conceptualize power as a theater. In fact, Silvan Tomkins, a Princeton psychologist and one of the seminal figures in the development of affect theory, began his career not as a psychologist, but as a playwright.[5] In the acting context, an actor's "instrument" comprises the body and not the script, with effective actors meticulously deploying every aspect of their bodies—voice, hands, face, posture, stride, gaze, gait, and muscles—to compose an affective symphony. Directors, too, use a nonverbal repertoire—including timing, staging, and perspective—to weave a thick knot of affects that runs through their script. The most expertly scripted play can be ruined by underwhelming acting, clumsy direction, or confusing staging. This is because the work of making bodies move is not accomplished by words alone, nor even primarily by words. Within affect theory, power is conceived in the same terms. As anthropologist Kathleen Stewart observes, "power is a thing of the senses" (Stewart 2007: 84). When viewed through the lens of affect theory, politics is conceived as a performance rather than a set of propositions that are thoughtfully considered by rational, choosing subjects (e.g., "Vote for x if you want bridges. Vote for y if you want bombers").

A few features of Ana Rosa's telling are specific to performance: to theatrical monologue. Thus, she remembered and spoke with words (oral memory), "drew" with sentences (displaying a map that she created for herself and her audience), and used her body to materialize her emotions. Some forms of nonfiltered and more immediate communication used by Ana Rosa crucially enabled her to express her memory in a more "complete way." Unlike her prepared speech presented before her peers, her nonverbal language could not, by definition, be prepared or mediated by reason. The body is a mirror for our emotions and feelings, sometimes clashing with what we think or say knowingly. It is a different form of communication that simply flows. This kind of language "completes" the memory transmission, and those who received this transmission felt as if they were receiving a global memory, not simply through listening to Ana Rosa's staged story but also by "watching" it. Images of/from memory, combined with gestures, succeed in reaching those areas of our history that we forget and cannot or dare not describe in words.

Languages across Generations

Ana Rosa's story gave voice to many generations. To speak means to convey a plurality of intertwined memories that link the speaker to those who came before and to those who will follow. Language does not belong to any one individual; via the selected languages, many other stories come to life and emerge from silence. The journey in this case study encompasses three sets of family members: Ana Rosa's Venetian parents, whose journey was conveyed through the map and the narration; her own and her son's journey; and that of her grandfather, which was only narrated orally. Below, I present translated excerpts from Ana Rosa's interview:

> My dad used to work in the shoe industry, and back then (the eighties), many Italians traveled to America and brought shoes, which were handmade. My dad was in charge of a company. He was always on the go; he would come to Italy for fashion shows and fairs and was engaged in import and export activity between Italy and America. My family's journey (on my dad's side) began in Venice; they moved [from there] to Brazil, and then came back to Italy. My grandparents [next] went to Venezuela, where they decided to stay: they had land, they could work, etc. Later, however, my dad came back to Italy with my grandma (his mother). She decided to stay in Italy, while my dad did his military service in the Alpine Units. He worked in a hotel, the Danieli, and when he went back to Venezuela, he met my mother, and after a while, I was born.

The above illustration is a good example of what the historian Marianne Hirsch terms "postmemory." According to Hirsch, postmemory can be defined as the relationship of the "generation after" with the personal, collective, and cultural trauma of those who came before them—that is, their connection to experiences that they "remember" only by means of the stories, images, and behaviors to which they were exposed while growing up. But these experiences were transmitted to them so profoundly and affectively that they seem to constitute memories in their own right. Thus, the connection of postmemory to the past is in fact mediated not by recall but by imaginative investment, projection, and creation.

This is apparent in the case of Ana Rosa. Almost all of the memory segments that she shared with us about her grandparents, parents, and their "migration itineraries" were not directly experienced by her; they were narrated to her in a way that was likely so vivid and detailed that she made them hers. Within the framework of her oral memory, and in her visual map, there were no significant stylistic or content-based differences between "personal" and "generational" memory, except perhaps her increased "emotional engagement" when she spoke about "I" rather than "those before me."

Words as an Act of Survival and Identity

As mentioned in the previous section, oral expression conveys discourses on politics and protest, belonging and identity. Deploying this communication channel, Ana Rosa not only conveyed a "family" memory marked by "domestic" keywords, but the *word* here was collectively applied and conveyed a *political* goal. It served as a means of denunciation and indignation for the collective and not just for individuals. In Ana Rosa's discourse, is it possible to find strong political and protest elements that are connected with her homeland (Venezuela) and the country of arrival (Italy). However, Italy for her is both the country of immigration and emigration; therefore, it is the country of her roots and origins, par excellence. Italy is where everything began, and her claim is "political": her story begins in and returns to Italy. Although she does not feel that she fully belongs to this country (because of certain events that will be revealed), in Renan's words, she yearns to "feel recognized" both by "descent" and by "election" (Renan 1882). Thus, Ana Rosa not only has Italian origins but she has also made a choice to live and work in this country, which she has chosen as her new home, and to contribute to its future. Ana Rosa spoke of Venezuela as follows:

> It was 1998; my son had been born. There were elections, and then the communist regime took over. I was twenty-six, and I had two restaurants with my father. The Venezuelan economy collapsed, so we had to close both restaurants, sell both houses and throw or give away everything we had. My son's father, who was an opponent to the government, was killed. The government had everything; they took away his lands after killing him. We were left with nothing, so that's why I couldn't finish university. I was studying journalism, and they threatened to kill us if we didn't stop the student newspaper.

Sometimes, words can be almost salvific. To remember becomes an act of survival as well as a political act; language and autobiographic and collective memory are intertwined. In their essay titled "Cultural Memory: A European Perspective," Fortunanti and Lamberti observe: "Sometimes, memory becomes an 'act of survival,' of consciousness and creativity, fundamental to the formation and rewriting of identity as both an individual and a political act" (2008: 129).

Ana Rosa narrated a painful incident that occurred in Italy, related to language, speech, and the subtle and devious link between language and discrimination:

> Not being able to speak Venetian, I lost some job opportunities in Venice. I was told: "You're not getting this job because you don't speak Venetian." . . .

This happened in 2007, in a very well-known bakery called XXX. . . . I worked for them for a week, after which they told me, "Bye-bye, you don't speak Venetian!"

Therefore, despite her sacrifices and compromises, Ana Rosa endured unjust discrimination. She accepted a job that did not match her qualifications, gave up her aspiration to become a journalist, and achieved fluency in Italian. But all of this was not enough because to be able to work, she had to speak Venetian. Given that she feels that she is more Italian than many Italians, she does not accept being labeled as "not belonging" and "foreign" in this country.

Therefore, her oral narrative also provides an important conceptualization relating to a sense of belonging: "I am Italian because I was born from Italian parents, by blood. I can choose whether to accept or give up on my being Italian. I am Italian twice: by right and because I want to [be]."

Visual Memory and the Geography of Emotions

Often, memories and thoughts are conveyed first in images and not in words. Individuals expressing a memory frequently succeed in conveying concepts much more effectively with images than with words. Sometimes, rationality takes over the oral telling, so that the narrative only conveys data, dates, names, and information. By contrast, discovering and reproducing an image allows for the expression of emotions and of a more intimate and private area of the memory. Mirzoeff elucidates this as follows:

> But above all, it is a different form of memory which can go beyond the written and spoken words. . . . A kind of memory to go beyond, to pierce the silence, to express ourselves in a way that would otherwise not be imaginable. The visual offers a sensual immediacy that cannot be compared to written or oral words. There is an undeniable impact at first sight that a text cannot replicate. (1998: 9)

Echterhoff also sheds light on this topic as follows: "Testifying to this account, Albert Einstein, clearly a man with a highly active mind, reported that his thoughts did not come to him in words and that he tried to express them verbally only afterwards" (2008: 265). This applies precisely in the next case study presented here. Hakima, who is from Morocco, and who was interviewed in Turin in December 2015, said very little in her oral memory (despite the presence of a cultural mediator who could have translated for her). All of her memory was entrusted to the weeping "bird-plane" image, and afterward, she expressed some of it in Arabic.

This drawing means that during my journey to Italy, I was both happy and sad at the same time. I was happy because I was going to start a new life with my husband in another country. I'd heard it's beautiful. I was sad because I had left my parents, my siblings, and all my family; and when I said goodbye to my mother and my little son, I cried, as I depicted in my drawing.

In Hakima's visual map, a process of "birdification" is apparent, conveying a double transition: from an inanimate object to an animal and from an animal to a person. The plane, which is one of the most widely used means of transport, is transformed into a living creature of the sky: a huge bird that is given human characteristics, such as the ability to cry in order to express sadness.

Hakima chose what is universally considered a means of transport, and, therefore, "cold" and "objective," transforming it and assigning to it a new codifying language and role signifying a brand new, daring, personal, and authentic task. In this rendering of memory, a means of transport, which is a mechanical machine, is "animated," thus enabling it to bear Hakima's "emotional transference." Only after drawing the plane, did she express herself with words, placing them next to her drawing.

Hakima traveled on a plane that became something else to help her convey all of the distressing emotions that she experienced while traveling to Italy. She needed a mediator to convey her memory that could not be adequately expressed in words. It is no coincidence that Hakima chose a migratory bird

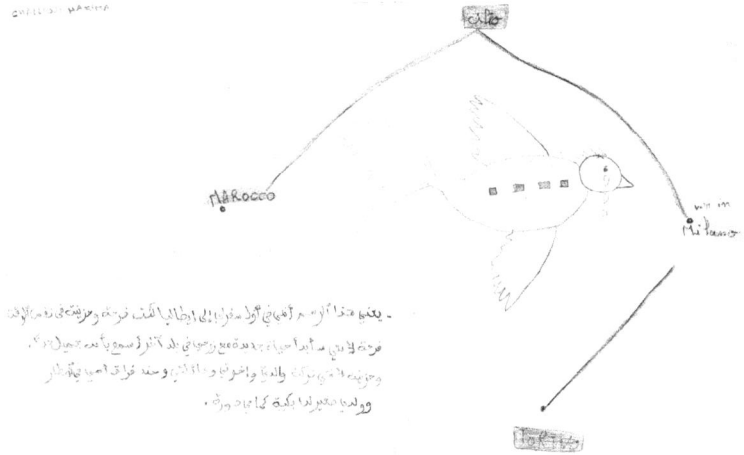

FIGURE 2.2. Hakima's Map: *Visual Memory, the Geography of Emotions, and the Mother Tongue.* Published with permission.

undergoing a long trip overseas as her "spokesperson." Migratory birds, just like people, move mainly to find better life conditions for themselves and their offspring. In fact, migration is widely acknowledged to be a crucial event in the lives of thousands of birds and is essential to their survival.

In 2015, the "Agrupación Señor Serrano" group won the Silver Lion award for innovation in their "Birdie" show at the Venice Biennale. The word "birdie" is both a diminutive and a golf score. This is the premise of the show that brings together two worlds, two horizons—those of mass migration, and of the consumer society and hyperprotection of its goods and lifestyle. The show draws inspiration from José Palazon's well-known photograph taken in Melilla of a golf course surrounded by a high net fence that is being scaled by black people about to trespass on to the golf course. This image provides a starting point for an analysis of visual perception, and of the deeper underlying meaning, to get to the migration of birds happening in the sky above us, our heads, and our "small" lives. We cannot stop birds from migrating, but we try to stop other humans from doing so.

Returning to Hakima, her visual map provided an entry point into her feelings. She did not say, "I was in pain"; instead, the drawing said this for her. However, Hakima was able to write in her own language, so, in the order of her memory, the drawing comes first, followed by the written mother tongue, and finally the translation of the mother tongue into a bridging language. Hakima chose not to rely on the cultural mediator (in spite of mutual trust), probably because she believed that what needed to be drawn had been drawn and what needed to be said had been said. While she wrote a few important words, the image she drew was incredibly impressive, rendering words unnecessary.

Between the Written Word and Figurative Expression

To what extent can written words be considered an exclusively "verbal" form of communication? If these words are part of a text that supports a figurative representation (as in Hakima's case), can they be considered and interpreted as part of the visual map? A hybrid form exists between the seen and the said, between the read and the observed. Although written words convey a different kind of memory to that conveyed by oral speech, because they are perceived through the same channel (eyes) and the same sense (sight), they are viewed as part of the drawing. This happens especially in the case of names of places en route (e.g., in Ana Rosa's and Hakima's drawings), or, even more specifically, when written words actually become a part of the drawing, as in the next case study.

Although written narratives are not works of art, they have such a significant visual connotation that they could be interpreted as "works" of visual memory. It is noteworthy that some scholars believe that written words play a significant visual role, which is sometimes essential to the completion and interpretation of the figurative element; at other times, they constitute both a complete form of expression and a complete visual form of reception. Madison Pass observes:

> The purpose of the writing and language that composes the entirety of Resilience is not to be readable; it is to convey a larger meaning than the words alone can. The purpose of the words in this piece is more symbolic, and that symbolism is tied more to the way the words create the image than their exact content, which is actually fairly repetitive. (2016: 9)

Hakima also applied text that was evidently accompanied by a translation and was external to the drawing. At first glance, this text may erroneously be viewed as tautological. It did not substitute the visual memory; it completed it. Whereas the drawing depicted the effect and symptom, the origin or cause was apparent in the text. Here, the text was not merely a commentary attached to the drawing; it was not an external, secondary, or peripheral memory.

The memory of the journey is constituted and conveyed through two fundamental processes. The first entails feelings at the surface that are immediate, impulsive, and visceral, expressed via the drawing. Following the expression of this memory, conveyed through feelings (profound sadness in this case), which is now more alive and intuitive, a second process occurs in which rational and more organized thought narrates its memory, now dual, being both emotional and rational, with written words.

The Mother Tongue, Identity, and Primary Communication

Hakima's sparse and carefully chosen words that conveyed probably the most important journey of her life were deliberately written in Arabic. Hakima succeeded in expressing emotions in her mother tongue that were first conveyed by the visual image. The researchers in the project observed that students' contributions shifted dramatically when they were told that they could express themselves in their language of choice. Here, Wittgenstein provides a valuable insight: "The limits of my language are the limits of my word, all I know is what I have words for: language was a cage for the memory" (1960: 115).

The use of their mother tongues enabled the students to better express what they wanted to say. For them, Italian was a second language in which they were not yet proficient at the time of the interviews. This is often the case with vehicular languages. It is also noteworthy that some words do not have their equivalents in other languages. A second and more important point to note is that engagement with memory contextually requires a privileged and preserved identity that often only uses the mother tongue.

Over the last forty years, studies on the neuropsychology of language have demonstrated that there are two kinds of memory: short-term and long-term memory (the latter is the memory considered in this chapter). These can be implicit (unconscious learning of motor and cognitive skills entailing the deepest structures of the brain, such as basal ganglia and the cerebellum) or explicit (e.g., semantic memory, which uses general knowledge of the world and is activated in the cortex of the left hemisphere, and episodic memory, activated in the deep structures of both hemispheres). Research on mnestic processes in bilingual subjects has demonstrated that depending on the times and modalities of acquisition, the types of memory involved differ. Paradis (1994) posits that a bilingual subject usually uses implicit memory in relation to L1 (the native language or mother tongue), whereas L2 (the second or foreign language) can be associated with implicit or explicit memory, depending on the contexts and modalities of contact with the second language (Fabbro 1996: 103, and Cardona 2001: 44–67).

Learning a foreign language does not simply mean adding one language to another. The learning process does not just entail addition; it is a process that involves a resignification of the entire language system and of the associative network that holds meanings together. A new name and a new word are not merely intellectual acquisitions; they are elements that modify the entire context of an individual's relationships with objects because emotional investments in particular words differ across languages.[6] The process of learning a second language entails an emotional distancing from words in the mother tongue that is uncomfortable. This is because it is necessary for adults learning a foreign language to question, if not renounce, some of the emotional aspects of language, which, together with other aspects, structure their identities.

Thus, remembering, writing, and expression in the mother tongue all have different meanings, values, and outcomes compared with those conducted in another language. Accordingly, the views of some scholars, activists, writers, and artists who are working and have worked on the importance of the mother tongue are discussed here. In her December 2012 "TEDx Beirut" talk titled "Don't kill your language,"[7] Suzanne Talhouk, a poet and advocate of deploying the Arabic language as a tool of power, pride, and unity, provides the following warning: "What's lost in translation is not just a word here and there, but a collective voice, a collective memory, a culture's presence in the world. Using your mother tongue, in short, is nothing less than a civic duty. . . . Language isn't just for conversing. Language represents specific stages in our lives, and terminology that is linked to our emotions."

For her TED audience in Beirut, Talhouk recalls the emotionally charged slogan of Lebanon's "Cedar Revolution" in 2005.[8] The chant "*Hurriyya, Siyada, Istiqlal*" ("Freedom, Solidarity, Independence") reverberated through the streets of the city, and, as Talhouk observes, continues to conjure up the scenes of mass protests: "Each one of you draws a specific image in [your] own mind; there are specific feelings of a specific day in a specific historical period." Talhouk further argues that the words, once translated, lose their emotional impact. She asks: "If your son came up to you and said, 'Dad, have you lived through the period of the "freedom" slogan?' how would you feel?" Moreover, she asks, pointedly, what feelings would be evoked in someone with English as a first language by a famous English expression, but with a substitute Arabic word—"God save the *malika*" instead of "God save the Queen." Thus, her point is that "this isn't just about language, but about culture, society, memory, community."

Referring to her time in Germany with her parents, Agota Kristof makes the following observations about the importance of language in her autobiographical novel: *L'Analfabeta* (*The Illiterate*):

> In the beginning there was just one language. Objects, things, feelings, colors, dreams, letters, books—they were that language. I could never imagine that there could be another language, that a human being could speak words I could not understand. . . . I was nine when we moved. We moved to a border town where at least a quarter of the population spoke German. To us, as Hungarians, it was the enemy's language, because it reminded us of the Austrian rule, and it was also the language of soldiers who were occupying our country at the time. (2005:54)

Subsequently, in France with her husband and daughter, she makes the following observations:

> We are refugees. . . . What's strange is that I have few memories of all this. As if everything took place in a dream, or in another life. As if my memory refused to remember the moment I lost an important part of my life. I left my secret writing diary, and my first poems as well in Hungary. I left there my siblings, my parents, without telling them, without saying goodbye or bidding farewell. . . . We all know what it means to end up in Hungary: jail for crossing the border illegally, and bullets [shot] by drunk Russian border guards. . . . This is where [the] desert begins. [A] social desert, [a] cultural desert. Silence, emptiness, nostalgia for home, family and friends replace the excitement about the revolution days and the escape. . . . I went back to [being] illiterate. I could read at 4. I know words. When I read them, I don't

recognize them. Letters do not match with anything. . . . The girl is about to turn six, and she's about to start school. Me too, I'm going back to school. At 27 . . . . This language, French, I did not choose it. It was forced on me by fate, by circumstance. I know I will just never be able to write like French-born writers. But I will write as best as I can. It's a challenge. The challenge of an illiterate. (Kristov 2005: 25–26, 36, 41–42, 50–52)

"Symbolic," Personal, and Collective Steps

Differing from his classmates, Moulay, a Moroccan student who was interviewed in Turin in 2013, decided to represent his journey figuratively through a symbolic drawing instead of a "map." He drew a suitcase, which is an exemplary symbol of and equipment for travel. Moulay used a sort of "visual grammar" that immediately activates connections in the observer's eyes. He chose to express himself through a universal symbol that is immediately codifiable and identifiable by all travelers, viewers, and especially migrants. As Tolia-Kelly points out, "These active connections with memories through visual and material cultures constitute processes of identification for a group" (2010: 2).

Many artists who have worked on migration have focused their attention on travelers. Among them are Victor López González and Bruno Catalano. López González created the "smuggler" image for the VIAPAC project,[9] which, as a symbol and allegory of a person who crosses all borders and exceeds these limits, can be deployed to deconstruct and interrogate the concept of borders. The protagonist, Antonio Giavelli, who is a former smuggler, recounts the problems and experiences he faced while smuggling between Italy and France in the Stura Valley located between Italy and France. In the temporal space of the video, he encounters a fictitious smuggler of our time, who tries with the help of donkeys, loaded with his "illegal goods"—an indefinite number of images—to transgress the boundary line.[10] Among these, a suitcase, the symbol of traveling, crossing borders, and moving goods, stands out.

The second artist is Bruno Catalano, who created a work called "The Travelers,"[11] which depicts two migrants or wanderers, both holding their suitcases. Men and women lack body parts and their "holes" come to be filled by the surrounding landscape, so that they merge and become one with the landscape. More tangibly, it is striking how the suitcase becomes the focal point of the sculpture, grounding it and serving as the cornerstone that keeps the travelers standing, in spite of their "holes."[12] Such travelers walk the streets of the world with suitcases full of dreams, disappointments, skills, and future opportunities. These works are almost surreal, wherein empty spaces weigh the same as filled spaces and where absence becomes presence. They are highly intersubjective artistic works that fully engage the viewer. Whoever

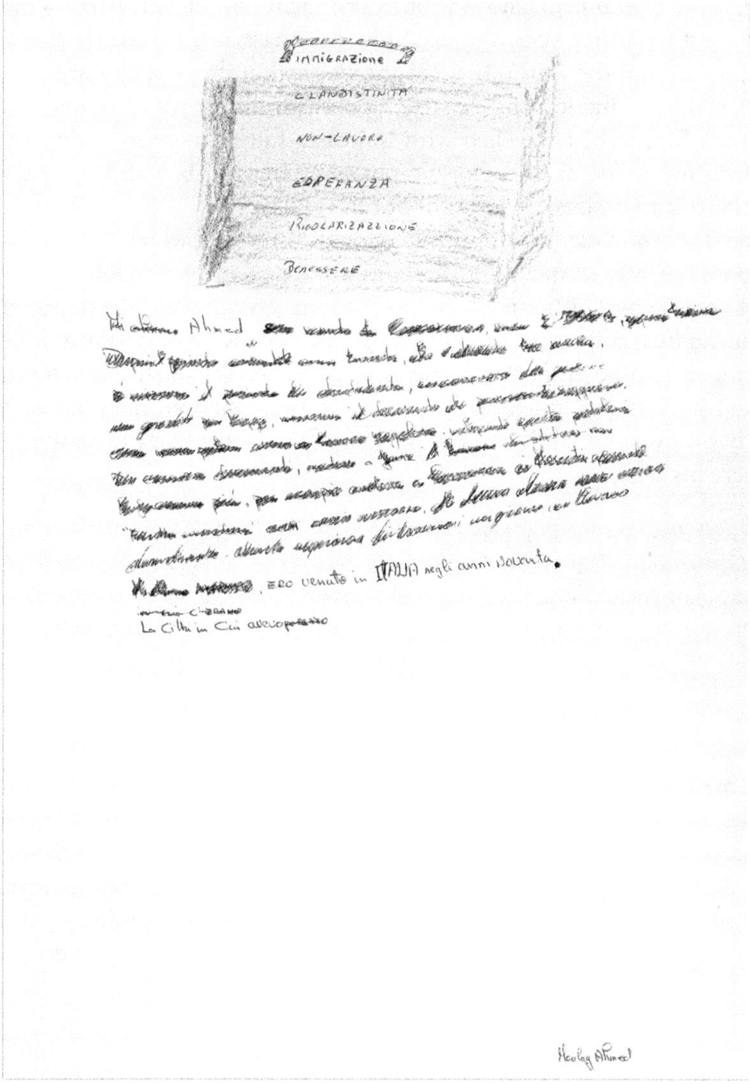

FIGURE 2.3. Moulay's Map: *Universal and Biographic Language; Words Said and Denied.* Published with Permission.

observes them can fill them in with whatever they want to see beyond the "shreds" or missing body parts. They are "broken" and nomadic human beings; figures that are inhabited by the places through which they have traveled, place that may welcome them if, after leaving other places, people, and lives, they want to or can stop and stay in them.

Sculptor Bruno Catalano was born of Italian and French parents in Morocco, and for thirty years, he lived like the characters he creates as a sailor traveling around the world. In 1975, he stopped in the port city of Marseille, which is the destination and departure point for thousands of people: "Coming from Morocco, I travelled with 'suitcases full of memories' that I often put into my work. It does not simply show images, but also my personal experience and desires: my origins, but in motion."[13]

The discussion can now return to Moulay's suitcase, which is abstract and composed of "steps," including difficulties and goals, dreams, and aspirations. These steps begin with arrival in a new country as an immigrant, culminating in the final step, which Moulay described as the yearned-for well-being. Here, it should be emphasized and kept in mind (for further developments and reflections) that in Moulay's drawing and explanation, the suitcase is not strictly his own; rather, it belongs to "many." He never said "I," as the travelers were his subjects.

> Here, I drew a suitcase as people tend to hold it when they travel. Here, I drew different steps. This is the illegal immigration step. You get here as an immigrant, but you're illegal and can't work because you're not allowed to stay here. You can only hope they [will] make a law to regularize this situation. After that, you can find your well-being, what you've been looking for after all this traveling.

While speaking, Moulay pointed to all of these steps, beginning at the top with the first, which was probably placed intentionally next to the suitcase handle, as if to suggest "taking our future and life into our own hands," "making sometimes risky decisions," and taking full responsibility for them. The steps depicted are immigration–illegality–no job–regularization–well-being.

In the drawing, a suitcase, broken in half through the middle by a straight line, can be seen. The first three steps are negative, but then "hope" somehow leads to regularization, that is, to recognition of a right. These steps represent the only way of reaching the bottom of the suitcase, its base, which is its deepest part where Moulay wants to put down his roots and find well-being. These steps make the gap between formal citizenship and the reality of living in a country, working, or studying there explicit, depicting what Sassen (1992) has termed "effective nationality" or "informal citizenship." The notion of effective nationality refers to a specific contemporary condition that Sassen conceptualizes as arising from years spent in a country living and functioning as a legal citizen, attending school there, holding a job, and raising a family—but without formal recognition. As Sassen (2000: 283) points out, immigrants' "identities as members of a community of residence assume some of the features of citizenship identities," with the only difference being that they were born elsewhere, or in the case of Europe, outside of the European Union. What emerges in the biographies of the informal citizens of *Speeches* is a far more complex notion of citizenship and identity, of people's relationship with the place they call home.

Although Moulay chose the suitcase, which is a very common object for migrants and travelers, he personalizes it with important autobiographical details in his "secret" writing, introducing language about himself. In a unique manner, Moulay wrote autobiographical text under the suitcase, of which only the first line: "My name's Ahmed" and the last: "I came to Italy in the nineties" are readable. He wrote, "The city where . . ." but then stopped writing and erased this text. He was either unable or unwilling to answer questions on why he did this, but he said that he wrote the very same words in his notebook, and, if we (the project researchers) wished, he could share them orally, reading them out to us and his classmates. Moulay read out his story for us, and it sounded like a narration of "life notes," a stream of thoughts giving meaning to and shaping the steps of the suitcase, fixing them in time and space and securing them in relation to a well-defined self.

> My name's Ahmed; I came from Casablanca to Turin, Italy, where I was allowed to spend three months as a tourist. After that, I would become an illegal immigrant, with no documents allowing me to stay here and work legally. Although I didn't meet those requirements, I had not lost hope that I could work, doing jobs I could never imagine I would do, like the porter at wholesale markets. I would start [out] at 2 in the morning, and would go there by foot; there was no means of transport so early in the morning.

What Applebee wrote in the 1980s sheds light on the relationship between Moulay and his writing: "Writing involves a number of recursively operating subprocesses (for example, planning, monitoring, drafting, revising, editing) rather than a linear sequence" (1984: 582). He wrote, erased, wrote again, planned, wrote on an external, intimate, reassuring medium, and transferred his memories from the sheet we gave him to his notebook. Eventually, he agreed to read it out but not to leave a written trace. Why? What are the reasons behind such partial silence? Behind a denied, erased word?

Denied, Unspoken, Interrupted Words

In the case of Moulay's memories, as for many other written memories that we collected over the course of this research, we can suppose that the process of writing in a second language is nowhere near as easy and immediate as visual expression. "Linguistic uncertainty" would appear to be the most likely reason behind the erasure or blacking out of words, and their inscription in a private notebook outside of the drawing. However, Moulay's choice not to share his full story, at least in the beginning, should not be underestimated. He wrote it down, but then had second thoughts and erased it, and in doing so, he did not simply erase words without a meaning; he erased words that carried his memory. Dealing with memory inevitably entails dealing with what is erroneously seen as its alter ego: silence.

What to say and what not to say, that is, words and silence constitute an inevitable topic in discussions about memory. However, remembering always implies a dialogue between memory and oblivion, memories and counter memories, the ethics of bearing witness, and the difficulty of telling and representing. According to LaCapra, "Writing trauma means acting it out in a performative discourse or in artistic practice" (2001: 86–187). Often, however, whereas other emotions can somehow be expressed, pain gets associated with silence. As Luisa Passerini observes, there is a huge difference between silence and oblivion. She emphasizes that silence is a choice, constituting a form of memory and narration:

> It is possible not to say something because its memory is being repressed—because of a trauma, because it clashes with the present, because of individual or collective conflicts—or because the conditions for its expression do not exist or are not yet in place. Sometimes a change in such conditions breaks the silence and lets memories out; some other times, silence lasts so long, it erases memory and creates oblivion. At the same time, silence is able to nurture a story and establish a communication. (Passerini 2003: 16–17)

Various reasons can be found for a total, partial, "rethought" silence, including shame, lack of self-esteem, or the inability to accord the "right value" to memory. What is important is the inclusion of silence as a form of speech that requires equal, if not more, consideration as a form of expression.

Conclusion

In many of the compiled maps, the students chose to express themselves through a series of different language types, portraying a sort of dance between memory conveyed by words and images, respectively. Even though the method applied could be questioned, and may sometimes appear forced, the diversity of linguistic expression enabled the interviewed students to take up precious and relevant memories. The languages we analyzed were intertwined with different processes of expression, each of which embedded a crucial component of memory that could not replace the others.

The case studies examined above demonstrate that languages used to express mobility need to be fluid, in motion, and continuously migrating. A tense relationship prevails between the self and the other, with the narration inclined toward an intersubjective relationship that determines and shapes its outlines.

The "personalization of visual language" by each of the three subjects was explored: Ana Rosa's personalization of symbols (the creation of a subjective legend), Hakima's personalization of the means of transport (the plane as a mirror for feelings), and Moulay's personalization of universal objects (a suitcase that is not carried but instead "carries" the stages of life). At the onset of the process of expressing their visual memories, all three individuals felt the need to make them "subjective," with their written and oral narration following their figurative representations. In the first case (the only one entailing a geographic "map"), human figures were required first for the itinerary of mobility, followed by crosses, then written words, and finally a rich oral narration. In the second case, the plane was drawn "on impulse," appearing to be the condition, sine qua non, enabling the subject to find the right words, which in fact were directly connected with the drawing. The subject was unable or unwilling to talk about her migratory experience without drawing a connection to that visual memory. The mental process of the third subject was similar to that of the first, but with two significant differences. First, the figurative part was defined as both autobiographic and as the common/collective (Moulay stated that "all travelers carry a suitcase.") Moreover, there was an objective difficulty in speaking of the self. First, there was an attempt at writing on the map, which was then erased and rewritten in a "personal" notebook, which was finally shared orally at the request of the professionals involved in the research.

Furthermore, a comparative consideration on the types of "journey" reveals that they differed from each other both in terms of the reasons for the departure (the political situation in Venezuela, family reunion, lack of employment, and the need to provide for the original family) and in terms of the modalities and kinds of journeys ("ordinary" or life-threatening). However, none of the three subjects reported mobility-related difficulties (not even Moulay, whose journey must have entailed danger given its "illegality"); instead, they all focused on "emotional difficulties." They revealed, respectively, real and figurative deaths (such as the unfinished university) that were left behind, nostalgia about the known and fear of the unknown (during the flight), and the "narration of life stages" in Italy (especially those relating to language, documents, jobs, and discrimination, as the stages drawn in Moulay's map).

In this regard, Ana Rosa and Moulay both engaged, importantly, in political and social condemnation, beginning with their biographic experiences and subsequently condemning the unsustainable and unspeakable life conditions commonly experienced by migrants. Another language was used to express memories: a "grammar of outrage" that constitutes an image of the dark side of migrant hosting.

Finally, the three case studies can also be seen to "dialogue" with each other in relation to similarities and differences regarding the choice of language, which is the first form of subjectification in the sharing of memories. Ana Rosa chose Italian as the singular language of expression of her memory; in Hakima's case, her mother tongue appeared only in writing; and Moulay wrote, erased, and rewrote "broken Italian words." The attempt in this chapter to shed some light on the mobility of languages reveals an intertwining of the mother tongue with the target language (Italian) and with a vehicular language (in this case, English). Members of our research team had an opportunity to observe how memory changes (first silent, then modified, erased, and returning) depending on the language used and the associated relationship (emotional, violent, forced, or painfully sought).

The three poles of language, mobility, and memory are intimately connected to the expression of self and, therefore, to identity. It is important to recall that the expression of self in a second language is itself the end point of linguistic mobility and also represents a "hybrid" outcome of an identity that entails and implies a form of communicative integration in the host country, and is, therefore, controlled and "artificial." In general, and from methodological, social, and political perspectives, languages in conjunction with free expression of the self and the sharing of memories are crucial for building a "new European identity." Such an identity should be pluricultural; culture does not only apply to those belonging to Europe but also to those "brought to Europe" by new nationals who want to be part of Europe and to help build a new "face"—a cosmopolitan identity that is the outcome of interactions between the local and the global. Such an identity is open to the world and available to those who are not European by birth or by education, but who choose to become so.

Giada Giustetto was a research associate on the BABE Project at the European University Institute. She teaches Italian L2 and coordinates educational programs in schools and voluntary associations, primarily aimed at women and children, and migrants with psychological disabilities. Her research interests include sexual memories in psychiatric inpatients, the boundaries between gender and body, and memories of asylum seekers in educational contexts. Her methodology has included the use of oral, visual, and written memories.

Notes

1. A language may be defined as "vehicular" when it is used to foster communication between members of different linguistic groups.
2. Within the educational system, L1 denotes the speaker's first language while L2 refers to a language learned later, usually a foreign language, but it could also be another language used in the speaker's home country.
3. In 1953, Luigi Bartolini, the painter and writer, was the first to acknowledge this meaning of this term.
4. This definition is a translation sourced from the Italian dictionary, *Il nuovo Zingarelli* (1990: 1,031), published in Bologna.
5. Tomkin's theatrical interest endured even while he was formulating concepts that would later evolve into affect theory. At heart, Tomkin was a dramatist, bringing this understanding of people and their relationships into his conception of affect theory. Dramatists know that acting is not about memorizing the words on a page. Although the task of learning three hundred lines of text may appear formidable, this is actually the easiest part of an actor's work. Acting is about taking those lines and packing each and every word—and the spaces between words—with emotional nuances.
6. Here, Lévi-Strauss' reflection that cheese and *fromage* evoke different thoughts is pertinent: "As for myself, who has spoken English exclusively during certain periods of my life without ever, however, becoming bilingual, *fromage* and *cheese* mean the same thing, but with different shadings. *Fromage* evokes a certain heaviness, an oily substance not prone to crumble, and a thick flavor. This term is especially suitable for denoting what dairymen call *pâtes grasses* (high in butter-fat content), whereas *cheese*, which is lighter, fresher, a little sour, and which crumbles in the mouth (compare the shape of the mouth) reminds me immediately of the French *fromage blanc*. The 'archetypal cheese,' therefore, is not always the same for me, according to whether I am thinking in French or in English" (Lévi-Strauss 1958: 110). This difference arises because emotional and sensory paths, as well as the relational roots that characterize the learning of a language and its vocabulary, differ for each individual.
7. See https://www.ted.com/talks/suzanne_talhouk_don_t_kill_your_language?language=en.
8. For details, see https://tavaana.org/en/content/cedar-revolution-lebanon-0.
9. Supported by the Piedmont Regional Authority, the VIAPAC project created a 200-km itinerary as a "route" for contemporary art connecting the alpine regions of France and Italy. Its aim was to enhance the uniqueness of the culture and nature of this region by displaying the works of major contemporary artists. For this international project, sculptures and permanent installations were created, in addition to the development of cultural tours for exploring cross-border areas between France and Italy. A novel aspect of this project has entailed its consideration of a rural and mostly mountainous area as an alternative area for exposition of and experimentation with an integrated cultural policy.
10. The video work uses a labyrinthine narrative strategy with various levels of "reality" to create a common space in the time between two figures. In the video installation, images from different geographical regions of the Stura Valley converge with shots of high-tech industries that are located there, which suggests a common cartography for both protagonists and a way of thinking about history.
11. See http://brunocatalano.com/sculpture-bronze/Le-Grand-Van-Gogh_2_.php, accessed 18 May 2020.
12. All twenty-five figures constituting an itinerant display in different European port cities include a suitcase evoking the journey for the viewer; a theme that is dear to the artist.

The bronze sculpture is fragmented, with no bright colors, giving it an old-worldly charm. Each figure is missing a body part; therefore, it appears as if these incomplete beings have left behind pieces of themselves in each of the places they went to, thus highlighting the true essence of the traveler. When we travel, we leave behind pieces of ourselves in the places we visit that stay where they are, timeless and spaceless. At the same time, we are marked by the spaces we cross, which in turn become part of us.
13. See http://www.racnamagazine.it/sculptures-for-a-world-in-transit-the-voyageurs-of-bruno-catalano3880/, accessed 18 May 2020.

References

Applebee, Arthur N. 1984. "Writing and Reasoning." *Review of Educational Research* 54, no. 4: 577–96.
Aronoff, Mark. 1985. "Orthography and Linguistic Theory: The Syntactic Basis of Masoretic Hebrew Punctuation." *Language* 61, no. 1: 28–72.
Barthes, Roland. 1982. "Il messaggio fotografico" ["The Photographic Message"]. In *L'ovvio e l'ottuso: Saggi critici* [*Image Music Text*]. Torino: Piccola Biblioteca Einaudi.
Bloomfield, Leonard. 1933. *Language.* Chicago: University of Chicago Press.
Cardona, Mario. 2001. *Il ruolo della memoria nell'apprendimento delle lingue: una prospettiva glottodidattica* Torino: Utet Libreria.
Echterhoff, Gerald. 2008. "Language and Memory: Social and Cognitive Processes in Media." In *Cultural Memory Studies: An International and Interdisciplinary Handbook*, edited by Astrid Erll and Ansgar Nünning, 263–74. Berlin: Walter de Gruyter.
Erll, Astrid, and Ansgar Nünning, eds. 2008. *Cultural Memory Studies: An International and Interdisciplinary Handbook.* Berlin: Walter de Gruyter.
Fabbro, Franco. 1996. *Il cervello bilingue: Neurolinguistica e poliglossia.* Roma: Astrolabio.
Fillmore, Charles. 1981. "Pragmatics and the Description of Discourse." In *Radical Pragmatics*, edited by Peter Cole, 143–166. New York: Academic Press.
Fortunati, Vita, and Elena Lamberti. 2008. "Cultural Memory: A European Perspective." In *Cultural Memory Studies: An International and Interdisciplinary Handbook*, edited by Astrid Erll and Ansgar Nünning, 127–37. Berlin: Walter de Gruyter.
Hirsch, Marianne. 2012. *The Generation of Postmemory: Writing and Visual Culture after the Holocaust.* New York: Columbia University Press.
Keim, Jean A. 1962. "The Picture and Its Frame." *Diogenes* 10, no. 38: 95–111.
Kristof, Agota. 2005. *L'Analfabeta [The Illiterate].* Bellinzona: Casagrande.
Lacan, Jacques. 1971. *Il seminario, libro XVIII: Di un discorso che non sarebbe del sembiante?* [*Seminar XVIII: On a Discourse That Might Not Be a Semblance*]. Torino: Einaudi.
LaCapra, Dominick. 2001. *Writing History, Writing Trauma.* Baltimore: Johns Hopkins University Press.
Lévi-Strauss, Claude. 1958. *Anthropologie structurale.* Paris: Plon.
Liu, Chang-Kang. 1996. *Research on English Composition.* Taipei: The Crane Publishing Co. Ltd.
Mirzoeff, Nicholas. 1998. "What Is Visual Culture?" In *The Visual Culture Reader*, edited by Nicholas Mirzoeff, 3–13. London: Routledge.
Paradis, Michel. 1994. "Neurolinguistic Aspects of Implicit and Explicit Memory: Implications for Bilingualism and SLA." In *Implicit and Explicit Language Learning*, edited by N. Ellis, 393–419. London: Academic Press.

———. 2009. *Declarative and Procedural Determinants of Second Languages*. Amsterdam: John Benjamins Publishing Company.

Pass, Madison, K. 2016. "The Relationship between the Written Word and Visual Art." Undergraduate Honors Thesis, Laramie, University of Wyoming.

Passerini, Luisa. 2003. *Memoria e utopia: Il primato dell'intersoggettività*. Torino: Bollati Boringhieri.

Renan, Ernest. 1882. *Qu'est-ce qu'une nation?* Paris: Presses-Pocket.

Sapir, Edward. 1921. *Language: An Introduction to the Study of Speech*. New York: Harcourt, Brace.

Sassen, Saskia. 1992. *The Global City: New York, London, Tokyo*. Princeton: Princeton University Press.

———. 2000. "Towards Post-National and Denationalized Citizenship." In *Handbook of Citizenship Studies*, edited by Engin F. Isin and Bryan S. Turner, 277–91. London: SAGE Publications.

Schallert, Diane L., Glenn M. Klelman, and Ann D. Rubin. 1977. *Technical Report No. 29: Analyses of Differences between Written and Oral Language*. Urbana: Center for the Study of Reading, University of Illinois at Urbana-Champaign.

Stewart, Kathleen. 2007. *Ordinary Affects*. Durham, NC: Duke University Press.

Tolia-Kelly, Divya. 2010. "Locating Processes of Identification: Studying the Precipitates of Re-Memory through Artefacts in the British Asian Home." *Transactions of the Institute of British Geographers* 29, no.3: 314–29.

Wittgenstein, Ludwig. 1960. *Tractatus Logico-Philosophicus*. London: Routledge & Kegan Paul.

Part II

SUBJECTIVITIES IN EDUCATIONAL SETTINGS

Chapter 3

REPRESENTED BODIES, BROKEN BODIES

Visions of Transnational Subjectivities and Memories among Italian Students

Graziella Bonansea

Convergences

In this chapter, my aim is to bring into convergence some streams of thoughts about the school environment drawn from my research conducted in several schools in northern Italy and in Palermo, Sicily. My research setting was strategic, enabling me to capture the views of both native and migrant youth. The chapter is an attempt to understand the languages through which fifteen- to twenty-year-old high school students understand and *recount* contemporary Europe at a time of transformative change. In particular, the chapter brings into focus the cultural landscapes, new geographies, and images arising from movements, crossings, and the settlement of masses of people arriving from different parts of the world.

My research, which emerged out of my interest in social changes linked to movements and crossings across countries and continents, itself engendered the production of a rich variety of sources.[1] Thus, I attended to dimensions of change born of relationships, exchanges, and encounters, and shared trajectories among students bearing diverse national and transnational identities. This approach closely follows the direction of the BABE research project, which has promoted a productive debate on diversity. The students' engagement with the project encouraged them to give voice to their expectations, emotions, and desires and to envisage new projects for the future. Consequently, the BABE research process facilitated intensive exchanges among students and their articulations of difference within the participating classes.

Representations of the body constitute a basic component of this relational dimension of change. Thus, the body, perceived in terms of its parts rather than as a whole, featured prominently in the photographs, drawings, and videos produced by the students. In this chapter, I will attempt to clarify how body parts (hands, torsos, and faces) symbolically represent borders and limits. In limiting space, these bodily segments themselves resemble borders and boundaries, depicting fragmented social space and mirroring media and communicative models (see Foucault 1978).

From 2013, students participating in the BABE Project were encouraged to express the patterns of their own subjectivity. Consequently, the students chose to foreground the body as the focus of their representations. These representations are integral aspects of a complex process and also represent a goal in the itinerary of the groups of students who were involved in the project.

At the same time, this thematic preference for the body can be seen as an indirect critique of the cultural strategies deployed by Italian schools, reflecting blindness to and concealment of the body. In my dual capacity as a teacher and a scholar, I have been a witness to the increasingly residual role of the body in education. This becomes increasingly apparent as children progress from kindergarten up to high school. In the educational context, with students' advancing ages, the body's role becomes increasingly residual. It becomes an object of their attention only through its imperfections during episodes of abuse, or in sex education. In schools, sex education is taught like any other subject, representing the loss of a unique opportunity to explore feelings and emotions. Accordingly, the body is rarely engaged with as a tool for knowledge production and a site for intersubjective exchanges between the sexes, and between generations, and, above all, as a site of resistance to codified translations within cultural and symbolic systems. The latter role in particular was foregrounded in the perceptions of migrant children.

Between Regression and Immobility: The Italian School Context

Over the course of many years of high school teaching, I have adopted a double role as a teacher and researcher, blending pedagogy and the transmission and study of individual and collective identities of male and female students (Bonansea 2000). In this dual capacity, I have witnessed the increasing interventions of the Ministry of State Education, leading to the gradual bureaucratization of education. The effects of this bureaucratization on the relationship between schools and other educational agencies in Italy have been increasingly evident since the onset of the new millennium.

A gradual decline in cooperation between pedagogical institutions and national cultural associations, which is also linked to diminishing economic investments, has brought to a halt several initiatives attempting to foster dialogue among researchers, scholars, and others with an interest in innovative teaching methods and approaches. Therefore, teachers' own educational backgrounds constitute the only accessible pedagogical source for many schools. Consequently, highly self-referential and closed cultural patterns are evident in many institutes. In particular, the liberal arts have suffered as a result of this limiting perspective, while technical and professional disciplines that interface with the world of practitioners have fared better and gained exposure to some degree of pedagogical innovation.

Over the last fifteen years, the quality of various teaching-learning activities has significantly declined. Among these processes are those associated with experimental approaches that relate to the plural subjectivities of youth, encompassing their rich biographies, gendered identities, and their use of their bodies and gestures as sites of learning in their interactions within an educational context. Along with the limited focus on the rich biographies of students with diverse origins, teaching approaches increasingly demonstrate a partitioning trend that disallows connections between taught subjects—for example, history and geography, economics and literature, and art history and law. As a teacher, I observed that each subject was considered a delimited, uncommunicative universe in accordance with the established pedagogical order.

This confining trend is also evident in the teaching sources of individual disciplines, notably history. In historical textbooks, which are often the only source of learning about history for students, the histories of several countries get only a brief mention. This is evident, for example, in the case of East European countries that are the places of origin of a large proportion of children of both first- and second-generation migrants.[2]

Similarly, there are no specific references to historical events in the Balkan countries (Albania, the Republics of Macedonia and Romania, and the former Republic of Yugoslavia) or in the Maghreb countries (Morocco, Algeria, Tunisia, and Libya) in teaching materials on twentieth century cultural history. The histories of these latter countries are only mentioned in the context of Italian, French, and British colonialism. Otherwise, as for the Balkans, they are referred to solely as countries that emerged following the collapse of the Ottoman and Austro-Hungarian Empires after World War I. It seems that such countries are being denied the right to their own histories that are independent of colonialism or neocolonialism within textbooks. This raises the question of what this absence might mean for Albanian, Romanian, Moroccan, and Tunisian students. Moreover, how might this void affect perceptions of history and European memory, understood as a cultural heritage? Further, how is it possible to examine history more generally from this space of emptiness? This issue brings into question the entire edifice of school subjects and prompts an urgent global call for revisiting the thematic articulation of the educational transmission process beyond just inclusion of content within school syllabi. Moreover, this concern is not limited to historical topics.

This impoverishment of school education, which is part of a process of rationalization and assimilation through which otherness is translated into specific schemes, also entails an assessing gaze directed at students' skills and competences. Assessments tend to classify, codify, and render their subjects visible. Students' cognitive development conveys a transmitted knowledge that is being increasingly fragmented, disciplined, and partitioned. In the course of my teaching experience, I have witnessed the difficulties undergone by many students from different parts of Eastern Europe, particularly Romania, coping with this system designed to assess their knowledge and competences. It is a deterministic system, influenced by a taxonomic approach derived from an Anglo-Saxon, neopositivist-inspired tradition within the social sciences that has prevailed from the end of the 1970s. The transmission of content is increasingly controlled and monitored under this system (Bloom et al. 1956), which does not consider students' backgrounds and is, therefore, increasingly disconnected from their diverse cultural identities. In such an educational setting, the process of acquiring knowledge becomes technical and rigid.

In my own teaching work, I observed how an assessment system based on indicators for the reception, comprehension, application, and organization of learning material affected students' behavioral patterns. Students undergoing a process of observation, measuring, decoding, and assessment (Mager 1984) demonstrate behavioral patterns that express a loss of personal independence and constrained critical skills. As this chapter shows, students' own representations of broken and fragmented bodies can be linked to the processes of rationalization and transmission that they experience at school. Moreover, in such a context, the accumulated wealth of knowledge and experience of each succeeding generation becomes increasingly unacknowledged and unsupported. Thus, the experimental methodological approach developed over the course of the BABE Project was aimed at recovering this cultural repository of knowledge and skills.

The Specificity of the School Case

Notwithstanding the significant contradictions inherent in the Italian school system, it is important to acknowledge that many teachers are still able to conduct long-term projects aimed at linking pedagogy and research. These projects are the outcomes of their advanced skills, their development of well-structured methodologies, and their considerable professionalism, illustrated by their care and attention to their students and to their stories. When gathering sources and materials in schools, I targeted such teachers. Applying strategies that are characteristic of the oral history, I attempted to forge diverse relational networks in southern and northern Italy. This strategy enabled me to gain access to different high schools. Between 2013 and 2016, I worked intensively with two hundred students aged fifteen to twenty years, attending schools near Turin and in Palermo.[3] From the outset, I attempted to integrate the cultural themes of colonialism, post-colonialism, and the phenomenon of new migration that students were grappling with and that constitute the underlying core of the BABE research. I next considered the trajectories of migrants from the African continent who moved to Europe from the 1990s up to 2016. During our discussions, including those held within small groups, we spoke of the wars, social conflicts, and forms of poverty that prompted the departures of their families from their countries of origin.

The issue of time and its allocation was a distinctive and prominent feature of my work with high school students, given that students spend more time at school than students at the Centri Territoriali Permanenti (permanent territorial centers—CTPs). Migrant students attend classes and training courses of short duration to learn the Italian language at the intercultural centers of the CTPs (see Giada Giustetto's chapter in this volume on this topic). By contrast, teaching–learning activities at schools extend over nine months of the year, providing opportunities for the production of sources, including drawings, photographs, texts, videos, and objects of various kinds. Thus, the time students spend at school, comprising different phases for the acquisition of competences and knowledges, is longer than that spent at CTPs and could be synchronized with teaching activities in the production of the research sources.

The duration of time that students spent at school facilitated their deep engagement with the main themes of the BABE Project—representations of migration, cultural mixing, exchanges, new spatial configurations, and a geographic perspective that is linked to feelings and emotions—in the teaching of school subjects. Within the working groups that were formed, the subjectivities of students with migrant backgrounds were not experienced neutrally. They had some influence initially on students' interactions and subsequently in the framing of questions relating to historical, literary, economic, and artistic topics.

Moreover, throughout the research process, a lot of questions were raised directly by teachers and indirectly by students regarding the content of school subjects and the teaching–learning approaches applied. The biographies of the students who were the children of migrants implicitly influenced such questions. They recalled the learning methods in their countries of origin, and their cultural relevance as part of their educational experience, the roles of their teachers, and their relationships with their families. However, this attempt to rethink teaching strategies in combination with a theoretical consideration of the cultural bases, which are the foundations of the subjects themselves, proved challenging.

I can affirm, based on my experience, that the BABE Project has supported and strengthened the pedagogical models developed over the last twenty years (Biagioli 2008; Cambi 2001; Demetrio and Favaro 2002; Porteria 2003; Ricca 2013) that a few teachers have experimented with. Such models have been premised on welcoming and endorsing diversity, emphasizing the need to develop new views in the present and to imagine original ways of relating to the public and private spheres. Accordingly, subjectivity itself is valued as an open and ongoing process entailing exchanges and relationships between figures and roles in the school setting: teachers and students and the teaching strategies that constitute the basis of the education offered by every school. Simultaneously, across the horizon of cultural memory,[4] the Project gave voice to prejudices and stereotypes that were transmitted and acquired (Assmann 2011). Such aspects of cultural memory are linked to networks, family structures, contexts, and referential groups. Social and collective realities convey sentiments and emotions as well as removals and silences that reflect feelings of loneliness, abandonment, fear, nostalgia, and of being wounded. Thus, from its inception, the BABE Project engaged with dimensions targeted for transformation that are of significance in relation to school policies while simultaneously influencing students' awareness, which was expressed in their representations of the body.

The Dialectic between Sources and Visuality

From a methodological perspective, the sources in this study comprised students' productions in response to a series of video sequences[5] produced by artists whose works engage with migration, passages, transits, and border crossings of escaping bodies but also with the rejection of individuals and of groups through forms of deletion and silencing. The artistic research productions shown to the students directly convey representations of marginalization and rejection,[6] simultaneously portraying the need to construct particular kinds of identities and social relationships in European countries. In particular, students' responses were shaped by their perception of the push for change conveyed in the video sequences. On the one hand, the videos served at a methodological level as an *aide mémoire*, eliciting personal thoughts and memories; on the other hand, they revealed a cultural heritage that belonged to migrant youth, prompting them to recount their personal stories. This experience gave rise to debates among the students centering on new patterns of citizenship and considering transnational identities and relationships between the public and private spheres.

After viewing the videos, videotaped interviews were conducted with individuals and groups before the students embarked on their productions of different types of sources. As previously mentioned, the students developed a wide variety of sources: video productions, photograph collections, captions, collages, and objects, such as a little paper house constructed by a female student from Palermo titled "Ciò che porti con te" ("What you bring with you").

A particular focus of attention was on visuality at the beginning and at the conclusion of the research itinerary, which encouraged the students to articulate images of their lived experience. In addition to the images, and considering the phases of youth that are marked by "transitions" from one age to the next, students' patterns of self-representation alternated, frequently signifying a need to be manifest and seen but also a need to hide and be silent (Boltanski 1999). These are patterns that cross the languages of oral, written, and visual traditions, supporting choral and dialectic memories resulting from continual interactions between familial cultures, class membership, gender, and exchanges within groups in the classroom. Evidently, the sources produced by students within their networks of relationships, contacts, and patterns of sharing were strengthened because they themselves constituted a platform for accumulating recollections, pictures, traces, and languages.

Parallels between Experiences and Narrative Patterns

In 2014 and 2015, the efforts of the students of two high schools located near Turin to connect different visions of Europe gave rise to intensive dialogues concerning the characters featured in the videos they saw. This dialogue prompted the drawing of parallels between the stories depicted in the films and some of the migrant children's biographical events. In their descriptions, the students focused in particular on the characters' bodies. They described the faces of men and women in Adrian Paci's videos, namely *Centro di Permanenza Temporanea* (2007) and *The Column* (2013), as well as the face of the young Senegalese girl who was the main protagonist in Ursula Biemann's "Coumba's Boat Passage" (2006–2007). One student observed that the faces of the Moldavian children in Ed Moschitz's *Mama Illegal* (2011) were marked by pain.

In March and April 2014, the students in two classes at the Scientific High School near Turin took several photographs focusing thematically on both inclusion and exclusion. The first scenes are of the exclusion of two female students, Asia H., whose mother is Somalian, and Sara P., who is of Nepali origin, by their classmates. In the following scenes, these students are successfully integrated within the class and begin a dialogue with their classmates. The final scenes depict the whole class forming a tight circle around Sara and Asia, mimicking a dance that unites them all. The moving bodies symbolically convey a barrier and its overcoming.

I now turn to an analysis of particular cases relating to this theme of inclusion and exclusion that allows me to explore more deeply the visual languages used by the students. I begin my analysis with a photograph comprising two sequences taken by students from Vittorio Emanuele II, a grammar high school located in Palermo, in April 2016.[7] This source is drawn from a night scene, depicted in *Mama Illegal* (2011), in which a woman, man, and their child are walking toward a bus that transports men and women from Moldavia to Austria and Italy. The lights of the bus cause the figures to appear like shadows.

This aesthetic pattern also appears in the students' photograph depicting the shadows of two young girls standing next to each other. It is important to note that the focus of attention in the picture is on these children. The students were moved by the plight of the Moldavian children in Moschitz's film, deprived of their mothers who had departed for different European countries. Consequently, the children experienced loneliness and abandonment, living with their grandparents and rarely seeing their fathers.

Although the students watched several artistic video productions, their collectively produced photographic sequence does not focus directly on migrants. Instead, it highlights the *removal* of the gaze that is directed away from them (figure 3.1). This picture critically introduces a narrative strand relating to the perception of social space as emptiness, distance, and otherness. The caption written by the students that accompanies the picture states that migrants do not have any rights; they are just shadows, mere appearances. They are powerless and uncared for, faced with the indifference of so many European citizens.

The picture, which has been subtly edited, comprises two photographs taken from different perspectives. In both of the photographs, the gaze and its relation to the positioning of the body effectively portrays a closed attitude of unavailability toward people in the vicinity of the subject. This attitude may convey the inability to respond to external solicitation with anything other than indifference. The title of the photograph, "*Ragazzo ombra*" ("Boy shadow"), is also revealing, indicating the boy rather than the stylized figures of the little girls is actually the shadow.

FIGURE 3.1. *"Ragazzo ombra"* – "Shadow Boy." By Giovanni P., Ginevra C., Gaia D. F., Leonardo B., Maria Laura T., and Rebecca A. Palermo, 2016.

In May 2016, at an exhibition of the drawings, photographs, and videos produced by the students in Palermo who participated in the BABE Project,[8] I asked some of the students to comment on this sequence of photographs in the context of the sources themselves. Some of them highlighted the relationship between the picture and words like *marginalization*, *border*, *exclusion*, and *imagination*. Others focused on an image conveyed in "Don't Ask Me for Words," a poem by Eugenio Montale that they had studied and subsequently used as an aesthetic frame for the photograph. In the students' picture, not only is the boy unable to see the shadows around him, but also—with reference to Eugenio Montale's poem, an extract of which is cited below—he does not even care about the shadow of his own body on the wall behind him.

> Ah, that man so confidently striding,
> friend to others and himself, careless
> that the dog day's sun might stamp
> his shadow on a crumbling wall! (Montale 1994)

As I will show further along in this chapter, the students frequently mentioned that the inspiration for their productions also came from poems they had studied. This linkage to such texts was highly empathetic, indicating that lyrical poems may be more effective than other artistic languages in representing certain aspects of the living conditions and experiences of youth. This case study provides valuable insights into existing tensions around the themes of rejection, indifference, and deletion from gaze at different levels.[9] According to the students, these themes have a close bearing on social attitudes and practices of isolation and segregation toward groups of migrants that are characteristic of Palermo's urban context.

Wall-Bodies

Given such a perspective whereby a young body becomes (willingly or not) a mirror of rejection and an object of disinterest as a social attitude, it would be useful here to draw parallels with two other pictures. These comprise a photograph (figure 3.2a) and a drawing (figure 3.2b) within a collection produced by students from Marie Curie Science High School in Pinerolo, a town located near Turin. The photograph in figure 3.2a, which was taken by Selene M.,[10] evokes the image of a wall, even if the surrounding purple light detracts from the harshness and inviolability of the barrier. In the photograph, a young woman (Selene) stands against a grilled window that obstructs her. Light penetrates through the window but beyond it, nothing is in sight. It appears that the girl is reacting to the grid by performing a dance step that challenges the barrier, opening up a path going forward and upward. This suggests that breaking pressure and overwhelming tension can emerge from and within the body. The gap between the picture and the window grid is represented in an exemplary way by a pair of ballet shoes abandoned on the floor.

The same theme of an obstacle and barrier can be seen in figure 3.2b, which depicts a drawing by Chaima C.,[11] a female student of Moroccan origin. The drawing shows a young woman inside a glass case. The female body within this enclosed space attempts to break out through a Herculean sprint that engages the whole body from the feet to the hair. In both pictures, the jump enacted by each of the bodies signifies the search for a way out. However, in both cases, the bodies are stuck. Contrasting with the unaware and indifferent act of the "Boy shadow " in the previous photograph, Chaima's drawing depicts the female figure enclosed within a glass case/cage that is a tangible element imprisoning the body.

In Chaima's drawing, this element of closing in/exclusion is of particular significance, as depicted in the polyhedron hive, made up of cells, beside the case. The cells are thick and black and, as Chaima explains in the caption accompanying the drawing, they represent spaces around which borders are drawn, closing them off from the outside. As Chaima notes in the caption, "Borders are thick and this prevents a lot of things." The implicit reference here is to the condition of those attempting, unsuccessfully, to cross borders. The bee will not be allowed to enter the cells.

In this case too, there is a literary reference, namely a poem by Giovanni Pascoli titled "Il gelsomino notturno" ("The Night Jasmine"), from the collection *I Canti di Castelvecchio* (1907) in Baruffi (2017) that the students studied at school during the period of the research. In the poem, the parallelism between the drawing and the following lines is highly effective and persuasive: "A late bee murmurs/ finding all taken the cells." The text of the entire poem (written by the poet in celebration of his friend's wedding) conveys an

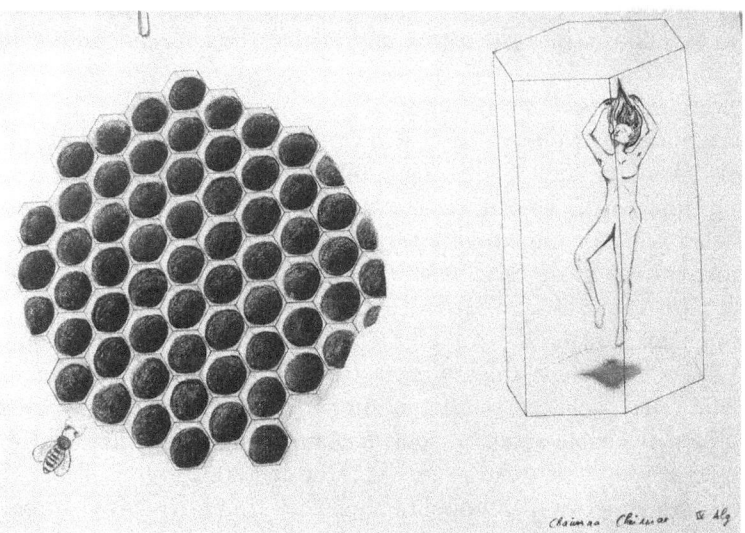

FIGURE 3.2. The imprisoned body and exit strategies: photograph (Figure 3.2a, by Selene M., Pinerolo, 2014) and drawing (Figure 3.2b, Chaima C., Pinerolo, 2014).

erotic metaphor along with symbolic imagery of limits; the obstacle that prevents an individual from overcoming the conditions in which he or she lives.

As previously discussed, the students' productions reveal the intertwining of visual images and *didactic* and literary content sourced from the students' school subjects. On an iconographical level, the sources simultaneously highlight the relationship between social beliefs, collective tensions, and the personal changes and memories that students themselves bring with them.

Narrative Forms

The narration of walls and borders through images of bodies that are always connected to the lived conditions of youth, and to their levels of communication, is also evident in the captions accompanying the pictures. This narrative was shared by students of different nationalities. In the captions of the photographs and the drawings, the unaware students naively highlighted the relationship between the walls erected by European countries to stop migration flows and those reproduced, for example, in the context of relationships between adults and young people, which also reflect internal psychological situations.

In the students' texts, both of these levels, which are not distinct from each other, are consequential. As Selene writes, "The wall is what can stop a flow of people, but it is also the border one has inside." Chaima similarly observes that the cells of the polyhedron are so thick that they obscure a view of others and their differences. The thickness thus becomes a barrier and leads to feelings of aversion toward those who are different because individuals cannot see beyond their cells.

During the period of production of the sources, being aware of the complex relationship that youth have with written compositions and with media models (Ortoleva 2009; Stefinlongo 2006), I emphasized the importance of writing different kinds of text. The writings of native students reflected a particular tendency to neutralize social complexity and cultural images. The narrative forms that reveal discomfort with features of written languages often do not take into account the passages, links, and mediations that are necessary for showing the complexity of the represented social conditions. As I subsequently show, this is a characteristic not only of writing but also of oral narration. Therefore, schools need to engage more with approaches and methods that enable access to tools encompassing vision, knowledge, and collective as well as personal awareness (Mattozzi 2002).[12]

Thus, students' sources should be situated within integrative patterns that bring together forms of mass media communication (of spoken more than written language), interpreted as immediate translations of the given reality that are considered to be "spontaneous." What emerges in the texts is not an institutional memory linked to the country and to the territory but a memory pattern (De Cesari and Rigney 2014) that comes from the territorial context of belonging (groups, friends, and families) and extends to the horizon of the self, considered as unique and nonreplicable. In their narratives, students commonly used the expression "wanting to be themselves" at any cost.

It would seem that neither female nor male students conveyed awareness—from the perspective of generational belonging—of their heritage of narratives, imaginaries, models, narratives, and figurative patterns. In light of this finding, the process of building stereotypes should be analyzed as the basis for understanding phenomena like migration, diaspora, and the crossings of people.

The Building of Stereotypes

When engaging with the theme of stereotypes, which are present in both oral and written traditions, it is helpful to maintain a tension between the students' own narrations and the narratives promoted by schools within textbooks, particularly those on history and geography. A narrative pattern of events and situations is constructed through the linking of several kinds of writing, including those encountered at school. In this context, it is important to note the absence of a narrator in textbooks that record and communicate a definite pattern of cultural transmission following a chronological order of events. This communicative pattern lacks an order founded on the narrating "I." Consequently, the forms of intersubjectivities required to structure the patterns of imagination and of personal narration in the interlocution are absent.

From this perspective, discomfort relating to communication and the transmission of cultural content in the school context can be linked to discomfort relating to the narration of history. Memory appears to be frozen in a communicative function that is deprived of the "I," leaving space for neutral, abstract, and universal statements. This absence of the "I," which is also evident in mostly formal exchanges between teachers and students, prevents the occurrence of a mirror trick between emotions and *logos*, enabling the interlocutor to represent the event from a creative/imaginary point of view (Bonansea 2002).[13] Together with several other factors that are linked to social, cultural, and territorial belonging, this absence produces a feeling of loss and discomfort, if not aphasia (Ruml et al. 2000; Shapiro and Levine 1990; Wepman and Jones 1966), which is reflected in the young person's language. It is a language that often presents pauses, silences, a search for words, and connections in which stereotypes become reservoirs of pictures and representations. They become "cages of the language" rather than the expression of closed, still thought. In the absence of structure and complex narrative patterns, stereotypes serve a useful communicative purpose, revealing discomfort as opposed to expressing models and patterns that are desired and deliberately chosen.

Reflecting on my experiences as a teacher, I have considered how this communicative and narrative *displacement*, connected to an impoverished acquisition of the Italian language, is very strong and limiting, particularly in the context of relationships formed between generations and between teachers and students. There are multiple factors relating to this displacement that entail for natives family conditions, the schooling process, and, above all, separation from the languages and traditions of the cultures to which they belong. What I have observed is that a broader level of communication has gradually been replaced by a highly self-referential jargon linked to the specific world of young people; a kind of clan language.

From this perspective, what emerges in schools beyond the span of more or less extensive meanings joined to the cultural baggage of individuals are overlapping codes, registers, and languages. My observations point to an often-contradictory connection between different types of languages rather than a monolingualism. I have further observed that these languages, both in more formal school situations and in peer exchanges, frequently reflect patterns and models of media communication entailing verbal and nonverbal codes. The characteristics of this communication are increased speed, contracted word usage, a pronounced synthesis of content, reduced passages in the articulation of messages, and continual references to common images. This is a form of communication that uses words related to contexts that are not only national but also local, incorporating codes expressed by students within the school environment.

These forms of language directly intervene in the construction of oral memory. As the next chapter will show, nonarticulation of the language and the production of a broken and fragmented orality encourage easy slippage into prejudices and forms of exclusion. Moreover, in their interviews, many migrant students pointed to the difficulty of having to learn a language at two levels. The first level entails shared and formal communication, and the second level is linked to the youth universe. Without any knowledge of the latter, the likelihood of a student's admission into the peer group is reduced.

Feelings, Emotions, and Prejudice

I will now present the case of Lorenzo C.[14] that shows how stereotypes and prejudice should be read as a whole within the stories that students produced. Gazes, sensibilities, and behaviors, which are at the foundation of attitudes of being closed and unavailable, can be interpreted only through the networks of relationships and exchanges with friends and mates of different nationalities, both within and outside of school.

Following the same procedure for all of the students, I first interviewed Lorenzo in a group and then alone, asking him to comment on the abovementioned videos of the artists. He immediately expressed his opinion about migrants, whom he perceived as a threat to European youth, depriving them of assured employment and future opportunities. As highlighted in the excerpt from his interview, presented below, the rhythm of his speech was fragmented and the images entailed common opinions, lacking coherence and strung together in the absence of any linker. For instance, an allusion to the horror and violence of a terrorist organization like ISIS was immediately linked to his perception of a safety risk associated with migration. He referred to migrants as "people with other cultures," who were opposed to a "we" that could denote "we Italians" but also, more broadly, "we Europeans" and even, if not willingly, "we, the young generation of the present."

> Let's say that anyway I see that our cultures are closed . . . but I think they are not so closed. Now I see with ISIS . . . what is happening in the world, and I understand it is hard to unify two societies that have such very different views. And in my opinion, also talking to people with other cultures, they also tell me that it is almost impossible . . . because they have things. . . . Also violence, some things are usual to them; they are not [seen in] the same way as we see them.

Again, in a group interview, Lorenzo insisted on this opposition between "we" and "they" (an unnamed entity). For Lorenzo, this opposition was reflected in the tension around national governmental policies in Italy, which he perceived as favoring migrants over the youth of his generation. His view was that when one social group receives something, another one is deprived of something. He observed: "The system is thinking of these people [migrants] a lot and it is thinking of us a bit. We are on the margins of society. . . . I feel like I am an Italian who is subject to discrimination."

But as he continued talking and as the questions probed deeper, Lorenzo revealed two streams of thought. Running closely parallel with his speech that directly articulated social prejudice and stereotypes ("migrants steal Italians' jobs" and "they bring a violent culture with them"), was a second articulation that was linked to his personal experience. When he began describing this experience, he became more attentive and sensitive regarding the people who come to Italy with the desire to improve their living and working conditions. A lengthy section of the interview focused on the life of a seventeen-year-old Romanian boy whom Lorenzo knew at primary and secondary school and who later died tragically: "He did not have a lot of friends. I noticed he was always alone, playing . . . in the square, so he . . . never mixed with us. However, it was difficult for him."

Following his recounting, Lorenzo dwelled on events and circumstances related to this boy: how difficult he found it to be part of a group of youth both inside and outside of the school; his vulnerability relating to the contexts at the limits of legality in which he was engaged; a social and political system that "makes people go from one country to another" without caring for the actual conditions of hosting; and feelings of uncertainty and fear that can originate from the instability of family conditions.

In the interview in which silences and pauses were frequent, Lorenzo began speaking indirectly to his "lost" generation living in a historical age in which doors are closed to everybody: both migrants and natives. The iconography of Chaima's drawings of the enclosed girl and the bee that tries to enter the cells appears to epitomize the situation of youth looking for escapes.

Lorenzo also mentioned a poem he studied at school by Giuseppe Ungaretti titled *In Memoria* (1916). The poem is about Mohammed Sceab, the poet's friend, who committed suicide in Paris in 1913. He is caught between the nomadic culture of the desert that he brings with him and the horizons of a modern age, unable to get closer and understand the wealth of differences between them. In his reference to Mohammed Sceab, who represents a people without a homeland, Lorenzo mirrors the situation of his Romanian friend. Further, the poetic device operating in this case is full of empty spaces and silences, resembling the communication of young people (Traversi 2016). The sensorial perception, the power of the visual, and the shades of poetic lines allow for acceptance and empathy.

Stereotypes entailed in this experiential pattern become narratives within a dialogue that is also linked to processes of deletion. The memory captures them in a moment of displacement when the right connections or words cannot be found. From this perspective, stereotypes are like tracks of a broken language in which the layers and levels of different meanings get mixed up and in which the prevailing meaning is of emptiness and loss.[15]

Thus, the research highlighted the need to involve native students as part of a story and memory. From that position of belonging, they could observe the reality of migration. Consequently, the telling of the story takes precedence over general declarations of principle, providing space for attitudes entailing greater awareness and a sense of social responsibility. Further, the introduction of subjectivity brings forth a perspective that leads to relationships and exchanges. Speaking from a position of "belonging," Christian C., a student at the "Michele Buniva" Higher Education Institute in Pinerolo near Torino, who was born in 1995, expresses this process of change as follows:[16]

I am glad I am here now for this interview to tell you how I have changed. I mean, you cannot keep on being narrow-minded. My girlfriend is Romanian, and my best friend is black . . . from Nigeria. My girlfriend, Daiana, lived alone in Romania until she was six; her grandparents brought her up. I was shocked when I discovered this. I felt sad when I got to know that they came here—people who are subject to discrimination, honest people—they came here to find a job, to help their families.

Bodies and Geographies

Stereotypes are useful for representing the body, which can never be separated from mass media models, reproducing a fragmented social space that reflects self-centered and clear-cut cultural attitudes. This occurred independently of the will of individual students, who demonstrated a need to develop and link social projects to exchanges in their productions of videos, maps, drawings, and photographs. Such projects entail the students' envisioning of their own bodies as narrative vehicles of emotions. In fact, body, hands, and faces may be marked by the resulting emotion. Thus, in her video, inspired by *Mama Illegal*, Elisa C.[17] shows her classmate writing words like "fear," "loss," "joy," and "change" on her (Elisa's) cheeks, forehead, and hands with a brush.

The body thus becomes a geographic space that brings to mind a wider symbolic social space. The parts of the body, which themselves mark space, denote borders and limits. This conceptualization prompted the production of a series of photographs by the students depicting hands, feet, torsos, backs, and faces almost like mechanical body parts. These sections are associated with colorful or dark stripes, lines, or barriers that imprison the body within claustrophobic or limiting situations. In some photographs, hands are depicted behind the bars of a jail cell. The light, shining on them, emphasizes their proportions, confusing genders and notions of the masculine and the feminine. These are hands that welcome migrants' preserved memories of the homes they have left behind. As revealed by the sequence of images in figure 3.3, the students who produced this series were deeply inspired by the works of artists that they had examined as a group. The image of "crowded hands" on the column brings to mind Adrian Paci's (2013) film, *The Column*,[18] emphasizing the centrality of the theme of work in this artistic production. In fact, the Palermo students decided to change the color of the column from white to a dark shade, placing dirty, red, and seemingly callused hands on it. The accompanying caption states, "It is easy to observe the completed work of art without looking at the hands that made it." They are conveying the

FIGURE 3.3. A series of pictures depicting hands and feet. Creators from left to right: Rebecca A. (Palermo 2016), Alessandra M. (Pinerolo 2014), Maria A., Rebecca A., Ginevra C., Isabella L., Katia M., Federica Z. (Palermo 2016); Asia H. I, Veronica R., Massimo M., Denisa B. (Pinerolo 2014).

view that the process of globalization of art itself entails a symbolic and actual agenda of subjection and enslavement.

The photographs of the hands are followed by a series of photographs of feet marking the land with their steps but brought to a halt in front of a line that they cannot cross. The drawing of Asia H. I. is particularly representative of her history, bringing into focus a world of visions, expectations, and projects of children of second-generation migrants. The daughter of a Somalian mother and an African father of undeclared nationality, Asia was born in 1996 in a little town near Turin. In her rich and lengthy interview, she testifies to the balance of those who stand between two transnational cultural universes; the original universe of her mother and the Italian one in which she was born and raised.

Asia produced the abovementioned drawing-map for the BABE Project, which represents the journey of her young mother traveling from Mogadishu to Italy along the northeastern Mediterranean coasts. Her testimony, which also includes her commentary on the drawing, focuses attention on the conditions of her mother's journey; the fear and suffering produced by the deaths of friends and companions at sea: ". . . I do not know how my mother made a journey like this . . . I do not know how . . . ." In the drawing, Asia's mother's footsteps are thick and black, indicating the harshness of her itinerary and her struggle to survive. Asia's footsteps are contrastingly colorful and light. They cross the Atlantic and reach Canada, where possibly Asia would like to live.

In search of a complex and strong social subjectivity, Asia extends her itinerary beyond Europe to encounter other cultures, other worlds. As the daughter of migrants, and as a citizen looking for a national identity that represents her, Asia shows a strong desire for inclusion. This desire stems from her awareness of just beginning to belong as a young Somalian woman, having repeatedly experienced forms of disparity, discomfort, and injustice within different social settings. Her story conveys her desire to combine aspects of the Somalian tradition and her future expectations as a young woman. It is precisely these expectations that lead her to imagine an increasingly active and invigorated bond—almost a form of social redemption—forged with the mother's origin and, by extension, with the entire African continent. "My dream is to become a doctor and volunteer in the poorest countries. And as a goal, I have in mind especially Africa; I really want . . . to realize also how my mother lived."

For Asia, as for other offspring of migrants, such footsteps in her drawing tangibly mark a contrast with the sufferings of these young people's parents along with the need for social rescue. Therefore, she and other classmates would like to "leave traces" in other countries, particularly in the ones that are the outcomes of the significant imbalances and inequality, as she stated earlier. These students demonstrate an engagement that is simultaneously a kind of compensation relating to the homelands of their parents, deprived of their youth and energy through migrations.

Bodies, genealogies, and social planning are thus closely linked from a perspective of personal and collective change.

From Decomposition to Dissolution

What is striking in the sequences of photographs taken by the students is the representation of parts of the body as symbolic barriers (e.g., the bare back shown by Madalina M.—figure 3.4),[19] but also the fact that frontal or direct images of the body are entirely absent. Not even faces are shown directly. The only face photographed by the students is veiled, revealing only eyes that are piercing and lively, conveying expressive power. The subject of the photograph is Chaima C., who decided to be portrayed wearing the veil typically worn in Morocco, where she comes from. The narrative, associated with Chaima's photograph, conveyed through pictures, focuses on the body, beginning with single parts, then images of the body being shielded and seen from faraway, and finally its fragmentation into inconsistent proportions that almost reach a stage of dissolution.

This distancing is also evident in Marco G.'s[20] photograph, which was taken from a bridge on the Po River—the bodies of men and women seen

FIGURE 3.4. From the body perimeter to the shadow body. Creators from top to bottom, then left to right: Massimo M., Pinerolo, 2014; Madalina M., Pinerolo, 2014; Marco G., Pinerolo, 2014; Photo y Chaima C., Pinerolo, 2014.

from high above are blurred, appearing like a vague stain. The picture is aimed at recalling the first scenes of the crowded fish market in Mbour, Senegal, in Ursula Biemann's film, "Coumba's Boat Passage," as Marco G. notes on the photograph itself.

Representations of the body fluctuate between what is visible and what is invisible; what is close and what is distant. This fluctuation prompts Massimo M., another student, to "build" a photograph (figure 3.4) that is technically edited and comprises several scenes in which a faint, almost silhouette-like figure of a young man surmounts a ruined wall, producing a large shadow on the wall of a house to the front. The symbolic aspect of overcoming the wall is evident. The photograph integrates the two narrative threads that I have examined so far: those of social space and of a multifaceted body. This is a body considered in terms of its separate parts, which, seen at a height, loses its consistency and becomes shadow-like. Thus, a parabola that the body veils and reveals itself in a play of light and shadow in which the density of the visual experience slowly dissolves, giving rise to almost evanescent figures (Perretta 2017). This imagery would seem to be reminiscent of the "shadow migrants" described by the Palermo students in the caption attached to the picture of the boy whose gaze appears to be focused solely on his mobile phone.

Concluding Remarks

The theme of the shadow raises questions about the students' cultural representations. In their photographs, the shadow assumes different values. First of all, it signifies a spatial reduction of the migrants' public and social profiles. Thus, at a symbolic level, they become mere stylized figures. This perspective was particularly prominent among students in Palermo, a city that hosts but also segregates migrants within defined and delimited spaces.

The shadow is not only a metaphor for obscurity and deletion but is also a mold and an image of an inner silence (Trevi 2009). In the photographs taken by children of both migrants and natives, several overlapping and mixed up layers were apparent: those linked to the border condition and those linked to perceptual and visual models and patterns of young men and women who are living an age of transition from adolescence to maturity. From this perspective, the shadow can be seen to be part of a complex narrative language that paradoxically focuses mainly on the body. As previously noted, it is a body that is fragmented, reflecting breaks, wounds, and human and social discontinuities, perhaps eventually dissolving and losing its centrality and unity. This path therefore encompasses the social and existential world, revealing a space in which these generations act and move. It is a floating space that is increasingly devoid of patterns of representation and self-representation that are coherent and uniform.

Therefore, the visions of these young people appear to be emphasizing the image of the threshold and of the precarious balance that they seek within this apparently floating space. It is an image infused by feelings, emotions, and perceptions, which is itself influenced by a profusion of didactic and cultural suggestions encountered at school. Notwithstanding the apparent contradictions of educational agencies, school is the central institution where students experience the transmission of cultural contents. In the captions accompanying the photographs, videos, and drawings, the students often refer to writers and poems that they studied during the research period. The poetic texts convey fragmentation, gaps, separation, and distance, which are also conveyed in the fragmented representations of the body and which assume the function of a real "objective correlative" that roots fears, uncertainty, and a sense of isolation and loneliness. Such feelings are commonly experienced by those who cross between national and transnational belonging.

The visual sources (photographs, drawings, and videos) take on strength and efficacy only through a process of sharing and in a time that expands and widens. When they encompass the heritage of familiar, genealogical, and collective memories, they constitute a cultural trail. In the practice of intersubjectivity, the richness of "heritage" becomes the creative force driving relationships among students of different nationalities. Thus, belongings fostered through a process of exchange are transformed into an active resource for engendering cultural pluralism as a positive dialectic.

The relationship between these young people with the visuality calls for analysis from a long-term perspective that takes into account social class and cultural systems and the stereotypes, prejudices, and images that they unknowingly transmit. Only then will it be possible to witness the manifestation of the desired mobility conveyed in the students' productions. Moreover, through these highly visual languages, these desires may be translated into hybrid patterns of citizenship entailing public as well as private subjectivity.

In conclusion, the BABE research found a place within these unprecedented projects in an unexpected context, namely the Italian school system, which generally lacks the capacity to grasp the challenges of cultural complexity. With the aim of fostering a new "human" and social awareness, the project encouraged and supported cultural memories, readings of a changing social landscape, expectations, desires, and dreams that rendered visible the individual and collective itineraries of these representatives of a young generation that is itself positioned at the edge.

Graziella Bonansea is a historian and writer and a member of the Italian Historical Society. She was trained in oral history with Luisa Passerini at the University of Turin and Michelle Perrot in Paris, where she earned her PhD in History and Civilization in 1991. In 1996–97, she was the recipient of a Jean Monnet Fellowship at the European University Institute in Florence. She has published numerous essays on subjectivity, oral memory, gender, and generations in relation to key historical moments in the twentieth century, such as Fascism, the World Wars, and the 1950s. Her research has delved into visual and imaginary representations of the body in the context of Italy's industrial life and total institutions (hospitals in particular), with special focus on the female body in Italian and European Protestant religious imaginary.

Notes

I would like to extend my special thanks to the principals of the various institutes and high schools who provided me with the opportunity to engage with classes and groups of students during the period 2012–2016. This exposure and the connections that they fostered enabled me to weave a rich tapestry of reflections and cultural itineraries gathered from multiple sources. Specifically, I would like to thank Velia Alletti, Marco Bolla, Danilo Chiabrando, Lina Coscarella, Virginia Tamone, Giovanni Trinchieri, and Carmelina Venuti.

I would also like to thank the following teachers: Francesco Berta, Antonella Bonetto, Lorella Pogolotti, Renata Racalbuto, Erminio Ronco, Silvia Silvestri, and Patrizia Troina, whose care, attention, and helpfulness facilitated the production of drawings, photographs, videos, and texts in the participating schools. I am deeply grateful to all of them for supporting the relationship between pedagogy and research within this study. This perspective is crucial for exploring and advancing changes and new horizons within and outside of educational institutions.

1. In this chapter, the term "source" has two specific and key meanings in relation to the subject matter discussed. On the one hand, it refers to the visual productions of artists (videos and figurative materials) that students engaged with during different phases of the work. On the other hand, "sources" refers to the productions of the students themselves and can be viewed as active responses to the former, which were intended to evoke their memories through a process of "induced reception." These latter sources comprise photographs, videos, drawings, texts, and individual and collective interviews.
2. The school context is challenging us to reconsider the languages that define subjectivities and different national and transnational identities. Words and codes are not always appropriate for translating and transmitting the cultural complexities and connections relating to each student's educational process. Conversely, they often tend to crystallize and obscure exchanges among those with different identities. While acknowledging the risk of making belonging the basic constitutive element of an individual's subjectivity, I nevertheless found that the labels "migrants' children" and "natives' children" offered possibilities for forging a common path for children that is linked to the roles of families, groups, genealogies, traditions, and national and transnational cultural imageries.
3. Of the two hundred students with whom I worked, I conducted individual videotaped interviews with twenty-six students, of whom sixteen were children of migrants.
4. Here, I would like to clarify my use of the term "cultural memory," which appears frequently in my chapter. In my analysis, the cultural memories of the groups with whom I worked (children of migrants and natives) comprised intertwined memories that arose in the sources and in the pictures and representations to which they referred. These memories are very significant and provide insights into the roles of peer-groups, family contexts, networks and, more broadly, social patterns.
5. The students watched the following videos: *Felix in Exile*, 1994, directed by William Kentridge, South Africa; *Sahara Chronicle* ("Arlit Uranium Mine," "Iron Ore Train," and "Coumba's Boat Passage"), 2006–2007, directed by Ursula Biemann, Switzerland; *En Camino – On the Way*, 2009, directed by Mirta Kupferminc and Mariana Sosnowski, USA: GitterArts; *Mama Illegal*, 2011, directed by Ed Moschitz, Austria: Golden Girls FilmProduktion and Film Services; *Moldova Children Express Their Views on Migration through Cartoons and Movies*, 2008; *The Mapping Journey Project* ("Constellations" and "I Crossed the Libyan Border"), 2011, directed by Khalili Bouchra; *Centro di perma-

nenza temporaneo, 2007, directed by Adrian Paci (http://vimeo.com/69536830); and *The Column*, 2013, directed by Adrian Paci (http://vimeo.com/69613425).
6. Some of the best-known photographs from Eva Leitolf's collection titled *Postcard for Europe* (2015) were shown in the classrooms. These images aesthetically blended marginalization and imagination. See Haeckel (2015).
7. The picture was the collective work of the following students at Vittorio Emanuele II Grammar High School, who actively participated in the BABE research project in 2016: Giovanni P., Ginevra C., Gaia D. F., Leonardo B., Maria Laura T. and Rebecca A.
8. The exhibition was held from 28 May to 9 June 2016 at Palazzo delle Aquile, which is the site of the City Hall. It was introduced by Leoluca Orlando, the mayor of Palermo.
9. These levels refer to the intertwining of lyrical and poetic language and the representation of the existential condition of youth.
10. I interviewed Selene M. in 2014. She was born near Turin in 1996 and was attending the Marie Curie Scientific High School at the time of the interview.
11. Chaima C. was born in Morocco in 1996 and came to Italy with her family when she was very young. I interviewed Chaima in 2014 at her school, Marie Curie Scientific High School.
12. On the relationship between historical time and teaching models, see Celli (2003) and Sorcinelli and Varni (2004).
13. For a discussion of the transmission of history, see also, Bonansea (2005, 2010).
14. On 4 March 2015, I interviewed Lorenzo C. (born near Turin in 1995) at Michele Buniva High School in Pinerolo.
15. Ann Stoler has written about memories of colonialism. She describes "aphasia" as "an occlusion of knowledge as a difficulty generating a vocabulary that associates appropriate words and concepts with appropriate things" (Stoler 2011: 121).
16. I interviewed Christian C. on 17 March 2014 at Michele Buniva High School in Pinerolo near Turin.
17. Elisa C. was born in Palermo in 1998 and attends Vittorio Emanuele II, the local grammar school. With the assistance of Renata Racalbuto, her history and philosophy teacher, Elisa made three videos in 2016.
18. The work titled *The Column* was exhibited at the Jeu de Paume National Museum in Paris in February 2013 and subsequently at a personal exhibition titled "Vite in transito" ("Crossing Lives") held at the PAC gallery in Milan in 2014.
19. The image is reminiscent of Caspar David Friedrich's paintings on canvas titled *Woman before the Setting Sun* (1818–20) and *Wanderer above the Sea of Fog* (1817–18), which the students analyzed with their art teacher during the period of the study.
20. Marco G. was born near Turin in 1996, and in 2014, he was in his fourth year at Marie Curie Scientific High School in Pinerolo, near Turin.

References

Assmann, J. 2011. *Cultural Memory and Early Civilization: Writing, Remembrance, and Political Imagination*. Cambridge, UK: Cambridge University Press.
Baruffi, A., ed. 2017. *The Poems of Giovanni Pascoli. Translated in English, with Original Italian Text*. Philadelphia: Literary Joint Press.
Biagioli, R. 2008. *La pedagogia dell'accoglienza: Ragazze ragazzi stranieri nella scuola dell'obbligo*. Pisa: ETS.

Bloom, B. S., M. D. Engelhart, E. J. Furst, W. H. Hill, and D. R. Krathwohl. 1956. *Taxonomy of Educational Objectives: The Classification of Educational Goals. Handbook I: Cognitive Domain*. New York: David McKay Company.

Boltanski, L. 1999. *Distant Suffering: Morality, Media and Politics*. Cambridge, UK: Cambridge University Press.

Bonansea, G. 2000. "Generazioni: la dimensione mutante." In *Nuove parole, nuovi metodi: Soggettività femminile, ricerca e didattica della storia*, edited by A Delmonaco, 81–92. Corso Interdirezionale di Aggiornamento per Docenti, Ministero della Pubblica Istruzione, Quarto (NA): Tipografia "Baiano," 87.

———. 2002. "Verso la scrittura, oltre il manuale": "Diritti e Privilegi." *Genesis: Magazine of the Società Italiana delle Storiche* 1–2: 192–94.

———. 2005. "Tradire la narrazione, rispettare la storia." In *La biblioteca della memoria*, edited by Vincenzo Campo, 40–49. Milano: Fondazione Arnoldo e Alberto Mondadori.

———. 2010. "Sulla soglia dei linguaggi: tra storia, memoria e narrazione." *Quaderni di Gruppoanalisi* 16: 35–44.

Cambi, F. 2001. *Intercultura: Fondamenti pedagogici*. Rome: Carocci.

Celli, M. 2003. "Le misure del tempo storico." *La vita scolastica* 6: 36–47.

De Cesari, C., and A. Rigney, eds. 2014. *Transnational Memory: Circulation, Articulation, Scales*. Berlin: De Gruyter.

Demetrio, D., and G. Favaro. 2002. *Didattica interculturale: Nuovi sguardi, competenze, percorsi*. Milano: Franco Angeli.

Foucault, M. 1978. *The History of Sexuality*. New York: Pantheon Books.

Haeckel, J. 2015. "An Aesthetic of Absence: Critical Counter-Narratives of Journalistic Story-Telling in Eva Leitolf's Photography." *Image & Narrative* 16, no. 1: 45–56.

Mager, R. F. 1984. *Developing Attitude toward Learning*. 2nd ed. Atlanta: The Center for Effective Performance Inc.

Mattozzi, I. 2002. "La formazione del pensiero temporale." In *La storia: Istruzioni per l'uso*, edited by Ernesto Perillo Napoli: Tecnodid.

Montale, E. 1994. *Cuttlefish Bones 1920–1927*. Translated by William Arrowsmith. New York: W. W. Norton.

Ortoleva, P. 2009. *Il secolo dei media*. Milano: Il Saggiatore.

Perretta, G. 2017. *La densità del vuoto*. Ancona: Fondazione Cassa di Risparmio of Jesi.

Portera, A. 2003. *Pedagogie interculturali in Italia e in Europa*. Milano: Vita e Pensiero.

Ricca, M. 2013. *Culture interdette*. Torino: Bollati Boringhieri.

Ruml, W., A. Caramazza, J. R. Shelton, and D. Chailant. 2000. "Testing Assumptions in Computational Theories of Aphasia." *Journal of Memory and Language* 43, no. 2: 217–48.

Shapiro, L. P., and B. A. Levine. 1990. "Verb Processing during Sentence Comprehension in Aphasia." *Brain and Language* 38: 21–47.

Sorcinelli, P., and A. Varni, eds. 2004. *Il secolo dei giovani: le nuove generazioni e la storia del Novecento*. Rome: Donzelli.

Stefinlongo, A. 2006. *I giovani e la scrittura: Attitudini, bisogni, competenze di scrittura delle nuove generazioni*. Roma: Aracne.

Stoler, A. L.,2011. "Colonial Aphasia: Race and Disabled Histories in France." *Public Culture* 23, no. 1: 121–56.

Traversi, A. 2016. "I giovani e la poesia." *Cultural Magazine online of Livorno*.

Trevi, M. Romano, A. 2009. *Studi sull'ombra*. Milano: Raffaello Cortina.

Ungaretti, G. 1916. *Il Porto Sepolto*. Udine: Stabilimento tipografico friulano.

Wepman J. M., and L. V. Jones. 1966. "Studies in Aphasia: Classification of Aphasic Speech by the Noun-Pronoun Ratio." *British Journal of Disorders of Communication* 1, no. 1: 46–54.

Chapter 4

TRANSCULTURAL ITINERARIES AND NEW LITERACIES

How Memories Could Reshape School Systems

Emmanuelle Le Pichon-Vorstman, Sergio Baauw,
Debbie Cole, Suzanne Dekker, and Marie Steffens

We currently live in a space–time dimension that is pervaded and constructed by a discursive genre known as "globalization talk" (Agha 2015). Globalization talk is a contemporary way of representing human migration flows in the present and recent past as patterns of contact and movement that are qualitatively and quantitatively different and distinct from those in the past. It is used in tandem with other terms such as "diversity talk" and "superdiversity talk", all of which are used to conceptualize the multiplication of differences, borders, border crossings, and hybridity, both as the outcome of this contemporarily specific or "new" era of globalization and as a problem or challenge that must be faced and solved (Pavlenko 2017). However, the phenomena under discussion in contemporary globalization talk are neither new nor necessarily more intense than they have been in other times and places in relation to the current nation–state hubs within the Global North. Several scholars across a wide range of disciplines in the humanities and social sciences who have long reflected on and engaged with migration, contact, and border crossings of various types, especially within locations that are spatially and temporally distant from these hubs, share this view. The following observation by a linguistic anthropologist helps to elucidate our approach, adopted in this chapter, of viewing the mobility of memory through the lens of language:

So much for the imperial and colonial peripheries at which we who work in relatively local, small-scale language communities have long confronted these problems. I think that we live today in a world in which these very processes have been in effect noticeably spreading to the politico-economic metropole, causing consternation in many organizational sites—for example, educational, medical, legal—that administer in one or another domain of contemporary mass social life, but therefore necessitating a thorough revision of the tacit reliance on the Enlightenment mapping of language community into polity. Multiple factors are responsible for the breakdown felt perhaps most acutely within Europe as the languages of the peripheries of former empires are practically experienced at home, not just in scholarly settings, thus setting up new dilemmas widely experienced as social forces in any First World post-imperial metropole. (Silverstein 2015: 16)

In this chapter, by attending to the languages and school biographies of students with multidimensional and heterogeneous memories of languages and learning, who have recently traveled to a European metropole, we participate in this contemporary genre of globalization talk. Many students attending schools in contemporary Europe have acquired new memories as a result of their travels across national boundaries that add to their understanding of education and of themselves (Herzog-Punzenberger, Le Pichon-Vorstman, and Siarova 2017). Through our study of these children's experiences, we address a dilemma facing European educators that centers on questions of whether and how to adapt current school systems to best educate their diverse and changing student populations.

We draw on data generated through the EDucation of International Newly Arrived migrant pupils (EDINA) project, which supports municipalities, schools, and teachers in rethinking and reshaping education for students with transcultural memories. Consequently, this article represents an attempt to understand why contemporary school systems, primarily created and maintained by individuals who grew up within a single memory culture, do not usually entail a conception of schools and schooling that is based on an understanding of transcultural complexity. In doing so, we respond to Erll's exhortation that "the overall aim of transcultural memory studies must consist in complicating the notion of 'single memory cultures'" (Erll 2011: 8). We argue that didactic practices should be adapted to increasingly prevalent transcultural itineraries. In this chapter, we view students' migration memories as a starting point for redefining concepts such as school language proficiency (Clark and Dervin 2014). We show that the willingness of school stakeholders to engage in translingual practices (Canagarajah 2013) may depend on their capacity to reflect upon and connect their own memories to the transcultural memories and multiliteracies of their students (Hornberger and Link 2012; Cole 2014).

We begin by laying out the various elements of the categories and categorization processes, focusing on languages that matter for newly arrived students in Dutch classrooms to demonstrate the institutional momentum of these processes. Subsequently, we reveal how an intervention focusing on the flexible use of multiple languages in education, also called "translanguaging" (see, for instance, Creese and Blackledge 2010), enabled some teachers and administrators to gain an awareness of their own experiences and competencies that defied easy categorization. This awareness resulted in their willingness to experiment with a different approach in answering the question of "what to do" for themselves and for their students. We conclude with a short overview of relevant sociolinguistic theory that points to the inescapability of categorization processes, which we hope will stimulate the efforts of teachers and researchers to better understand and acknowledge the difficulty entailed in categorizing their own memories and competences.

Mobility: Old Story, New Chapters

Although migration flows are not new, the number of people leaving their home countries has reached an all-time high, leading to increasingly complex migration flows. Jackson (2014) has labeled these groups as "border crossers", distinguishing between voluntary and involuntary border crossers and between permanent and temporary border crossers. We use the term "migrants" to indicate people who move to another country, either voluntarily or involuntarily and for political or economic reasons, and who settle in the new country for a sufficiently long period to enable their participation in the host society. Children of migrants whose first language is not the school language of the new society are henceforth referred to as "newly arrived students" in line with the EDINA project terminology. Many factors, ranging from the compulsion to flee because of life-threatening situations to seeking employment, play a role in explaining why people are leaving their home countries in large numbers. Within the Dutch school system at least, the characteristics of this influx of newly arrived students differ in several ways from those that have been previously documented (Banks 2008; Heineke et al. 2012). These characteristics are described below.

First, the current arrival rate of migrants, including refugees, in the Netherlands is unprecedented. Out of a total of 31,200 refugees who arrived in the Netherlands in 2016 (Sociaal-Economische Raad 2017), 25 percent were minors (VluchtelingenWerk Nederland 2016). A total of 6,416 children and adolescents between the ages of 4 and 17 and another 1,779 children between the ages of 0 and 3 are living in asylum centers scattered across the Netherlands (Centraal Orgaan Opvang Asielzoekers 2017). Of these minors,

1,200 arrived without their parents. In the Netherlands, as in other European countries, education is compulsory between the ages of 5 and 18, which means that the majority of these students enter the school system as soon as possible.

Second, the countries of origin of newly arrived children are considerably more diverse than those of children who arrived earlier (Le Pichon-Vorstman, van Erning, and Baauw 2016; Vertovec 2007). In addition to an examination of the composition of the population of newly arrived students in schools, a closer look at their migration trajectories can provide useful insights. In our data, the students' countries of birth frequently differed from the countries of provenance of their parents, which often did not correspond to the students' nationalities. For instance, students may have been born in refugee camps located along the migratory path traveled by their parents from their countries of origin to their current country, and they may have remained in the intermediate country for several years. Their parents may have met in these refugee camps, possibly belonging to different cultures and speaking different languages themselves. Evidently, such trajectories have shaped the students' linguistic repertoires and cultural experiences. From a purely linguistic perspective, identifying which language can be considered the first languages of these students is a difficult task.

In many cases, newly arrived students not only have complicated, multinational trajectories prior to their arrival in Europe, but they are also likely to be confronted with several more postarrival transitions. These transitions are likely to occur in relation to different European countries as well as different regions or cities within the latest host country. At the start of the EDINA project, refugees in the Netherlands were being moved from one refugee camp to the next every three months, even though protesting NGOs successfully pushed for the establishment of regulations that should have resulted in a reduction of these moves to an average of two a year in the initial postarrival years (Werkgroep Kind in AZC 2013). The practice of moving migrant families every three months was in fact a violation of the regulations established two years previously. By contrast, Dutch citizens move homes on average once every ten years in the Netherlands (Werkgroep Kind in AZC 2013).

Additionally, complicated migration laws may prompt increased movements of migrant families from one country to the next, even after prolonged periods of preliminary settlement in some cases. Between the school years 2014–15 and 2015–16, the increase in the total number of classrooms was nominal in Rotterdam, changing from thirty to thirty-one. However, a closer examination of the division of classes by the total number of schools reveals very little stability in numbers of classes held in each school. According to municipality authorities, these fluctuations can be attributed to the inflow and outflow of students (Le Pichon-Vorstman, van Erning, and Baauw 2016). For instance, during the period of our research, two young students left for the United Kingdom two years after their primary settlement in the Netherlands. After their arrival in the Netherlands, these students had worked hard to learn Dutch and acquire fluency, but then they suddenly found themselves in a country where knowledge of Dutch is not a useful asset. How, then, does this experience contribute to their memories and to their experience of literacy? Will they be deemed functionally "illiterate" again when entering the new country/school system? Thus, increased mobility raises complex questions. For instance, should these students be schooled in the local language, in their own language, or in the language of their last school? Further, how are their own memories and literacy experiences taken into account in their schooling?

Single Memory Culture Schooling Practices

The Organization of Schooling

Proficiency in school languages is seen as a prerequisite for success in school subjects, and, ultimately, for professional success. This perception has led to language policies that only allow for the use of the school language(s) in the school environment. Therefore, at the preprimary and primary school levels (ages 4–12) and at the secondary school level (ages 13–18), depending on the district in which they live, most newly arrived students are schooled separately from other students because they lack proficiency in the school language. There are, in fact, three options for primary school students. The first option entails their attendance at a school located within a refugee center until they receive a response regarding the acceptance or rejection of their request for asylum. The second option entails their integration into a school or classroom that is specialized and equipped to receive such students. After one or two years of schooling, these students would be integrated into a regular primary classroom, usually within their own neighborhood. The final option is to place the children directly in a regular classroom in district schools located in the countryside. However, whether or not this last strategy is really an option is debatable as it entails no further special arrangements made for the students.

In light of the implementation of a national policy, with only minor variations among municipalities in the Netherlands, at the level of secondary education, classes are held for newly arrived students in specialized secondary schools under the International Transition Classrooms (ISK) program.[1] However, this separate school system attended by students during their initial postarrival years may raise various challenges relating to their integration. These challenges include, for instance, the imposition of an extra transition on this already vulnerable population and a focus on monolingual proficiency in the school language. Clearly, the underlying rationale for separate schooling is the belief that insufficient proficiency in the school language would prevent students from participating in regular classrooms (Le Pichon-Vorstman, van Erning, and Baauw 2016).

The Role of the Dominant Language in Social Participation

The role of language proficiency in relation to economic progress has been studied in different countries. For example, one study examined the relation between migrants' proficiency in Spanish and their earnings in Spain, revealing that proficiency in Spanish mainly had a positive effect on the earnings of highly educated migrants but not on those of less well-educated migrants (Budría and Swedberg 2015). Sanford (2002) reported similar findings for his study on Mexican migrants in the United States; only migrants with at least a high school education benefited from proficiency in English. This implies that "English language deficiency prevents [highly educated] migrants from making use of their acquired human capital in the U.S. labor market" (Sanford 2002: 19). Similarly, a study conducted in Norway on "Third World immigrants" found that proficiency in Norwegian did not lead to higher earnings (Hayfron 2001). Whereas it appeared to help migrants to procure jobs, other factors determined the levels of their earnings. Moreover, "Third World immigrants are usually found in low-skilled and least-paid jobs in the Norwegian labour market" (Hayfron 2001: 1978) for which advanced Norwegian language skills are not required.

The findings of these studies indicate that proficiency in the host country's language is an important factor, but only if other academic skills have been developed too. This insight has important consequences for the education of newly arrived students. Because of their limited proficiency in the school language, these students are often assigned to practical levels of secondary education (Le Pichon-Vorstman, Baauw, and Vorstman 2016), leading to their procurement of jobs that do not require high levels of school language proficiency. Thus, not meeting the required language proficiency levels harms these students in two ways: it prevents their admission into academic levels of secondary education,[2] which give students access to higher education, and in turn, this barrier constrains their access to jobs for which high levels of proficiency in the school language matter.

Language Assessments

Another symptom of this single memory culture is the Common European Framework of Reference for Languages (CEFR), aimed at standardizing the process of evaluating language proficiency. Created to promote the mobility of Europeans as well as their social integration and professional development abroad, the CEFR distinguishes between individual general skills, communicative skills, language activities, and the domains into which these skills and activities fit (Council of Europe 2001: 15–18). These skills, activities, and domains can be categorized according to three user profiles and six reference levels, ranging from A1 to C2 (Council of Europe 2001: 25), along with specific descriptions of the tasks to be accomplished to achieve these levels. By applying these levels in place of traditionally defined levels (basic, intermediate or independent, and expert levels) that are intuitively perceived but defined in a fuzzy and heterogeneous way, the CEFR clarifies and rationalizes systems of teaching and assessing linguistic competences. Accordingly, a procedure and external evaluation criteria have been established that are independent of the evaluating body, the language taught, the first languages spoken, and the linguistic-cultural background of learners. The CEFR has gradually emerged as the referential guide for designing placement tests conducted for admission into language courses (for the formation of learning groups), final course tests (e.g., the language tests for assessing Dutch proficiency), as well as the actual content of the courses (e.g., ISK curricula).

However, the challenges entailed in teaching languages in environments that often include vulnerable learners, some of whom have had very little schooling in their countries of origin, highlight the fact that the CEFR is more appropriate for highly educated publics. Starting from a threshold level, the tasks to be conducted rely more on intellectual skills than on linguistic skills (e.g., text synthesis, argumentation, and evaluations). Many learners are unable to perform the typical tasks assigned at levels above B1 either in the target language or in their mother tongue. As a corollary, only a small fraction of native speakers will ever attain the C2 level. This is because the competencies targeted by the CEFR are generally the kinds of skills whose acquisition in the first languages develops among students undergoing long-term schooling as opposed to skills that can be acquired outside of formal education contexts. Learners with little or no education will not succeed in advancing beyond the B1 level in the CEFR, even if their language skills are equivalent to those of a native speaker with an equivalent amount of schooling. Thus, learners who are unable to read, understand, and summarize a complex text or to construct structured argumentation in their mother tongues may never become "independent users" in relation to the new language that they are learning.

Two scenarios can be distinguished. In the first, there is no match between learners' academic competency in their mother tongue and in the new language(s) they are learning. In the second, there is a match between these skills. Accordingly, learners in the first scenario require a language course in the target language to meet language requirements. In the second scenario, if the learners are not able to summarize academic texts in their mother tongue, their capacity to do so in a new language will be even weaker. In this case, the problem is not a linguistic one that can be dealt with in the context of a language course. If the academic competence of learners in their own languages is not very strong, then no language course, regardless of its quality, will enable these learners to overcome a lack of academic preparation and to acquire such skills in a new target language. A troublesome misunderstanding remains. If considered as what they in fact are, CEFR levels are excellent indicators of mastery of language-based intellectual skills among proficient speakers of a particular language. However, when considered as indicators of the language level of learners of a second language, they are misleading. This is because they center on skills that are unattainable by most second-language learners, and even by those who are proficient in their first languages but lack the requisite academic background.

In sum, the single, monolingual memory culture that continues to form the basis for assessments of language proficiency profoundly impacts on the ways in which policies at local and national levels direct the organization of newly arrived students' schooling. The process of integration of these students is guided by assessments and schooling structures and content that reflect monolingual perspectives in relation to the students. Ultimately, these policies may prevent schools and educators from implementing initiatives that favor multilingual approaches.

Teachers' and Children's Voices: The EDINA Project

Teachers' Needs

The important task of introducing and integrating newly arrived students into the society of the host country mainly lies with primary and secondary school teachers. This task is not without challenges. A survey conducted by the Organisation for Economic Co-operation and Development in 2010 revealed teachers' aspirations to professionalize themselves in order to teach in diverse and multicultural classrooms. Between 85 and 95 percent of teachers surveyed in European countries such as Iceland, Ireland, Italy, Malta, Portugal, and Spain expressed their need for professionalization in this area. In 2016, a study by the Dutch governmental research institute, Dienst Uitvoering Onderwijs (DUO) found that 84 percent of Dutch primary school teachers experience severe work-related pressure and high stress levels. The teachers mainly attributed this pressure to compulsory administrative tasks and to the behavioral problems of their students (DUO 2016). Dervin, Simpson, and Matikainen (2016) reported another issue relating to the education of newly arrived students in Finland: namely that teachers in Finnish basic education demonstrate a lack of interest in students as they have not received the necessary professional preparation, and many are unaware of the policies that they are supposed to follow. Even though specific knowledge is required to successfully integrate newly arrived students, teachers do not receive specialized training in this area. In Flanders, the Dutch-speaking area in Belgium, as well as in the Netherlands, schools for higher vocational education confer a degree (comparable to a bachelor degree in education) on primary school teachers. However, at the time that the EDINA project was initiated, there were no specific prerequisites that a teacher was required to meet before teaching newly arrived students, mainly because of the lack of complementary training (Le Pichon-Vorstman, van Erning, and Baauw 2016). In the Netherlands, further professional courses on teaching newly arrived migrant students are offered by a wide variety of institutions and at different levels, but there is no legal requirement for teachers to enroll in them. In short, it could be said that teachers in the Netherlands, Flanders, and Finland do not have adequate opportunities to professionalize and prepare themselves to teach in multicultural and multilingual classrooms. Further, there is a need for effective policies to strengthen the inclusion of newly arrived migrant students.

The EDINA Project as an Attempt to Counter Single Memory and Deficit Perspectives

With the objective of addressing gaps relating to the single memory and deficit approach, a group of researchers, policy makers, and school board members from the Netherlands, Belgium, and Finland collaborated together within the framework of the transnational EDINA project. Under this project, professionalization material was developed and workshops were organized for primary and secondary school teachers who teach in multicultural and multilingual classrooms. The project was initiated in accordance with the desire expressed by school principals, teachers, and policy makers in the educational field to acquire more expertise and insights relating to the organization of newly arrived students' schooling. A multitude of academic studies have been conducted on this topic, but this information usually does not reach teachers and educational policy makers. Thus, the central objective of the EDINA project was to support municipalities, schools, and teachers by developing research-based professionalization material.

At the outset of the project, we interviewed teachers, school principals, and board members to determine their expectations for the project. During these interviews, conducted within an informal setting, we collected information on the current needs and concerns of primary and secondary school teachers regarding the education of newly arrived students. One of the main frustrations expressed by virtually all of them was the discontinuity of their students' school trajectories. In the project context, we interpreted this frustration positively because we believed that it provided an entry point for discursive negotiation. Moving individuals from country to country, and from school to school, impacts their multilingualism and the continuity of the learning process, affecting their literacy potential as well as their competences in wider school-based skills. As proposed by a large number of scholars, we started with a conception of newly arrived migrants as multilingual (Cummins 2001; Garcia, Skutnabb-Kangas, and Torres-Guzmann 2006; Piccardo 2013). This multilingualism is not the sum of separate languages; rather, it entails unbalanced competences in different languages. The first interviews conducted in the winter of 2016 revealed that the schools' stakeholders were attempting to cope with an overwhelming number of newly arrived migrant students with very different school backgrounds who needed to be integrated into school classrooms as soon as possible. According to the schools, the educational experiences of these students ranged from having no school background at all—for instance, in cases where they were born in a refugee camp where their parents had met—to those with a regular school background. Even if teachers and principals were acutely aware of the important issues of understanding children's experiences and their education, or lack thereof, in different settings, they prioritized traumatic experiences, needs, academic gaps, and poor academic skills. "We come across everything, ranging from ADHD to children who cannot get used to school; who are rebellious in the beginning, especially older children, which is very understandable. Children come here often . . . they are pretty much left alone" (school teacher interviewed in January 2016). Given these unprecedented circumstances, while the expressed sense of urgency appeared justified, the teachers perpetuated a deficit model and negative narratives.

Multiple, Situated, Evolving Memory as the Norm

To facilitate a better understanding of the current situation, we first examine the history of multilingualism and multiculturalism in the Netherlands, showing how it has influenced the current climate. As observed by Winter (2010: 174–83), the Netherlands, which has a discontinuous history of ethnocultural inclusion of incorporated groups, was one of the first countries to implement multicultural policies to promote the integration of newly arrived minority groups, defined in religious-ideological terms. However, in the early 2000s, a shift in policy had dramatic consequences. In the field of education, it resulted in the termination of funding for the education of migrant minorities in their native languages in 2004. Before 2004, part of the instruction was conducted after school in the official languages of the states of origin of their parents. Notably, instruction in Kurdish or Berber was not supported as these languages are considered "nonofficial languages." Once more, students' emergent bilingualism was viewed through a monolingual lens that attributed one official language to one country or well-defined geographical location. Previously, financial support had comprised after-school classes held by teachers familiar with particular languages, usually Turkish or Moroccan Arabic. The impact of this policy change on the Dutch educational landscape was analogous to that of an earthquake, and, as is often the case, an earthquake may be followed by a tsunami. In this case, the "tsunami" was a complete rejection of the students' own languages. Since 2004, the prevailing view of school authorities and teachers in the Netherlands has been that the use of minority languages is detrimental to students' development. Thus, the struggle to enact educational practices that accommodate the complex linguistic realities of students continues.

The field of linguistics could inform the policies that guide the practices of educators in this regard. As a discipline, linguistics includes a wide range of methods and theories that can be broadly categorized as generative, social, and applied approaches. This range of approaches is the result of different areas of focus within which researchers debate what constitutes language itself. These differences in methods, theories, and practices can make it difficult to determine which models and methods would be most useful for application in educational domains. Emerging plurilithic models of language that attempt to account for the observed complexity of language-related phenomena within both the cognitive and social domains may have a better chance of offering relevant insights for multilingual classrooms than prevailing monolithic models of language (Hall 2013). In monolithic approaches, a conception of language, culture, and memory, each assumed to be singular, serves as a basic foundation for understanding what language is. Historically, this concept of language has dominated much of linguistic research, and it fits well with everyday understandings of how languages work in the world (for instance, Dutch people speak Dutch and Japanese people speak Japanese). Plurilithic models of language, however, start from the recognition that language is inherently variable: not only is every language made up of dialects and varieties that change over time and across regions, but every individual speaker's grammar is idiosyncratic and can change over the course of the lifespan. Despite the variable and varying facts of language, resistance to plurilitihic models within the wider field of linguistics is ongoing. When variation is accepted, it is often evaluated as relying on evidence that is peripheral to the central, monolithic truths of language. For example, code switching between Spanish and English or hybrid language practices within border communities in the United States is taken as emblematic of what happens in exceptional cases and places when people from each side of a border come into contact. The received norm is that English speakers speak English and Spanish speakers speak Spanish. The easily observable and widely documented data demonstrating how speakers regularly blur these boundaries are often considered by some linguists to be exceptional cases. Recently, however, some scholars have acknowledged that such examples are illustrative not of exceptions but of a rule that all human languages (what people say and how they store their language systems within their brains) are individual, partial, fragmented, multiple, context-bound, and shifting even as their acquisition and use are social (Anzaldúa 1999; Blommaert 2010; Hall 2013).

In a recent review, Hall outlined how a view of language that reconciles the individual, social, and political facts of language could inform our linguistic practice in the area of language education and learning. In light of his attempts to reconcile the various subdisciplines of linguistics by foregrounding the multiplicity of languages, and their multiple dimensions, Hall offered the following summative statement: "All language learning and use is determined by the local experiences (and goals) of individuals who are non-conformist mental appropriators of external social practices" (Hall 2013: 227). Our attempts to collect language biographies from students who recently arrived in the Netherlands, and who are learning Dutch in local schools, are grounded in this observation and general orientation. We suggest that lessons emerging from interdisciplinary scholarship in the field of linguistics may offer some conceptual tools for rethinking movements of memories across borders, for redefining the interpretative categories we need to make sense of our consistently complex social and linguistic landscapes, and for coming to terms with our individual agency in the making and representation of shared memories.

Changing School Practices

Valuing Students' Multiple Memory Cultures and Literacies

In order for teachers and students to create new shared memories, newly arrived students must be allowed to develop their academic skills without being hampered by their limited proficiency in the school language. This will grant them, for instance, access to a wider spectrum of jobs, including those requiring higher education levels. At the same time, a high degree of proficiency in this language is necessary, particularly for job positions requiring higher education levels. Crucially, studies show that the development of students' proficiency in their first languages is important for their academic success.

Reintroduction of Students' First Languages within the Schooling System

Prevoo et al. (2016) analyzed eighty-six studies that explored the relationship between students' oral language proficiency in their first languages and in the school language, and their school outcomes. They found strong intralanguage relations between oral proficiency and reading outcomes, indicating that oral proficiency in the school language is strongly related to reading performance in this language, while oral proficiency in first languages corresponds to reading performance in these languages. The latter correspondence was observed within bilingual programs that were less common in the study. There were also intralanguage correlations between language proficiency and early literacy as well as between language proficiency and spelling, math, and general academic achievement, though these correlations were weaker. Notably, cross-language effects were observed in the study; there was a (weak) positive cross-language relation between students' oral proficiency in their first languages and early literacy and reading in the school language. As Prevoo et al. (2016) note, this finding is in line with Cummins' (1979) interdependence hypothesis, which states that a transfer of skills occurs between the first languages and the school language. These authors conclude that "stimulation of both L1 [first language] and L2 [school language] can be supportive for immigrant background children's [sic] educational achievement, which could contribute to narrowing the achievement gap with native-born children" (Prevoo et al. 2016: 265).

The positive influence of first language proficiency on school development can serve as an argument for considering the inclusion of first languages in the school program. This practice has been found to be effective (Seals and Peyton 2017). It can take the form of bilingual education or, alternatively, "translanguaging," which entails strategic deployment of the different languages represented in the classroom (e.g., Garcia and Wei 2015). This can facilitate continued development of students' linguistic skills, while supporting their academic development. There is thus sufficient evidence indicating that the entire language repertoire of students, including all of the languages that a student has previously encountered, and without reference to the degree to which these languages are developed, should be supported in schools (Herzog-Punzenberger, Pichon-Vorstman, and Siarova 2017).

School Assessments

The focus of the earlier financially supported education in foreign students' home languages was on ameliorating educational delays for these students. In light of the abrogation of the law supporting students' education in their home languages in 2004, current school practices reveal a unilateral focus on improving students' proficiency in the school language. The influx of newly arrived migrant students in Dutch schools has demonstrated the limitations of an exclusive focus on developing proficiency in the school language as a second language among these students without considering their often-rich language repertoire. When we launched the EDINA project, all of the school stakeholders in each of the three countries unanimously held the view that the school language should be the only language used in the school context. There were rigid rules in place disallowing students from using their first languages in class unless this was to the teacher's advantage. A study by van Waalbeek, conducted in the realm of EDINA, showed that when questioned whether they would ask students to translate formal or informal communication for their parents during interactions, all the teachers said they would do so at least occasionally (van Walbeek 2017). This response from the teachers implies that the students' multilingualism was considered legitimate in situations that potentially entail a breakdown of communication (e.g., during meetings of parents and teachers or when facilitating the integration of new students in the classroom), but not in others.

It is also possible to identify a common core set of skills shared by all native speakers of a language, regardless of their schooling levels. This is confirmed by Hulstijn, who distinguishes between "basic language cognition," which is common to all native speakers, and "higher language cognition" (2015: 46). Hulstijn also distinguishes between the "heart" (linguistic skills in phonetics, morphology, lexicology, and pragmatics) and the "periphery" (e.g., communicative skills, interactional skills, communication strategies, metalinguistic knowledge, and knowledge of types of speech) (2015: 42). Whereas basic language cognition includes most of the heart content, higher language cognition includes the content of the rest of the heart and that of the periphery. This perspective could lead to the development of learning methods that are better adapted to second-language learners.

Helping Teachers Apply Socially Oriented Theories of Language and Identity

Language Planning

Language planning is a research field that emerged in the 1960s. It mainly focuses on the macrolevel of language-related interventions within a community or a state. Such interventions can relate to the social status of different languages spoken in a region, the acquisition of these languages (languages taught as part of the curriculum, teaching material, and teacher training), or the language system itself, with its particular norms, units, and structures (Diaz Fouces 2010: 285; Kaplan and Baldauf 1997). Sociological studies suggest that every corpus planning action entails a status dimension (Fishman 2004). Modification of a language affects inclusion/exclusion processes within a society (Klinkenberg 2001) and individuals' representations of the language. An example is a debate held in France on gender-inclusive writing, with the Académie française arguing that such writing jeopardizes the very existence of the French language.³ Recent studies have pointed to the value of also considering microlevel language planning, depending on the choices and representations of civil society actors, individuals, and companies (Baldauf 2006). At the micro level, minority languages can be maintained in spite of macro policies because they federate, identify, and distinguish micro social groups, as in the Afrikaans versus English debate in South Africa (Dyers 2008). Deployment of such microlevel mechanisms explains why minority languages that lack legitimacy retain their vitality as home languages, even if another language is used in higher status contexts. Consequently, "it [the minority language] remains a powerful index of micro-networks, in-group identity, and the possible exclusion of those who do not speak this variety" (Dyers 2008: 67). The education system is the site where macro and micro levels are most intimately interconnected. To be effective, macro planning requires implementation at the micro level. Therefore, on the one hand, teachers and the students have key roles to play in language policy development (Payne 2006; Ricento and Hornberger 1996), and on the other hand, language policies implemented in schools have the greatest societal impact (Delarue and De Caluwe 2015; Liddicoat 2013). Teachers' professional identities along with their social relationships and the curriculum determine whether they resist or accept new teaching policies (Baldauf 2006: 157). To increase acceptance of language policies and avoid their erratic implementation, the policies must respond to local needs (Baldauf 2006: 163). Ideological conflicts may also play a role in the diffusion of language policies. For example, monolingual ideologies lead to the promotion of only the standard school language, despite a growing literature indicating the positive results of multilingual education initiatives, as in the case of Flanders (Delarue and De Caluwe 2015).

Addressing Beliefs and Ideologies

Following the same line of reasoning, it can be argued that differences in teachers' perceptions may also influence the effectiveness of instructional approaches. Already at the turn of century, Musumeci (1997) showed that failing to address teachers' belief systems could potentially impede pedagogical change. Schultz (2001) endorsed this view, further insisting on the importance of reducing potential conflicts between instructional practices and students' beliefs about their own learning. Hence, the strategies implemented in the EDINA project importantly entailed giving students a voice as well as elucidating teachers' perspectives. Ultimately, our aim was to apply this knowledge to develop improved instructional practices.

To elicit students' perceptions, we asked them about their views on education and obtained detailed information about the itineraries of thirty primary and secondary school students throughout the project. Some of the students described a lack of cognitive challenges, monotonous activities in the language class, and their desire to join regular classes with same-aged peers (Le Pichon-Vorstman and Cole 2017).

We engaged twenty-seven third-year students, aged nine to fifteen years old, in an exercise conducted within the Dutch component of the EDINA project. This exercise entailed an identity-related activity that was adapted from an online activity featured on Pinterest. Identity texts were used to explore students' memories and their social, educational, and/or emotional realities. These texts usually encompass a wide range of modalities—for instance, stickers, colors, and written and oral texts—to give students sufficient space and flexibility to demonstrate their skills in their different languages. Cummins et al. suggest that "effective educational responses to underachievement among students from marginalized communities imply the implementation of pedagogies that promote identity affirmation" (2015: 556).

In the two examples depicted in Figure 4.1, students were presented with a pattern that began with "me" depicted in red at the top of a pyramid, which then gradually extended to "my languages," "my friends," "my schools," "my cities," and "my countries." To accommodate students' transcultural memories, we decided to apply the plural forms of these nouns. In these examples, both students clearly explained how their mobility not only preceded their arrival in the Netherlands (encompassing, for instance, Syria, the United Arab Emirates, and, for the first student, the Netherlands), but it also continued after their arrival in the Netherlands, as both students were about to move to another Dutch city. Both students presented themselves as world citizens: the first included English, Dutch, and Arabic as his own languages, and additionally expressed a desire to learn Italian. The second student cited all of the countries she had visited, describing four languages—namely Thai, Dutch, English, and Laotian—as "my languages." This student also wrote down the name of the city in which she lived in the home language, demonstrating writing skills in a different writing system. These students' identity texts were representative of those of virtually all of the students with whom we interacted, indicating rich repertoires, trajectories, and experiences, as well as the ability to project themselves into an imagined future entailing new languages, new travels, new houses, and more. This visualized activity may support not only their own academic development and identity affirmation, as suggested by Cummins et al. (2015), but it may also help to avoid the use of a deficit approach in relation to these students. By giving them a space to voice their realities and to demonstrate their rich linguistic and cultural repertoire, supported by transcultural memories and new literacies, we may successfully facilitate the substitution of hegemonic and assimilative ideologies (Ruiz 1984) that all too often prevail in receiving countries, particularly in educational contexts.

To explore the school stakeholders' perspectives, we not only elicited their visions on current policies and pedagogies relating to newly arrived children,

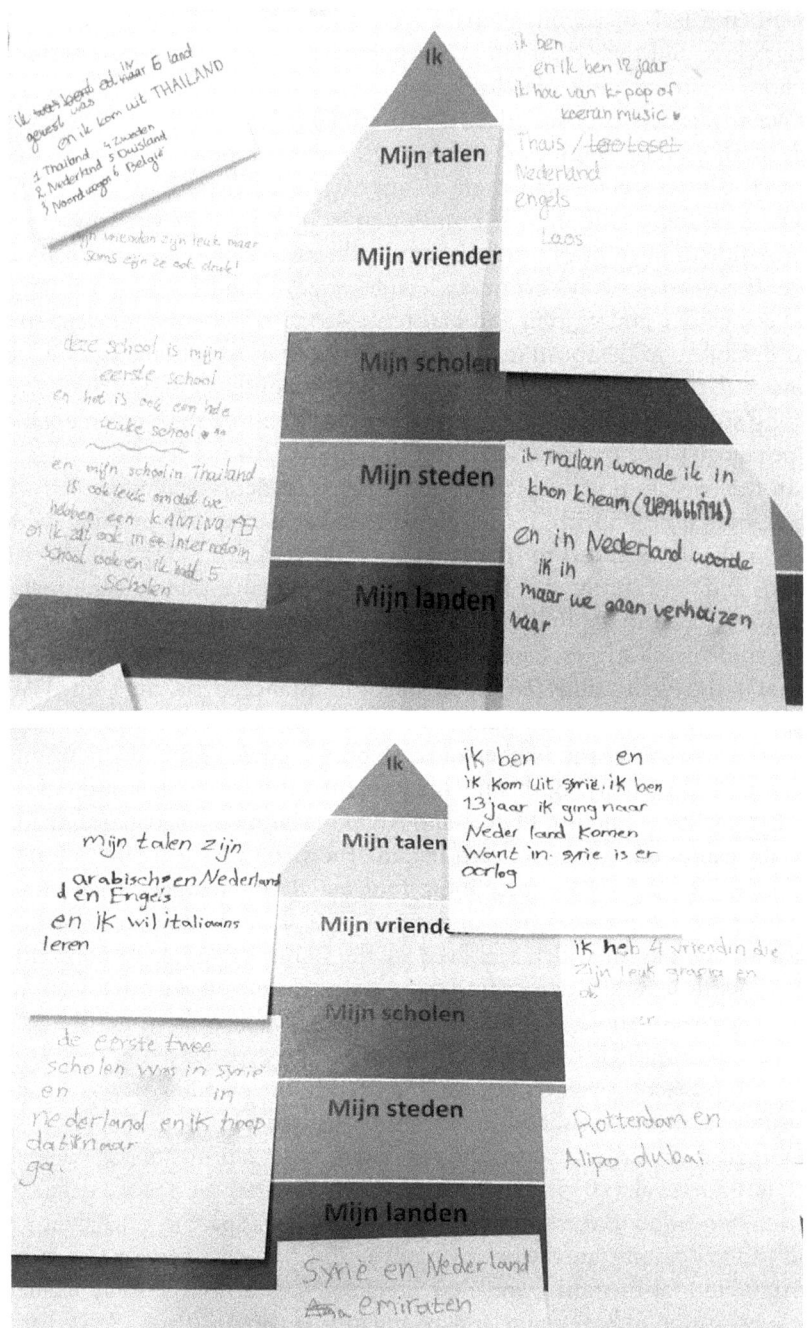

FIGURE 4.1. Two representations of the same activity conducted with students in the Dutch project component. Photograph by the authors. Published with permission.

and their desires and ideas for improving instructional practices for this group, but we also invited them to present their own personal language biographies. Interestingly, presenting their own students' perspectives to teachers and other stakeholders during the workshops had a profound impact on the perspectives of the latter. They gradually began to conceive of the students' agency within their own lives. Moreover, they felt compelled to question their existing beliefs regarding language learning, ideology, planning, and multilingual pedagogies. The revelation of student's perspectives along with inputs entailing occasional clarification of the presented concepts and highlighting efficient multilingual pedagogies when needed greatly contributed to advancing discussions through the gradual blending of academic insights with personal experiences (both of students and teachers) relating to (second) language learning. This approach of combining personal experiences with academic knowledge in an open and loosely structured setting yielded fruitful discussions without excluding more politically controversial pedagogies as possible solutions.

It is noteworthy that the use of this approach often led participants to share their own educational trajectories with each other. The results of this process strongly indicated that ultimately, a future teacher's own learning experience may be more impactful than what this same teacher may have learned formally during the training process (Graus and Coppen 2016). Interestingly, the act of sharing personal life stories itself prompted the group to address stereotypes and ideologies linked to the languages of newly arrived students (Holliday, Hyde, and Kullman 2010: 64; Canagarajah 2013). For instance, they became aware of the incongruence entailed in forbidding the use of first languages in the classroom after some of them realized that they too had suffered because of such policies. One of the participants explained how she was confronted with her own experiences of school and migration during the workshop. This shared story served as an eye-opener for her, and as a result, her school began implementing translanguaging principles as an educational objective the following school year. This example illustrates how this individual's shared memories mediated between her beliefs and teaching practices. This strategy, which was used within the EDINA project, therefore appears to be a beneficial and effective one, indicating that new venues for educational strategies and principles may be effective in a transnational context if the following conditions are met:

- School stakeholders/policy makers become aware of their own individual language biographies and itineraries from a translingual perspective. In particular, this process of becoming aware may be advanced by inviting stakeholders to reflect on their memories of their own school trajectories.

- Insights should focus not only on the needs of the students from the perspective of the educational system (Baldauf 2006), but also on their own perceived needs and beliefs about learning. This information can be used subsequently to increase stakeholders' understanding of students' perspectives.

In fact, through the application of the above strategies within the EDINA project, a burgeoning of alternative, more effective linguistic strategies have been apparent within classrooms. Diverging from their earlier descriptions of the use of first languages and language planning at the start of the EDINA project, many teachers reflected that they had earlier thought of students' first languages as a problem to be solved rather than a resource to be utilized. One primary school teacher, interviewed in April 2016, noted: "Children are not supposed to use their own languages in class. Sometimes a new pupil will arrive, and then the children will start speaking their own language to each other again. We haven't found a solution for that yet." However, after participating in several EDINA workshops, these same teachers and school leaders introduced several initiatives to incorporate students' first languages within their lessons and consequently noted a marked increase in students' participation and in their oracy and comprehension skills. In March 2018, schools partnering with the project presented the activities they had developed based on EDINA tools to a wider audience of primary and secondary school teachers, researchers, directors, policy makers, and teacher trainers from across the Netherlands.

At the primary school level, as its goal for the year, one of the schools implemented translanguaging practices, consequently setting up a language buddy system and regularly organizing translanguaging activities. For instance, on Valentine's Day, students played word games with hearts and identified as many words associated with love in their own languages as they could. At the secondary school level, with an overall goal of improving oracy in the school language, teachers experimented with the use of first languages during reading and listening comprehension sessions. They paired up students according to shared or similar home languages. Subsequently, the students watched a movie and were asked to negotiate the video's meaning with each other in their own languages. Next, the teachers repeated the video and asked them questions in Dutch. The teachers reported increased participation, animated responses from less confident students, and a level of listening comprehension skills far above the expected level for that class. In light of our experiences with the project, we suggest that eliciting memories of and beliefs about learning from the most important actors within education (students and school stakeholders) may contribute to a more sustainable shift in educational pedagogies.

Conclusion: "Complicating the Notion of 'Single Memory Cultures'"

In this concluding section, we return to Erll's idea of "complicating the notion of 'single memory cultures'" (Erll 2011: 8). The stated purpose of memory studies is precisely to grapple with the realization that our conceptual cartographies are in need of revision (Erll 2011; Kennedy and Nugent 2016). The experiences of those of us who previously felt a sense of comfort and familiarity with our old school maps of languages, people, and places are now ones of discomfort induced by a perception of increased complexity—a kind of vertigo whereby we feel dislocated at home. Interestingly, the answers to questions of what to do when engaging with real people whose experiences do not fit into our already established categorization processes lie *in between* the categories with which we have learned to work so comfortably. They exist along a continuum of possible answers and require us to cobble together solutions from different domains and to accept the existence of unfamiliar configurations of identity, competence, and historical trajectory markers.

Teachers intuitively know this. They are also often trained to make adjustments to accommodate students with different competencies, learning styles, and/or levels of prior knowledge. However, they are also charged with a task that requires them to assess students and classify their behaviors into predetermined categories. We have argued that teachers, school administrators, and policy makers find the courage and the willingness to seek answers to the question of "what to do?" that lie along a continuum situated between preestablished categories when they are able to personally connect to the experience of not fitting into particular categories themselves. In other words, school stakeholders may come to appreciate the multiple memory itineraries and language biographies of their students when they can connect their students' memories and itineraries with their own.

The EDINA Project (Project: 2015-1-NL01-KA201-0088) was cofunded by the EU ERASMUS+ program from 2015 to 2018. It brought together a network of organizations, researchers, and experts from the Netherlands, Belgium, and Finland to provide school stakeholders with the skills needed to support the integration of newly arrived migrant students from different language backgrounds. At the time of this project, the contributing authors, Emmanuelle Le Pichon, Sergio Baauw, Debbie Cole, Suzanne Dekker, and Marie Steffens, were researchers in language, communication, and education at Utrecht University and members of the Utrecht Institute of Linguistics.

Emmanuelle Le Pichon-Vorstman is Assistant Professor at the University of Toronto, OISE, head of the Centre de Recherches en Éducation Franco-Ontarienne (CRÉFO). Since 2009, she has led several projects on the inclusion of minority students in education. Her keen interest in migration policy has led her to conduct research studies on issues related to multilingual education. Emmanuelle was the Principal Investigator of the EDINA project.

Sergio Baauw is Assistant Professor at the Spanish Language and Culture program, and is also active in the master programs Intercultural Communication and Multilingualism and Language Acquisition. His research is focused on first and second language acquisition, multilingualism and language impairment. Sergio Baauw was a member of the EDINA project.

Debbie Cole received her PhD at the University of Arizona. Her work in semiotics combines research in linguistic, anthropological, and literary approaches to the study of language. Areas of interest include ideological and interdisciplinary constraints on socialized human categorizing, learning, and communicating. She also translates poetry from Bahasa Indonesia into English.

Suzanne Dekker is a PhD candidate at the University of Groningen, the Netherlands. Her research focuses on multilingualism and education. Suzanne was a research assistant for the EDINA project.

Marie Steffens is a lecturer in the French language and culture program of the Department of Languages, Literature and Communication at the University of Utrecht. Her work focuses on discourse analysis, historical linguistics, and semantics.

Notes

We would like to thank Manouk van Den Brink for her supportive inputs in the EDINA project during her internship for her master's program in Intercultural Communication at Utrecht in 2016–2017. We would also like to thank all the students and their families; the school teachers, principals, and counselors; and the policymakers who participated in the EDINA project.

1. The Dutch acronym, ISK stands for *Internationale SchakelKlas* in the Netherlands.
2. The Dutch educational system is an early tracking system, in which at the age of twelve, children are selected for either practical levels of secondary education (vocational training) or academic levels of education (preparing for higher education).
3. For details of the debate, see http://www.academie-francaise.fr/actualites/declaration-de-lacademie-francaise-sur-lecriture-dite-inclusive.

References

Agha, Asif. 2015. "Margins, Hubs, and Peripheries in a Decentralizing Indonesia." Discussant Paper for the Sociolinguistics of Globalization Symposium, Hong Kong. 3–6 June 2015. Hong Kong: The University of Hong Kong.

Anzaldúa, Gloria. 1999. *Borderlands/La Frontera: The New Mestiza*. 2nd ed. San Francisco: Aunt Lute Books.

Baldauf, Richard. 2006. "Rearticulating the Case for Micro Language Planning in a Language Ecology Context." *Current Issues in Language Planning* 7, no. 2: 147–70.

Banks, James. 2008. "Diversity, Group Identity, and Citizenship Education in a Global Age." *Educational Researcher* 37, no. 3: 129–39.

Blommaert, Jan. 2010. *The Sociolinguistics of Globalization*. Cambridge, UK: Cambridge University Press.

———. 2015. "Commentary: Superdiversity Old and New." *Language & Communication* 44: 82–88.

Budría, Santiago, and Pablo Swedberg. 2015. "The Impact of Language Proficiency on Immigrants' Earnings." *Revista de Economía Aplicada* 67, no. XXIII: 63–91.

Canagarajah, Suresh. 2013. "Negotiating Translingual Literacy: An Enactment." *Research in the Teaching of English* 48, no. 1: 40–67.

Centraal Orgaan Opvang Asielzoekers. 2017. *Antallen en herkomst* [Numbers and provenance]. Accessed 25 March 2018. https://www.werkwijzervluchtelingen.nl/feiten-cijfers/aantallen-herkomst.aspx.

Clark, Julie, and Fred Dervin. 2014. "Introduction." In *Reflexivity in Language and Intercultural Education: Rethinking Multilingualism and Interculturality*, edited by Julie Clark and Fred Dervin, 1–42. New York: Routledge.

Cole, Debbie. 2014. "Mobilizing Voices across Representational Boundaries: Some Considerations for Local Values and Functions." *International Journal of the Sociology of Language, Special Issue on Language and Borders: International Perspectives* 227: 175–92.

Council of Europe. 2001. *Common European Framework of Reference for Languages: Learning, Teaching, Assessment*. Strasbourg: Council of Europe.

Creese, Angela, and Adrian Blackledge. 2010. "Translanguaging in the Bilingual Classroom: A Pedagogy for Learning and Teaching?" *The Modern Language Journal* 1, no. 94: 103–15.

Cummins, Jim. 1979. "Linguistic Interdependence and the Educational Development of Bilingual Children." *Review of Educational Research* 49: 222–51.

———. 2001. *Negotiating Identities: Education Empowerment for a Diverse Society*. 2nd ed. Ontario, Canada: California Association for Bilingual Education.

Cummins, Jim, Shirley Hu, Paula Markus, and Kristina Montero. 2015. "Identity Texts and Academic Achievement: Connecting the Dots in Multilingual School Contexts." *TESOL Quarterly* 49, no. 3: 555–81.

Delarue, Steven, and Johan De Caluwe. 2015. "Eliminating Social Inequality by Reinforcing Standard Language Ideology? Language Policy for Dutch in Flemish Schools." *Current Issues in Language Planning* 16, no. 1–2: 8–25.

Dervin, Fred, Simpson, Ashley and Matikainen, Anna. 2016. Country report, Finland. Accessed 25 March 2018. https://edinaplatform.eu/en/edina/research/country-reports.

Diaz Fouces, Oscar. 2010. "(Eco)linguistic Planning and Language-Exchange Management." Translated by Robert N. Baxter. *MonTI* 2: 283–313.

DUO [Dienst Uitvoering Onderwijs]. 2016. *Onderwijsonderzoek: Werkdruk in het basisonderwijs* [Educational research: Work pressure in primary education]. Accessed 25 March 2018. http://cmsawt.ncrv.nl/data/files/bijlages/Rapportagepercent20-percent20Werkdrukpercent20Leerkrachtenpercent20POpercent20-percent20DEFpercent20VERSIE.pdf.

Dyers, Charlyn. 2008. "Language Shift or Maintenance? Factors Determining the Use of Afrikaans among Some Township Youth in South Africa." *Stellenbosch Papers in Linguistics* 38: 49–72.

Erll, Astrid. 2011. "Travelling Memory." *Parallax* 17, no. 4: 4–18.

Fishman, Joshua. 2004. "Ethnicity and Supra-Ethnicity in Corpus Planning: The Hidden Status Agenda in Corpus Planning." *Nations and Nationalism* 10, no. 1/2: 79–94.

Garcia, Ofelia, Tove Skutnabb-Kangas, and Maria Torres-Guzman, eds. 2006. *Imagining Multilingual Schools: Language in Education and Glocalization*. Toronto: Multilingual Matters.

Garcia, Ofelia, and Li Wei. 2015. "Translanguaging, Bilingualism, and Bilingual Education." In *The Handbook of Bilingual and Multilingual Education*, edited by W. E. Wright, S. Boun, and O. Garcia, 223–40. Chichester, UK: John Wiley & Sons.

Graus, Johan, and Peter-Arno Coppen. 2016. "Student Teacher Beliefs on Grammar Instruction." *Language Teaching Research* 20, no. 5: 571–99.

Hall, Christopher. 2013. "Cognitive Contributions to Plurilithic Views of English and Other Languages." *Applied Linguistics* 34, no. 2: 211–31.

Hayfron, John. 2001. "Language Training, Language Proficiency and Earnings of Immigrants in Norway." *Applied Economics* 33, no. 15: 1971–79.

Heineke, Amy, Elizabeth Coleman, Elizabeth Ferrell, and Craig Kersemeier. 2012. "Opening Doors for Bilingual Students: Recommendations for Building Linguistically Responsive Schools." *Improving Schools* 15, no. 2: 130–47.

Herzog-Punzenberger, Barbara, Emmanuelle Le Pichon-Vorstman, and Hanna Siarova. 2017. "Multilingual Education in the Light of Diversity: Lessons Learned." *NESET II Report*. Luxembourg: Publications Office of the European Union.

Holliday, Adrian, Martin Hyde, and John Kullman. 2010. *Intercultural Communication*. New York: Routledge.

Hornberger, Nancy, and Holly Link. 2012. "Translanguaging and Transnational Literacies in Multilingual Classrooms: A Biliteracy Lens." *International Journal of Bilingual Education and Bilingualism* 15, no. 3: 261–78.

Hulstijn, Jan. 2015. *Language Proficiency in Native and Non-Native Speakers: Theory and Research*. Amsterdam: John Benjamins.

Jackson, Jane. 2014. *Introducing Language and Intercultural Communication*. London: Routledge.

Kaplan, Robert, and Richard Baldauf. 1997. *Language Planning from Practice to Theory*. Clevedon: Multilingual Matters.

Kennedy, Rosanne, and Maria Nugent. 2016. "Scales of Memory: Reflections on an Emerging Concept." *Australian Humanities Review* 59: 61–76.

Klinkenberg, Jean- Marie. 2001. *La Langue et Le Citoyen* [*Language and the Citizen*]. Paris: PUF.

Le Pichon-Vorstman, Emmanuelle, Romée van Erning, and Sergio Baauw. 2016. *Country Report: The Netherlands; Education of Newly Arrived Migrant Pupils*. www.edinaplatform.eu.

Le Pichon-Vorstman, Emmanuelle, Sergio Baauw, and Jacob Vorstman. 2016. "School Development of Newly Arrived Migrant Pupils." European Conference on Educational Research, Dublin, Ireland. 26–28 August 2016.

Le Pichon-Vorstman, Emmanuelle, and Debbie Cole, 2017. "Giving Voice to the Newly Arrived Migrant Pupils." International Conference on Multilingualism and Multilingual Education, Braga, Portugal. 11–13 May 2017.

Liddicoat, Anthony. 2013. *Language-in-Education Policies: The Discursive Construction of Intercultural Relations*. Bristol: Multilingual Matters.

Musumeci, Diane. 1997. *Breaking Tradition: An Exploration of the Historical Relationship between Theory and Practice in Second Language Teaching*. New York: McGraw.

Pavlenko, Aneta. 2017. "Superdiversity and Why It Isn't." Edited by S. Breidbach, L. Kuster, B. Schmenk. Sloganizations in language education discourse, Bristol, UK: Multilingual Matters.

Payne, Mark. 2006. "Foreign Language Planning in England: The Pupil Perspective." *Current Issues in Language Planning* 7, no. 2: 189–213.

Piccardo, Enrica. 2013. "Plurilingualism and Curriculum Design: Toward a Synergic Vision." *TESOL Quarterly* 47, no. 3: 600–14.

Prevoo, Marielle, Maike Malda, Judi Mesman, and Marinus van IJzendoorn. 2016. "Within- and Cross-Language Relations between Oral Language Proficiency and School Outcomes in Bilingual Children with an Immigrant Background: A Meta-Analytical Study." *Review of Educational Research* 86, no. 1: 237–76.

Ricento, Thomas, and Nancy Hornberger. 1996. "Unpeeling the Onion: Language Planning and Policy and the ELT Professional." *TESOL Quarterly* 30, no. 3: 401–27.

Ruiz, Richard. 1984. "Orientations in Language Planning." *NABE: The Journal for the National Association for Bilingual Education* 8, no. 2: 15–34.

Sandford, Jeremy. 2002. "English Language Proficiency and the Earnings of Mexican Immigrants." Senior Honors Project. Bloomington: Illinois Wesleyan University.

Schulz, Renate. 2001. "Cultural Differences in Student and Teacher Perceptions Concerning the Role of Grammar Instruction and Corrective Feedback: USA-Colombia." *The Modern Language Journal* 85, no. 2: 244–58.

Seals, Corinne, and Joy Peyton. 2017. "Heritage Language Education: Valuing the Languages, Literacies, and Cultural Competencies of Immigrant Youth." *Current Issues in Language Planning* 18, no. 1: 87–101.

Sociaal-Economische Raad. 2017. "SER vraagt in Tweede Kamer aandacht voor snellere integratie vluchtelingen" ["SER requests attention in the House of Representatives for faster integration of refugees"]. 25 January. Accessed 24 March 2018. https://www.ser.nl/nl/.

Silverstein, Michael. 2015. "How Language Communities Intersect: Is 'Superdiversity' an Incremental or Transformative Condition?" *Language & Communication* 44: 7–18.

van Walbeek, Kim. 2017. "De communicatie in de samenwerking tussen ouders van nieuwkomersleerlingen en medewerkers in het primair en voortgezet onderwijs" ["Communication between Parents of Newly Arrived Students and Education Staff in Primary and Secondary Schools"]. Master's Thesis, Utrecht, Utrecht University.

Vertovec, Steven. 2007. "Super-Diversity and Its Implications." *Ethnic and Racial Studies* 30, no. 6: 1024–54.

VluchtelingenWerk Nederland. 2016. "Vluchtelingenwerk in Getallen 2016." 25 August 2016. Accessed 24 March 2018. https://www.vluchtelingenwerk.nl/sites/public/u895/Vluchtelingen ingetallen2016_nieuw.pdf.

Werkgroep Kind in AZC. 2013. *Ontheemd: De verhuizingen van asielzoekerskinderen in Nederland* [*Displaced: The removals of asylum seekers' children in the Netherlands*]. Accessed 24 March 2018. https://www.unicef.nl/nieuws/2013-02-14-ontheemd-de-verhuizingen-van-asielzoekerskinderen-in-nederland.

Winter, Elke. 2010. "Trajectories of Multiculturalism in Germany, the Netherlands and Canada: In Search of Common Patterns." *Government and Opposition* 45, no. 2: 166–86.

Part III

DIASPORIC MEMORIES AND ARCHIVAL TRAJECTORIES

Chapter 5

CONCEPTUALIZING DIASPORIC MEMORY

Temporalities and the Geography of Emotions
in Eritreans' Oral Tales

Gabriele Proglio

In this chapter, I seek to illuminate silenced narratives from the Global South. Specifically, I conducted interviews with individuals who came to Europe from the Horn of Africa, which is the region where former Italian colonies are located. The role of intersubjectivity was prominent in the semistructured interviews entailed in my methodology, and a geography of emotions (Proglio 2019) emerged during dialogues with respondents. The interview topics were wide-ranging, covering colonialism, the postcolonial condition, relationships with parents and friends, cultural identity, the journey, deaths in the Mediterranean, the place of arrival, and Fortress Europe. Empathy played a central role in facilitating my understanding of voices and silences (Proglio 2018b). In this chapter, I focus exclusively on interviews that I conducted with individuals from Eritrea, or those with cultural roots in that country—that is, individuals from second or third diasporic generations with at least one Eritrean parent in Italy or elsewhere. My aim is to theorize diasporic memory and its operation, demonstrating the relevance of memories and of the different temporalities entailed in the construction of identities.

Seeking "New Times"

Stuart Hall has described the production of diasporic narratives as a process entailing "a unity of two different elements, under certain conditions. It is a linkage that is not necessary, determined, absolute and essential for all time" (Grossberg 1996: 142–43). This conceptualization usefully draws attention to the continual and permanent movement of two parts in relation to each other. On the one hand, new narratives about categories of European subjects are constantly generated from the archives on Europeaness and citizenship; on the other hand, diasporic subjects invent new significations and deploy various strategies to assemble narratives and meanings that at first sight appear incompatible.

Another insight offered by Hall (1989) relates to subject positionality and subjectivities. In his discussion of the cinema of the Caribbean, he introduces the concept of articulation, suggesting that there are two different ways of thinking about "cultural identity." The first one entails a definition of cultural identity as a shared culture, a sort of collective "one true Self," reflecting a common historical experience such as colonialism or slavery. Conversely, the second approach highlights internal differences within the above described unity. He specifies that the difference relates to "what we really are . . . and what we have become" (Hall 1989: 75).

Hall's theorization of cultural identity enables transcendence of the canonical idea of the subject, which is necessary to understand the contradiction between "unity" and "difference" of ideas or groups that is entailed in the process of belonging. In addition, in "Minimal Selves," he affirms that identity is "formed at the unstable point where the 'unspeakable' stories of subjectivity meet the narratives of history, of a culture" (Hall 1967: 44). He points to a paradoxical dilemma: at the moment of understanding oneself to be "an immigrant," "one recognizes [that] one can't be an immigrant any longer: it isn't a tenable place to be" (Hall 1967: 45). Moreover, "constituting oneself as 'black' is another recognition of self through difference" (Hall 1967: 45). Thus, identity is conceived as a fiction; the product of a self-reflexivity that constitutes "politics in the recognition of the necessary arbitrariness of the closure around the imaginary communities" (Hall 1967: 45).

A methodological insight derived from Hall's theorization is that some identities, such as those connected with the idea of being black, should not be viewed as self-evident and given within the research process (Hall 1967: 45). Accordingly, diasporic subjectivity should be conceived as undetermined and always in process.

In "New Ethnicities" (1992), however, Hall shifts from a conception of difference as a way to recognize the self to the Derridian concept of *différance*, connoting an infinite sliding of the signifier.[1] Hall reframes the concept as a strategy for manifesting a process of meaning attribution based on a binary system, as described by Spivak, Fanon, and several other intellectuals. The term "diasporization," coined by Hall, signifies a cultural process relating to the politics of representation of black people in diaspora "and the consequences which this carries for the process of unsettling, recombination, hybridization and 'cut-and-mix'" (Hall 1992: 257). I would further suggest that the reshaping of memory—its mythologies, archives, and associated practices—is the outcome of the subject's new positionalities in the present. As Hall states, "There can be . . . no simple 'return' or 'recovery' of the ancestral past which is not re-experienced through the categories of the present" (Hall 1992: 258).

Theorizing Diasporic Memory

In theorizing diasporic memory, I would like to position this concept dialectically in relation to Hall's conceptualization. In doing so, my intention is to show that this memory is inherently unstable and can be drawn on in a variety of contexts and within different cultural processes. Examples include promoting recognition of individual and collective identities, constructing intersubjective life stories, and producing future layouts and practices of concealment, disguise, and mimicry connected with cultural identities and bodies.

Inherent to the diasporic condition is the will to return home and the simultaneous impossibility of doing so for several reasons (economic, political, and ethnic conflicts and wars). Another specific characteristic of this condition relates to the inhospitality of the country of arrival—or birth for second or third generations—and the resulting "betrayal" of expectations of being accepted and considered as an integral part of the national community. This exclusion is multifaceted, entailing territorial and political segregation, negative economic conditions, a labor market configured by race/gender/color/nationality (so called differential inclusion), and the impossibility of applying for and obtaining national citizenship. This is the *in between* condition under which diasporic memory operates. The denied desire for home is the other facet of betrayed expectations of a welcome and of hospitality. This experience of double denial invokes a subjective and collective condition of being out of place (Puwar 2004), out of history, and without a story that can be told.

The operation of diasporic memory enables the framing of strategic practices to resist the hegemonic narrative, which excludes, marginalizes, and dehumanizes people. As Hall points out, subjects move among several cultures and simultaneously hold many identities and beliefs. Diasporic memories—constituted through direct lived experiences or through the narrated experiences of friends who are in diaspora—are elaborated against a common cultural background, encompassing both the personal and public spheres from where positionalities are renegotiated. Thus, memory plays a role in the production of subjectivity, which, in turn, is involved in the production of memory. These mutual and simultaneous processes enable the elaboration of a shared imaginary and strategies for eluding dangers, border controls, identification, and depersonalization. Diasporic memory works to decontextualize and recontextualize topics and frameworks in the elaboration of new meanings, as theorized by Hall (1996a), who applied a Gramscian framework for the study of race and drew on the Derridian concept of *différance* to formulate a range of significations relating to the same topic. Drawing on Hall's insights, these narratives about diasporic memory that are at work in the decontextualizing and reconceptualizing of topics are not preconstituted; rather, they are actualized in the context of the diasporic condition. Hence, the aggregation of several discourses results from both the state of "inbetweeness" (Bhabha 2004) and adhesion to a community of people who embody and experience, in different ways, the same postcolonial condition. Last, the "cut-and-mix" practice is not a mere mechanical change of position of a single scrap-of-memory. In this movement of fragments, the entire archive is reshaped in terms of subjective and intersubjective ways of remembering and forgetting. The coherence of a narrative may result from meanings that extend beyond the scientific and historical roles of documentation, verification, and demonstration. Sometimes, the synthesis of various fragments and possible combinations is the outcome of strategies or ways of positioning the self, which would otherwise be flattened into a mere representation by the hegemonic discourse.

The positionality of diasporic subjectivity and relative memory is always characterized in relation to another narrative that is considered different. The divergence of the two narratives of hegemony and subalternity are in fact part of the same model; deconstruction of this essentially dualistic model illuminates a genealogy of power relations as well as possible ways of speaking and of silencing. Whereas history is linear, reflecting a *consecutio temporum* (sequence of tenses), the stories emanating from diasporic memory are discontinuous and characterized by asides, ellipses, and spiral narrative structures. As Hall (1989) notes, mapping their discourses may require a focus on disjuncture rather than on conjuncture.

Revisiting the colonial past, slavery—struggles for freedom against other nations/people (as in the case of the Ethiopian/Eritrean conflict)—may have relevance for the present by revealing connections with the progenitors of the subject's agency (e.g., resistance, subordination, and oppression). In line with the preceding argument, the storytelling may be regarded as a historical battleground in which several narratives about the past and concerning the present/future compete with each other. Diasporic memory works to elude these boundaries and prohibitions, proposing disallowed or inconceivable positionalities of historical subjects. If we think of history as a map, these stories are located both outside of and within its folds. They disclose transnational underground geographies that hegemonic narratives try to delete, hide, forget, make invisible, obscure, and fragment to the point of making the singular voice insignificant and unrepresentative of and for history. Such voices are dissolved within what is considered a "higher" history of humanity; they are personified and embodied within bodies that are considered remote from the culture, entitling history and the subject to write the past. Reshaping cultural roots and belonging to a diasporic community enables the subject to assume different positionalities. It is a strategy that works in the present while continually reconsidering both the past and the future.

Diasporic memory can thus be seen to operate on the edges of different spheres: individual, collective, and intersubjective. Moreover, it reveals another specific feature: namely, it ascribes new positionalities to the subject that are not those attributed by border identification devices. Narratives are shaped by a divisive border that is simultaneously generative of categories, such as "migrant," "refugee," "Tunisian," and "black," on the one hand, and of diasporic memories on the other hand. This process entails the strategic deployment of subjective practices and narratives, such as those of displacement, making others invisible, hiding and mimicry, doubling of the self, and multiplication of memories.

In light of the above discussion, it now becomes possible to problematize the question of temporality. Subjects who experience diasporic memory are suspended within several temporalities. Their condition of being in diaspora explains this condition. The first temporality is that of colonialism and slavery, the originating foundation for the production of the history of black and African people made by and in Europe. Usually, people in diaspora view these events as a *Moloch*;[2] that is, something that happened that changed forever the condition of not-white people. Such events are impossible to deconstruct; they are taken for granted even when they are forgotten or not written about. This is because the evidence and relevance of those past events are inscribed on their bodies in accordance with the archives of whiteness. This first temporality appears both as an act of "creation of the world" and its simultaneous division into parts. It is a primary denial of the subject, who feels and is always out of place because of his or her specific position within Europe, both in the past and in the present.

A second temporality relates to the present. The postcolonial condition of contemporary Europe is crucial in this regard. Because of international agreements, such as Dublin III, and existing regulations for applying for the status of refugee or asylum seeker, subjects arriving in Europe live in a suspended condition between denied rights and precarious conditions, hypervisibility and invisibility, differential inclusion and exclusion, ventriloquism by "humanitarians" and imposed silence. This iconic ambiguity simultaneously positions them at the center of the political scene—their lives and bodies serve as the screen upon which the anxieties of Europeans are projected—beyond any possibility of producing narratives in the public sphere. They live in a temporality marked by aporia. This term should be understood in two contrasting ways: as a lack of time that can be spent living and making choices and in the literal sense of an impossible passage from one condition to another that creates a situation of uncertainty. Both meanings generate antinomies in the sense of paradoxes, both from a narrative perspective, as pointed out by Ricoeur (1985), and in the determination of who is considered a human being, when and where, and who is not (Mbembe 2003).

The third temporality relates to the future, which is imagined to be positive—sometimes entailing mimicry of white European subjects—before departure from the homeland for Europe. The impact of encounters with border identification devices is significant. The future is reduced and compressed into an ongoing present without any possibility of moving beyond this state. If the possibility of creating an imagined new condition from narratives exists, this stage is characterized by aphasia. This term conveys the impossibility of people in diaspora expressing their subjectivity within the public sphere. However, the term also has a second meaning, signifying a desire to move beyond the present that is constantly betrayed.

From the perspective of subjectivity, the three temporalities represent three different typologies of an ongoing and enduring present that interact with each other within oral tales. When thoughts and feelings are conveyed in a European language, these appear fluent and linear within the narrative. However, a cultural analysis of oral sources brings to light various discontinuities and interruptions. All of the abovementioned characteristics featured constantly in the oral interviews I conducted with diverse Eritreans, male and female and of different ages, during my fieldwork in Italy (Bologna, Turin, Rome, Milan, and Padua). In the following pages, I will map the *différance* of diasporic memory emerging from these interviews. In light of the "geography of emotions" (Proglio 2018b) that this mapping reveals, I will focus on the relationship between feelings and temporalities in these narratives.

Eritreans in Italy: Mapping the *Différance* of Diasporic Memory

During my stay in the "Porta Venezia area" of Milan, which accommodates the greatest concentration of the Eritrean diaspora, I encountered several kinds of people. I was struck by the spatial distribution of the diaspora, reflecting different endings of migratory projects. First, there were people dressed in different attire walking down the streets. I asked about these differences in clothing during oral interviews. As Emy pointed out, those clothes originate in Lampedusa and in Italy's refugee shelters; they are markers of identity of recently arrived individuals. These people live on the street, which is the only space they are allowed to occupy: outside shops, bars, and building entrances. Then, there is another section of the Eritrean community working inside of the abovementioned spaces/places but living in other parts of the city. Their migration outcomes have been advantageous compared with those of their compatriots on the street. Most of these individuals did not arrive via the Mediterranean Sea but instead via other routes, and with the economic support of parents or friends in Italy. If the first condition entails a horizontal spatial orientation, the second evidences a vertical orientation, with several families residing in apartment blocks in Porta Venezia. Migratory projects have different outcomes. It can be assumed that successful migration is characterized by movement from horizontally occupied space—that is, from living on the street without any possibility of sedimenting lives lived on the ground—to vertically occupied space. Consequently, the subjects become a recognized and entropic part of the city, with a corresponding stratification of material memories inscribed in the territory, and in a place.

I met Aman on the street. He spoke only Eritrean and tried to explain to me that he had just arrived. "Libya, Mediterranean, Ciao," he affirmed. Having used these three words to map his crossing of the sea and his arrival in Italy, he touched his chest with both hands using two repeated movements that resembled a cardiac massage. I was struck by the fact that this was not a simple dialogue, and at the same time, I was fully cognizant of the meaning of the gesture: he was trying to convey to me the pain of losing friends. He continued to repeat the Italian word *morti* ("dead" in English). With this word, he assigned a name to those whose lives were lost below the waves of the Mediterranean Sea, using a term that embodies the memory of that past and marks the context in which the action happened, in Italy.

Winta is a twenty-year-old woman. She was born to an Eritrean family in Italy. She has not been to Eritrea, but she replied to my questions about Italian colonialism because she had an in-depth knowledge of Asmara and of the entire country.

> So, colonialism, in Eritrea, uh . . . is esthetically visible, that is to say, I could affirm that without Italians, many things would have been impossible. Asmara would not exist because all the buildings were made by Italians. . . . I don't agree with colonialism in general terms. Eritrea has always been kneeling to all [other countries]; she did not obtain her independence. So, as an Eritrean woman, I feel just a bit of partisan in giving my opinion. . . . I have never seen my country free, starting from Italy['s colonization of it].

I asked her what images Italian colonialism evoked in her mind. She replied, "Mussolini, the cathedral of Asmara, and the city." These images are derived from a diasporic archive because, as she informed me, she had never actually been to this African country. The visual memory of the diaspora appears to operate in parallel with the forgetting of "Eritrea's location within Africa" by younger Italians. In our interview, this topic served to introduce the theme of identity. In Winta's opinion, whereas Europeans could be considered good or bad, "foreign" only connoted something bad. She observed: "They are not ready to consider us the same as them. This is true also for those of us who have grown up here in Italy." At this point, I paused for a few seconds. I wanted to frame a question for her in positive terms. I asked her, "Why do they consider you different?" She responded without hesitation: "Because of my skin color. . . . If I was white, they wouldn't say the same things to me because I speak Italian as well as them." She explained further that it was the stranger they feared. "And of course," she added, "I am brown." "Black or brown?" I asked her. "Look, I always say I am black." As the extract cited below reveals, the distinction between "black" and "brown" signified the emergence of a double consciousness through an intersubjective inquiry that unfolded during the interview process.

> Gabriele: How do you define yourself? As Italian? Eritrean? Black?
>
> Winta: I define myself . . . as Eritrean, uh, yes, Eritrean, Black, and African, despite [my being] born [here] and growing up here. I speak Italian, I have Italian citizenship, but my heart is completely Eritrean.

Sara was born in Rome and when she was three years old, she moved, with her family, to Peschiera Borromeno, a small town not far from Milan. Her mother and father are former Eritrean freedom fighters, and she is proud of this. She was twenty-two years old at the time of the interview. I met her with Helen, an Eritrean woman, who is two years older than Sara. Contrasting with Sara, Helen arrived in Italy from Geshionsud, a small town in the Eritrean countryside. She has visited Eritrea four times.

They both spoke about Italian colonialism. According to Sara, "Some things are happening nowadays in Eritrea that are the consequences of colonialism . . . which is always bad." She added, "At the beginning, there was an illusion [she does not complete her enunciation of the word] . . . the division between white and black people. . . . White people imposed themselves on a land that did not belong to them."

Sarah's narrative appears to be intimately connected to her life. As a black woman, she embodies the experience of discrimination or exclusion from the community. She described this experience as follows:

> In my small town, I was the only woman of color. All of the guys were wealthy with stiff ideals. I can't say that I did not feel okay, because I had friends. But when I was a child . . . I remember when I was in class at the primary school . . .

there was a boy who called me "small nigger" [she used the Italian term *negretta*]. And immediately I started to cry.

She confessed that she felt embarrassed on behalf of another black woman, "the first one" she had met in her life. She attended high school in Milan. There, she met her in class: "I was the only colored woman. [Then,] I see this colored woman. For me it was an embarrassing moment. I felt ashamed. I was Italianized 100 percent; for me, Eritrea did not exist in my mind."

Helen noted that the stereotypical view of "Africa as a land to conquer and Africans as a people to enslave" could be traced back to the colonial era. She had been in contact with black people since her childhood, and her problematization of blackness differed from Sara's. She stated that she was not affected by racist comments about her skin. Notably, when she was in class, other students talked about migration and associated her with that phenomenon. She had no hesitation about returning to Eritrea if the possibility arose:

> If there was a possibility of choosing to live in Eritrea or remaining in Italy, and if the situation in Eritrea was positive, with peace and calm [restored] . . . I would immediately go back to Eritrea because, however . . . I mean, I feel Eritrea is my country, despite having grown up here. . . . I feel that it is my country. I don't know how to explain . . . perhaps this is because my father is there . . . perhaps [it] is the absence of my father, but I feel that it is my country, my place. . . . Before, and until the age of two or three, I thought perhaps that . . . Europe, Italy was my country. Now, I think it as a bad thing. So, I think something is missing in me, and I could find that part which is missing there.

At that point, as with Sara, I asked her about her identity. After a brief silence, she responded with these words: "I feel both Eritrean and Italian . . . but inside of me . . . my desire is to leave and to go live there . . . it is just a little bit strange . . . I feel both [identities], but I know that my place is there."

During my travels across Italy, I visited Padua several times. There, I conducted several interviews in the neighborhood of Arcella. This locality was constructed at the end of the nineteenth century as an industrial area and quickly became a working class neighborhood. During the Fascist era, hundreds of men from Arcella were enlisted in the Italian army and left their homes to participate in wars in Italy's colonies in Libya and in the Horn of Africa. This is the reason why some streets still bear the names of former Italian colonies and their cities (e.g., Via Somalia, Via Amba Lagi, Via Libia, Via Eritrea, Via Asmara, and Via Adua). In Arcella, I met Viviana Zorzato who lived there in an apartment with her family. Her father had been an Italian soldier who was sent to fight in the Eritrean conquest. When she arrived in Italy, she began to seek information about the history of Eritrea:

My political interest began with the history of my country. I started to collect documents and every kind of material on colonialism. I was looking for books and reviews of the period that talked about what was a part of me; a part that hurt me a lot. And I felt involved in the bad treatment . . . so terrible . . . talking about Eritreans, Blacks as people to . . . educate, to correct; as primitive and uncivilized people.

After a long silence, she resumed talking and began to speak about her father. "This interest led me [on a quest] to know my father, even if I was unable to recognize him in the narratives on colonizers. I was not able to recognize him because the thought in my mind was *No, my father is not like that!*" During her inquiry, she discovered new meanings for words such as "slavery" and "subjection." She began to critique the term "colonial adventure" because of the violence that was imposed on African people. Her imaginary relating to her father was of a man who decided to desert the army and marry an Ethiopian woman (Eritrea had not yet come into being at the time). The Italian term for such individuals was *insabbiato,* which can be translated as "shelved people." From one perspective, all *insabbiati* soldiers can be viewed as those who decided to break with Fascism and war, discarding the military uniform for a "normal" life with a *bella abissina* ("Abyssinian beauty"), an expression that was in vogue in Fascist Italy and was used to describe the exotic esthetic attributed to Ethiopian women. She thought of him as an "outsider" in contrast to the colonial ruling class. When I asked her about her cultural identity, she connected this memory to her own subjectivity:

> I am Italian, yes, because that is what I write on documents. When we were children in Eritrea, they had to write down our names, surnames, and nationalities. One had to write the citizenship and Italian nationality.[3] So, yes, in forms and papers I am Italian, despite having the ID . . . the Eritrean citizenship. I understood my Eritrean part well, but I am not sufficiently . . . I have had a hard time recognizing my Italian part because I am not aware of what being Italian means.

I also had the opportunity to interview Enrico Zorzato, Viviana's brother. He was forty-seven years old at the time of the interview. He recalled how climbs and descents had "a metaphysical meaning" in his life. When he was growing up in Asmara, there was a hill that he referred to as a "climb/descent," known as Abraha Zucchini. The first name was that of a famous Eritrean man living on the street; the second one was Italian. He stated: "For each climb/descent, you can't see what there is behind."

When we started to talk about Italian colonialism, he introduced the word "myth." "I remember that fantastic world that my father talked about," he told me, "a world made through epic endeavors. You can tell a child what you want, but the child can perceive tragedies." His father spent a lot of time outside the house because he worked as a driver, and he considered himself a "white African." The father's experience of returning home to Italy after colonialism ended and before the launch of the civil war to split from Ethiopia was paralleled by Enrico's experience of returning home to Eritrea from Italy. When he returned to Eritrea, the world that he knew no longer existed. This sense of being lost and disorientated, albeit from two different perspectives—in Italy and in Eritrea—shaped the lives of father and son. His father continued to look for ghosts during the years following their arrival in Italy. By contrast, when Enrico was able to return to Eritrea, he chose to apply his memory differently:

> There is no place in the world where there is no Eritrean, no Eritrean community. There are many more Eritreans abroad than in Eritrea. Nowadays, in Eritrea, I think there would be a few million inhabitants; but maybe 10 million or more are abroad and are second generation. So, I did not find the people I had left behind, but I found places that I had to recompose in my memory and [I had] to combine their presence in my remembering . . . in my memory streets and avenues. Even if I travelled across the city and saw the world changed, everything remained in my mind as a fossil.

These memories remained in his mind as well as those of his life in Italy. When we started to talk about his positionality, he suggested that a new category was required. He told me, "I own to the concepts of fifty-fifty or mulattos, or creoles, or half-blood." This connotation evokes "the beginnings of a strong sense of bewilderment." In this state, "people try to elaborate an identity as a half-blood, using a certain language, a specific gesture, which is a mixture of both cultural contexts. So, we will never be [he laughed] either white or black." The laugh was followed by silence, which conveyed ambiguity to me: it was something I understood only from a position outside my body; an understanding of other bodies through intersubjectivity. But at the same time, it was something that originated from the whiteness that I also embodied.

The Eritrean language specifically has a word, *anfez*, meaning "half-blood." Enrico explained that this is an Eritrean imaginary. In Italian, this word has no meaning because "the average Italian needs to be sure, and you know if you are Eritrean or Italian." Therefore, it is not possible to be "half and half." "They [Italians] can understand this from a physiological point of view, not from a cultural one." According to Enrico, this is because "the black Italian does not exist, and nor does the white African, such as my father." Thus, Enrico is an *anfez*, mulatto, creole, and half-blood.

Sonia used the same term in another context; that of Bologna. Since 1974, which is the date of the first international Eritrean festival held in the Emilia region of Italy, the city has been one of the key sites for the Eritrean diaspora.

Bologna is home to three generations of Eritreans who were born there. Sonia belongs to the last one. She was thirty-five years old at the time of the interview. Asmara is the city of her "father and family," whereas her mother is Italian. Keren is her grandmother's place of origin. She visited the country only once. When she got off the plane, she felt "a tremendous sense of belonging." Her knowledge of Eritrean history is derived from some videotapes carefully hidden away by her parents. These videos depict the war activities of the Eritrean Liberation Front. In her opinion, Italy is responsible for the violence inflicted during colonization and for what is happening in the Mediterranean. "This is a legacy of the colonial period that endures within Italian institutions," she observed. We moved on from colonialism to talk about the postcolonial condition, focusing on her experiences. She explained that her identity has oscillated between two cultural poles: Italy and Eritrea. She defined herself as *meticcia* (*mestizia*) and as mulatto. "This is not linked to the cultural field but to the esthetic one; to the color of your skin," she explained, adding, "I am *anfez*." In her opinion, there is no equivalent Italian word for this term. She provided her own interpretation of the word:

> We can say that everything is caused by my fluctuating position, of feeling myself . . . my Eritrean part never made me feel I was a stranger in the community; my Italian part [did so] many times. . . . I position myself simultaneously near and far by feeling Italian, feeling Eritrean. As I said to you, it has never been a question of being half and half, or feeling partially one thing and partially the other. You feel yourself all at once; you feel as a whole, in a complete way, each of the parts.

At the end of the interview, she emphasized the fact that she was very proud of her identity: "It has many facets, and I would like to be more of my Eritrean part."

Salem, an Eritrean woman, was thirty-two years old when I interviewed her. She was born in a small town in Eritrea and moved to Italy when she was a child. At the time of the interview, she was working in a bank as a counter assistant. When I asked her about colonialism in Eritrea, she said, "Those people left our country," revealing that she had studied the history of her country. She continued, in a different voice, speaking of common people, such as her grandmother, who "doesn't consider Italians with anger because they invaded and conquered us." According to Salem, "We had two colonialisms, Italian and English. In Asmara we lived a sort of apartheid, in the sense that there was a part of the city where Eritreans where not allowed; it was only for whites." Echoing her grandmother's view, she added, "Italians are not bad at all. There are a lot of *meticci* (half-breeds)." She explained: "*Anfez* is a word that describes people who are half-Italians and half-Eritrean." In her view, *anfez* means "blended." It describes thousands of people living in Eritrea and Italy. However, she is not *anfez*. When I asked her about the identity, she described it as follows:

> Salem: I am Eritrean. I am aware of that [identity] from being involved in political groups and in the debate on migrants. I would like to defend my compatriots every time they are attacked . . . from that I understand I am more Eritrean than Italian. Bolognese.
>
> Gabriele: Also Bolognese?
>
> S: Yes.
>
> G: That's important. You are Bolognese-Eritrean!
>
> S: Bolognese-Eritrean doesn't exist, however . . .
>
> G: It might . . .
>
> S: We make it exist!

She added another word, *ambescià*, which is used in both Ethiopia and Eritrea to describe those who come from these two countries, focusing on the mythical land of origin. This division reflects a different geography that existed prior to the Eritrean war of independence, which was launched in 1961, and the Eritrean-Ethiopian War that began in 1998. *Abescià* are all people from, or culturally connected with (as second-generation people living in diaspora), the land of the ancient Ethiopian Empire. Speaking from this standpoint, she asserted, "Africa is the house; Africa is my house. I am Eritrean and African, in the sense that . . . it is my representativeness; it is what represents me, hence my Africa." Shifting her attention to *abescià*, she explained that this term conveys the identity of the Ethiopian-Eritrean people, both in the Horn of Africa and in Europe, and specifically in Italy. "My mother's friends were *ambescià*, but . . . I decided to live at a distance from the *abescià* zone. . . . After a certain period, I felt the need to be part of my community, and when you enter it, you cannot leave it."

Robert crossed the Mediterranean and arrived in Italy in 2004. He described the relationship between migratory routes and Italian military actions in Africa: Libya, Ethiopia, and Eritrea, which were former colonies. Moreover, prior to 1861, the Italian king approved a military mission in Sudan. When I asked him about Italian colonialism, he replied, "I was not there, but my grandfather was a soldier for the Italians." I immediately asked him if his grandfather was an *ascaro* (the term used for an Italian troop soldier in the colonies). He replied, "Yes, he was . . . he was like a slave for the Italians . . . but, we can also talk of slavery today and not only during colonialism." After he made this statement, my thoughts were wrapped in silence. First, I was immersed in a reflection of the overlap of memories between colonialism and postcolonial conditions; between Robert's grandfather and himself. He connected his story with that of his ancestor in his narrative, demonstrating how this kind of telling does not proceed in a linear and chronological manner; rather, it assumes a temporality that blends together different life experiences. A second reflection was on the possible existence of a constellation of stories around the word "slave": Robert and his grandfather as well as other Eritreans considered as *ascari* and "migrants." He confirmed this view with the following statement:

> I don't argue with Bossi or Maroni.[4] I argue with the person who doesn't know why I have come here. He thinks I have come to steal his job. There are many reasons [rooted] in colonialism. Italians have to understand that. If they understand, then it is better not only for us but also for them. If you understand things, then you are beginning to understand what you have to do.

At the Edge of History

Mignolo (2000: 52) showed how the colonial world system is at the core of "forgotten stories that bring forward, at the same time, a new epistemological dimension: an epistemology of and from the border of the modern/colonial world system." In a more in-depth investigation, Quijano (1997) examined this border from another perspective; that of the relationship existing between colonialism and its heritage. He used two key phrases, "coloniality of power" and "historicostructural dependency," to describe how the past impacts the postcolonial condition. Specifically, "both imply the hegemony of eurocentrism as epistemological perspective. In the contest of coloniality of power, the dominated population, in their new, assigned identities, [*sic*] were also subjected to the Eurocentric hegemony as a way of knowing" (Quijano 1997: 117). Along with the philosopher, Enrique Dussel, who is the author of "Eurocentrism and Modernity" (1993), Quijano advocated seeking a location that is beyond Eurocentrism and Occidentalism. Adopting a different perspective, Santos (2011) proposed the notion of "epistemologies of the South" as a way to "reinvent social emancipation on a global scale." In his opinion, "the global South is not a geographical concept, even though the great majority of its population lives in the countries of the Southern hemisphere. The South is rather a metaphor for the human suffering caused by capitalism and colonialism on the global level, as well as for the resistance to overcoming or minimizing such suffering" (2011: 18).

In the diasporic context of Europe, the orally transmitted memories that I collected can be considered as aspects of the Global South because they share a common framework and are analogous (for example, black people in a white-dominated and former colonial power such as Italy). Each narrative can be conceptualized as an assemblage of fragmented memories of an "archive-body" that is connected with the rest of the world and with the diaspora. From another perspective, individuals belonging to diverse diasporas combine their subjectivities within a collective struggle for rights and freedom (as in the cases of *banlieues* in France and *ius soli* in Italy, and campaigns launched against segregated camps in places like Lampedusa, Greece, Calais, and Ventimiglia). As Passerini (2000; and with Gabaccia and Iacovetta 2016) has noted, the intersubjective field is not merely generated through the simple connection and interactions of two subjectivities; it is an ongoing condition entailing the production of meanings within a shared space of communication generated by cultural backgrounds, positionalities, and identities.

This way of thinking about signification resonates with Deriddian *différance*, whereby meanings are viewed as changeable and unstable, as in the case of *anfez*, which assumed manifold meanings in respondents' stories. In Enrico's narrative, *anfez* denotes someone who is "half-and-half" and is, consequently, not fully defined and incorporated within the ambit of humanity. This "dis-," "not-," or "other-humanity" evokes the notion of necropolitics introduced by Mbembe (2003). Mbembe's notion may be pertinent in the sense that colonialism and slavery inflict a primary violence that is followed by the construction of an archive. A closer view indicates that the term is not translatable into European languages, namely the languages of colonialism and of the colonial archives. Hence, *anfez* is something altogether different: a consequence of and reaction to the same generative epistemic violence of the archive. The meaning of *anfez* is unmapped within the domain of European knowledge, and it is also a word used in Europe, even though it does not belong to any European language. It is a form of cultural resistance to the "order of discourse" and to governmentality (Foucault 1991) because it reveals possible meanings existing beyond the archive and the production of meanings in European languages. *Anfez* does not respect coherence: it means several different things (for example, a half-and-half subject for Enrico, a unique entity with polymeric meanings for Sonia, and a mixed and blended context for Salem). For Enrico, *anfez* is mythically and metaphysically conveyed in the figure of the father and in the metaphor of climbing/descending. For Sonia, the meaning of the word relates to a simultaneous fluctuation between her Italian and Eritrean identities. It resolves this fluctuation through a reinterpretation of the condition of being *meticcia* and mulatta. For Salem, *anfez* is the outcome of a mixing and blending of two or more cultural components of subjectivity, with the possibility of discovering new and nonexclusive positionalities, such as one of being simultaneously Bolognese and Eritrean.

An alternative envisioning of the process of assembling subjectivities and producing intersubjectivity allows for a discussion of embodied and incarnate memories that disclose a transnational geography of the diaspora. This gaze, directed through a memory that is able to connect subjectivities in various parts of the world, results in the renaming of space and in new positionalities for what is termed "self" and "other," which are substituted with a nomenclature that encompasses numerous other positionalities. When I use the term "substituted," I do not mean that one geography disappears, and another takes its place. Diasporic memory allows for the creation of a complex geography that overlaps a canonized geography of Europe which is based on lines (Ingold 2007) and divisions between what is and what is not European, modernity, white, and progress. In this sense, it is possible to conceive of the transnationality of a single place as an overlapping and intertwining of multiple geographies that exceed national, European, and continental divisions. Aman provided a clear example of this through his act of naming. His use of the word *morti* (deaths), taken from the language of the colonizer and of the land he has come to, attributes responsibility for those deaths. *Morti* does not make it possible to name all of the bodies scattered in the Mediterranean Sea, but it pinpoints a specific cultural space of significance to Italy/Europe. This is another facet—that of the Black Mediterranean, conceived as an empty space of connection between cultures, peoples, nations, and continents, evoking narratives of blackness that are productive of a new geography of black people in diaspora and of those who decided to cross the European border illegally (Proglio 2018a). In other cases, the body itself constitutes an archive, revealing other typologies deployed by the diasporic memory. These are illustrated by Aman's gesture of placing his hands on his chest to expel painful feelings associated with the Mediterranean crossing; Winta's image of Eritrea kneeling before other countries; and the metaphor of Africa as a black body that is the object of violence and conquest by white men and white countries. Moreover, Helen spoke of a body as a metaphysical entity that connects the idea of rape and something missed. In Viviana's and Enrico's narratives, the father's body signifies an Italian identity, which both find problematic. From this perspective, *anfez* can be conceived as a colored line composed of different shades of blackness corresponding to each type of subjectivity.

Diasporic memory is elaborated in relation to fluid and mixed identities, entailing different positionalities: Aman and Robert were both born in Eritrea and crossed the Mediterranean to reach Lampedusa. Sara was born to Eritreans in Rome, Italy. Her idea of home brings together Eritrea and Peschiera Borromeo. By contrast, Helen, who was born in Eritrea, evoked images of Asmara as the land of return, a future mythical place of peace. Viviana and

Enrico reflected on their mixed identities from two different perspectives. Whereas Viviana examined the past to better understand how to situate the figure of the father and his white Italian part, Enrique's inquiry focused on the mythical field, counterpoising the figures of the "white African" and the *anfez*. Sonia was born in Italy to an Eritrean father and an Italian mother. After a long period, during which she fluctuated between two opposite poles marking her identity (Italian and Eritrean), she moved beyond this separation and reconfigured her identity as one that was unique and whole while simultaneously being multifaceted. Salem was born in Eritrea and lives in Bologna. Her involvement with political groups opposed to the Eritrean regime made her identity simultaneously Bolognese and Eritrean. Considering all of these cultural identities, it can be affirmed that the diasporic condition allows for multiple positionalities and plural subjectivities. Hence, from the lens of diasporic memory, many cultural identities do not match the genealogy and terms such as "migrant," "Eritrean," "black," and "illegal" produced through border operations.

The three temporalities discussed here produced different narratives according to the subjectivity and positionality of each of the concerned individuals. If it is true that the mobility of memory constitutes a common trait associated with tensions among temporalities, then these movements can be associated with a range of emotions. In the case of Winta, colonialism serves as a foundational act for people she considers her own; the originating event that inscribed a genealogy of whiteness on not-white bodies. In this sense, as she observed, whereas European people may be good or bad, foreigners can only be bad. This peculiarity seems to apply to all temporalities. Skin color is the trace of a past that remains esthetically evident in the postcolonial condition. Therefore, the first temporality extends into the others. Winta's emotions moved beyond the initial rage she felt at being discriminated against as she elaborated a multiple identity that resignified "being black" as Eritrean, African, and brown. Sara and Helen lived in the same postcolonial context, but their background stories differed. Sara, who had never visited Eritrea, opined that the condition of the country was a consequence of colonialism. Hers was a memory of other memories obtained from a diasporic archive that she had come to know during her stay within the Eritrean community. At the end of her narrative (she did not finish enunciating the word "illusion"), she alluded to the possibility of peace prevailing between white and black people. It appears that she came up against this illusion in relation to racism, which she experienced in her life after moving from a small town, where a sort of whiteness was ascribed to as a result of acceptance by people within the community, to Milan. Therefore, in this case, the possibility arose for the reproduction of the same model or gaze applied to all temporalities. For those born in diaspora, memory becomes a heritage while also affirming belonging within a community or a group. Her feelings shifted from pain due to being called a "small nigger" to embarrassment and shame on behalf of the only other black woman in her class. Conversely, for Helen, colonialism marked the time of origin of all of the stories of black people. In reaching that awareness, she claimed that she was not touched by racist comments and she conceptualized her blackness in terms of her future return in Eritrea. Both Helen and Sara were involved in the same racialized process of memory production.

Viviana's and Enrico's insights on colonialism arose from their reflections on the figure of their father as a colonizer. They occupied two temporalities parallel to those of the father, in the sense that both of them sought to interpret their own lives in terms of their father's story. However, they adopted different strategies. Viviana searched for fragments of his memory within the framework of History (intentionally capitalized) to dispense with her sense of guilt for being involved, somehow, in colonization. By contrast, Enrico's approach entailed delving into the most spiritual part of his soul, seeking an image that could explain an apparent contradiction of being black and of "mixed race" while at the same time being indirectly involved with Italian colonization. Their temporalities generated an ongoing sense of indeterminateness and uncertainty, a sense of discomfort, clearly revealing the public and private dimensions of colonialism. Enrico's use of the climb/descend metaphor also alluded to a temporality that is not linear and includes ghosts (colonialism and his father) from the past that are not directly visible. Sonia described being "in between" in the present and moving toward the past—forged through the memory of colonialism—as well as the future relating to her status as a foreign-Italian in Italy. She chose another temporality that centered on her complex subjectivity, without needing to relinquish any of the components of her identity, and that led to the deactivation of other temporalities. Her emotions arising from her sense of being "out of place" and not fully accepted were consequently replaced by a sense of happiness that stemmed from her ability to be herself. In Salem's view, colonialism marked the onset of a regime of apartheid that has involved all Eritrean people up to the present. She used the word "us" to refer to Eritreans subjected to Italian violence. In this sense, she connected territorial segregation during colonialism to the condition of her people in Italy. Thus, all fields overlapped and provoked interactions and consequences in terms of acts of violence and liberation.

Through my analysis of the compiled interviews, I was able to map many instances of resignification of a language by applying my own subjectivities to (re)define their stay in diaspora. Diasporic memory works as a *politics of naming*, as in the case of Aman, to inscribe a name and place in History. At other times, as in the cases of other respondents, diasporic memories reveal how a historical fact may be (re)signified in the sharing of a memory relating to the postcolonial condition with friends and members of the community with whom the interviewee has a close relationship. Images of the colonial past remain vivid in the archive of the diaspora. These images are symbols of a genealogy of different subjectivities; at the same time, they are traces of a border drawn between colonialism and the postcolonial condition and between colonized people and black subjects in Italy/Europe. There is a tangential point located between two different archives that are in dialogue with each subjectivity: a colonial one that was used for conquering colonies and afterward for controlling migration flows and black bodies; and a resistant other, constituted by narratives, practices, and meanings in opposition to colonialism and Fortress Europe, and to racism, xenophobia, and islamophobia. An inquiry into this second space reveals an ongoing process of signification that crosses borders, dichotomies, spatial divisions, and any singular temporality. Such traces indicate that subjectivity (be it black, brown, Eritrean, fully Italian or Eritrean, or Bolognese-Italian-Eritrean) is multiply positioned. Accordingly, segments of meaning are located outside of the language of colonialism (e.g., *habescià* and *anfez*), with interruptions of temporalities (different silences) and temporalities of interruption (e.g., colonial representations remaining attached to the skins and bodies of black people in Italy-Europe). Thus, the place of memory exists where images, narratives, and practices of resistance during the colonial past inhabit the same space as new forms of opposition to border controls, racism, and discrimination.

Conclusions

Diasporic memory envisions a transnational space for the circulation of narratives that permanently cross borders. This space can be expanded through the tool of intersubjectivity. From this perspective, what these interviews brought out was also a consequence of my encounter with my own subjectivity. Accordingly, many other traits can be assumed to have remained hidden for the same reasons. This attempt to relativize was a result of my intention not to repeat the process within colonialism of importing into Europe something that was not considered European because it was perceived as indefinite and ambiguous and consequently assigned a name and position, that is, a definition, through culture and narratives. On the contrary, my aim was to show that other subjectivities are at work in a transnational and global context. This work is an attempt to provincialize Europe, to reconfigure its centrality as an entity comprising nations and borders, and to question the organization of time and space. Diasporic memory creates cultural movements that can shift the centrality of Europe and create a space for "new" Europeans. Starting from these narratives, we may perhaps have to engage, collectively, in the invention of other ways of living together in Europe, Eritrea, and everywhere.

Gabriele Proglio is an FCT researcher in the Centre for Social Studies at the University of Coimbra. He earned his PhD at the University of Turin, Department of History, with a research project on colonial imaginaries. He was a visiting scholar at the University of California, Berkeley, and assistant professor in History of the Mediterranean at the University of Tunis El Manar. As research associate on the ERC project BABE, he conducted oral history research on migrants from the Horn of Africa. His research interests focus on colonial legacies in Europe, postcolonial societies, borders, frontiers, mobilities, and memories of migration across the Mediterranean. His recent publications include *Border Lampedusa: Subjectivity, Visibility and Memory in Stories of Sea and Land* (Palgrave, 2018) and *Decolonizing the Mediterranean: European Colonial Heritages in North Africa and the Middle East* (Cambridge Scholars, 2016).

Notes

1. The Algerian philosopher, Jacques Derrida, introduced the concept of *différance* to enable an exploration of the relationship between text and meaning and to elucidate the difference and deferral of meaning.
2. *Moloch* is a French and Italian term denoting something that cannot be discussed or analyzed.
3. She was referring to dual nationality.
4. Umberto Bossi and Roberto Maroni are two politicians within the Northern League, an Italian xenophobic and racist right-wing party.

References

Alexander, C. 2009. "Stuart Hall and Race." *Cultural Studies* 23, no. 4: 457–82.
Arnone, A. 2008. "Journeys to Exile: The Constitution of Eritrean Identity through Narratives and Experiences." *Journal of Ethnic and Migration Studies* 34, no. 2: 325–40.
Bhabha, H. K. 2004. *The Location of Culture*. Abingdon, UK: Routledge.
Brubaker, R. 2005. "The 'Diaspora' Diaspora." *Ethnic and Racial Studies* 28, no. 1: 1–19.
Dussel, E. 1993. "Eurocentrism and Modernity." *Boundary 2* 20, no. 3: 65–76.
Foucault, M. 1991. "Governmentality." In *The Foucault Effect*, edited by Graham Burchell, Colin Gordon, and Peter Miller, 87–104. Chicago: University of Chicago Press.
Grossberg, L. 1996. "On Postmodernism and Articulation: An Interview with Stuart Hall." In *Stuart Hall: Critical Dialogues in Cultural Studies*, edited by D. Morley and K. Chen, 131–50. London: Routledge.
Hall, S. 1967. *The Young Englanders*. London: National Committee for Commonwealth Immigrants.

———. 1970. "Black Britons. Part 1: Some Problems of Adjustment." *Community* 1, no. 2: 3–5.
———. 1973. "Encoding and Decoding in the Media Discourse." Birmingham: Centre for Contemporary Cultural Studies, University of Birmingham.
———. 1983. "The Problem of Ideology – Marxism without Guarantees." In *Marx: A Hundred Years On*, edited by B. Matthews, 56–90. Dagenham: Lawrence & Wishart.
———. 1989. "Cultural Identity and Cinematic Representation." *Framework: The Journal of Cinema and Media* 36: 68–81.
———. 1990. "Cultural Identity and Diaspora." In *Identity: Community, Culture, Difference*, edited by J. Rutherford, 222–37. Dagenham: Lawrence & Wishart.
———. 1992. "New Ethnicities." In *Race and Difference*, edited by J. Donald and A. Rattansi, 253–59. London: SAGE Publishing.
———. 1996a. "Gramsci's Relevance for the Study of Race and Ethnicity." In *Stuart Hall: Critical Dialogues in Cultural Studies*, edited by David Morley and Kuan-Hsing Chen, 411–41. London: Routledge.
———. 1996b. "Minimal Selves." In *Black British Cultural Studies*, edited by H. A. Baker, M. Diawara, and R. H. Lindeborg. Chicago: University of Chicago Press.
Hall, S., C. Critcher, T. Jefferson, J. Clarke, and B. Roberts. 1978. *Policing the Crisis: Mugging, the State and Law and Order*. London: Macmillan Press.
Ingold, T. 2007. *Lines: A Brief History*. Abingdon: Routledge.
Mbembe, A. 2003. "Necropolitics." *Public Culture* 15, no. 1: 11–40.
Mignolo, W. 2000. *Local Histories/Global Designs: Coloniality, Subaltern Knowledges, and Border Thinking*. Princeton: Princeton University Press.
Passerini, L. 2000. "Discontinuity of History and Diaspora of Languages." *New Left Review* 1 (January–February): 137–44.
Passerini, L., D. Gabaccia, and F. Iacovetta. 2016. "Bodies across Borders: Oral and Visual Memory in Europe and Beyond: A Conversation with Luisa Passerini, Donna Gabaccia and Franca Iacovetta." *Women's Historic Review* 25, no. 3: 458–69.
Puwar, N. 2004. *Space Invaders: Race, Gender and Bodies Out of Place*. Oxford: Berg Publishers.
Proglio, G. 2018a. "Is the Mediterranean a White Italian-European Sea? The Multiplication of Borders in the Production of Historical Subjectivity." *Interventions* 20, no. 3: 406–27.
———. 2018b. "Silences and Voices of Mediterranean Crossings: (Inter)subjectivity and Empathy as Research Practice." *Revista Brasileira de Perquisa Auto-Biográfica* 3, no. 7: 67–79.
———. 2019. "Geography of Emotions across the Black Mediterranean: Oral Memories and Dissonant Heritages of the Colonial Past and Slavery." In *Dissonant Heritages*, edited by T. Lähdesmäki, L. Passerini, S. Kaasik-Krogerus, I. van Huis. New York: Berghahn Books.
Quijano, A. 1997. "Colonialidad del poder: Cultura y conocimiento en America Latina." *Anuario Mariateguiano* 9: 113–21.
Ricoeur, P. 1985. *Temps et récit*. Paris: Le Seuil.
Santos, Boaventura de Sousa. 2011. "Épistémologies du sud." *Études Rurales* 187: 21–50.
Stoler, A. 2010. *Along the Archival Grain: Epistemic Anxieties and Colonial Common Sense*. Princeton: Princeton University Press.

Chapter 6

EVA NERA RELOADED

An Archive in the Making

Liliana Ellena

Eva Nera is the title of two Italian films released in 1954 and 1976, respectively. The first, set in former Italian East Africa, juxtaposes a series of intertwined encounters between Italian men and African women before and during World War II and in the aftermath of the British mandate over Eritrea. The second film, set in Hong Kong and directed by Joe D'Amato (alias Aristide Massaccesi), is part of the Italian *Emanuelle Nera* soft-porn series, conceived to capitalize on and exploit the success of the French film *Emmanuelle*. The Indonesian Dutch actress Laura Gemser plays the leading role of a mixed-race woman in *Eva Nera*. Born in Java in 1950, Gemser moved with her family to the Netherlands, where she was raised and completed her schooling in Utrecht. In the 1970s, she relocated to Italy, where she became an international icon of the racially themed erotic subgenre and continues to be celebrated in magazines and on social media fan pages, even now. In the mid-1970s—a period marked by sexual liberation and black civil rights movements—her rise to iconic status was largely contingent on efforts to keep her ethnic background ambiguous, so as to feed, in Gaia Giuliani's words, "the dual role of object and subject of the exotic-erotic discourse, thereby reinforcing 'the postcolonial modernity' of the Italian male, capable of sampling the delights of a 'guilt-free' and sexually liberated interracial sexuality" (Giuliani 2018: 151).

The fate of the first *Eva Nera* film, a docufiction shot in the early 1950s in Eritrea, contrasts sharply with the hypervisibility of Laura Gemser's dematerialized "blackness." Directed by Giuliano Tomei[1] and produced by Phoenix

Film, the film is unavailable in Italian film archives. Little is known about its production and distribution and the nonprofessional actors and actresses recruited onsite. The main traces it left are those relating to the controversy surrounding its release and the cuts required by the Italian censorship board, as a result of which, the movie gained a reputation of being anticolonialist (Ellena 2015). The unraveling of the material and historical entanglements between blackness, colonialism, and sexuality in the Italian postwar period is the main focus of this chapter, which discusses the encounter with informal assemblages of *Eva Nera*'s archive as a space for exploring the connection between visuality and decolonization across the private/public divide.

Within the wider European framework, Italy's postwar trajectory has long been defined in comparison to and in contrast with the experiences of other former colonial powers. The roots of its peculiar decolonization process have been traced back to the loss of its colonies as a result of its military defeat in World War II and to the mandatory abrogation of racial laws following the fall of Fascism and the transition to a democratic republican order. This process nonetheless entailed a "return" to Africa in the form of the Italian Trusteeship Administration of Somalia (AFIS). The supposed absence of anticolonial struggles and the lack of debate on its colonial and racist policies and crimes have been regarded as the main processes affecting and shaping Italy's long postimperial transition (Andall and Duncan 2005). These historical processes have supported both ideas about Italian colonial exceptionalism—seen as limited in scope and scale and therefore less harmful and exploitative—and the eclipse of "race" from Italy's language and national history (Pinkus 2003). Along these lines, Cristina Lombardi-Diop and Caterina Romeo (2015: 369) have observed how the intertwined dynamics of these processes, the impact of transcontinental and internal Italian migrations, and the limited presence of colonial migrants in the postwar period produced a disjunction between decolonization and postcoloniality, confining "colonial history to the periphery of the process of national identity formation" and deferring the articulation of "an African postcolonial counter-discourse in Italian" to recent times.

Building on these insights, in this chapter I will discuss *Eva Nera*'s archive as a starting point for reconsidering the relationship between postimperial cinema and decolonization in Italy. What is meant by Italian decolonization? When and where did it take place? What kinds of insights can gender issues provide into the relationship between colonial memory and present-day transmediterranean migration? In addressing these questions, I will draw on current debates in the field of Italian studies as well as in feminist and visual studies, which have brought into sharp focus the intersection between racialized significations of gendered bodies and "coloniality" (Lugones 2010). Distinct from colonialism, coloniality refers to the matrix of power that ties visuality to an epistemic regime; one "that seeks to order and consists in ordering the visible world in a particular way, a mode of arrangement of the visible around the principle of *dominatio*" (Sanogo 2011: 227; see also Mirzoeff 2011). Within this framework, I argue that the disjunction between decolonization and postcolonialism depends upon an ordering and bordering of the visible both within and outside of Italy, and upon an understanding of colonialism as a political experience untouched by questions concerning subjectivity and sexuality. This implies to reconsider how the racialized representations of bodies and political spaces were articulated and resignified during Italy's post-imperial transition. Contesting the representation of a sudden and homogenous colonial amnesia following the formal demise of the Italian Empire between 1947 and 1952 recent research has started to shed new light on the specific ways in which colonial and racial categories informed both the self-representation of Italy as a modernizing and homogenous white nation and the construction of internal and external alterities during the 1950s and the 1960s. These changes took shape in a shifting configuration marked both by internal conflicts over the definition of Italian postfascist identity as well as the repositioning of Italy within Europe and the Atlantic world in the context of the Cold War. For the purposes of the argument developed in this chapter I therefore use the term post-imperial transition to refer to the cultural and political dynamics which marked the period between the end of World War II and 1960, the year in which the end of the Italian Trusteeship Administration of Somalia coincided with the "year of Africa" when seventeen sub-Saharan African countries managed to gain their independence from European colonial powers.[2] This intersected perspective allows to bring to light the impact of larger transmediterranean biographical trajectories and cinema production's networks usually whitewashed from the history of postwar Italian cinema. In this light the imbrication of *Eva Nera*'s visual codes and discursive constructions with a larger set of political, gender, and cultural positionalities that affected its production and circulation configures its archive as a battleground for anticolonial contestation and postcolonial reconfigurations.

An Archive in the Making

The questions addressed in this chapter are part of a larger research project exploring *Eva Nera*'s archive, which was prompted and shaped by several unexpected encounters that challenged my previous writings on the movie (Ellena 2015). The first of these encounters involved a scene from *Eva Nera* on the website of Eritrea's state television. The clip was originally aired in November 2014 during Asmerom Habtemariam's morning talk show, *Merhaba*.

The journalist, a former fighter in the Eritrean People's Liberation Front,[3] introduced the movie as a "curious story" harkening back to the years of the British administration, which, although supposedly tasked with "freeing" Eritreans from fifty years of Italian rule, in fact allowed forty thousand Italian residents to remain in the country, continuing to run their businesses, and even shooting a movie (ERi-TV 2014). The scene revolves around an Italian soldier who flees to the Dahlak Islands to escape British troops after the fall of Massawa and is given refuge by a girl called Hassina. What makes the broadcast even more compelling is the presence of Tiblez Tesfamichael, who played the role of Hassina, in the studio audience. The camera zooms in on the octogenarian actress, but when Habtemariam introduces her, she stands up but remains silent, apparently because of health- and age-related issues, as images from her youth scroll across the screen. The living body and past images of Tiblez Tesfamichael, as viewed from Italy, enact a disturbing "return" of colonial subjects who would otherwise have remained unnamed and unknown. The African actresses were listed by their first names only in *Eva Nera*'s credits and reviews, or under the heading "Ragazze d'Africa" ("African girls").

Another crucial encounter that I had was with Giuseppe Sieber, whose role was instrumental in enabling me to access a digital copy of the movie. I first met Giuseppe after I came across an old message that he had left on an online cinema forum, where in 2008, he was looking for a copy of *Eva Nera*. His search was prompted by his desire to help his mother, Pia Cemulini Sieber, piece together her fragmented childhood memories. The daughter of Gino Cemulini, one of the nonprofessional actors in *Eva Nera*, Pia was born in Asmara in 1949. In 1960, she lost her memory in a car accident in which her mother died. When she returned home after her long stay in the hospital, her father decided to send her to Switzerland, where his sister had migrated from Friuli. He later married an Eritrean woman and prevented Pia from spending her summers in Asmara as she was accustomed to doing, eventually severing their relationship (Sieber 2017).

Both encounters led me to various copies of the movie circulating within informal social media networks. Despite Tiblez Tesfamichael's silent appearance, the clip from the ERi-TV talk show sparked interest across the Eritrean diaspora. Several comments mentioned that Tesfamichael was a well-known figure in Asmara, where she used to run a bar near the university. Her nephew, who lives in Bergamo, posted several more images in which pictures of himself and Tesfamichael are juxtaposed with stills from the film.[4]

The surfacing traces of *Eva Nera* draw forth an informal assemblage of objects, private and public pictures, moving images, and individual memories that blur the boundaries between subjective and cultural narrations, historical research, and public/political discourses that mark contemporary

FIGURE 6.1. Pia Cemulini with her father, Asmara 1954. Courtesy of Pia Cemulini Sieber.

processes of memory-making. The transnational and digital networks that characterized my encounter with the movie and its nonprofessional actors and actresses point to the dense and multilayered intersection of affective and personal attachments on one hand and geopolitical relations on the other, bringing to the fore the complex matrix that ties contemporary migration between the Horn of Africa and Italy to the aftermath of Italian rule. On the one hand, despite the dramatic increase in Eritrean asylum seekers reaching Italian shores since the late 1990s, Italy's sixty-year rule in Eritrea and the role that Italians played in the country after 1945 hardly ever became matters of concern in public debates. The same can be said of the almost century-long history of Eritrean migration to Italy for different reasons and purposes. On the other hand, the tragic shipwreck that occurred off Lampedusa on 3 October 2013, resulting in the deaths of 360 Eritreans sparked international outrage and thrust Eritrea's authoritarian regime under the spotlight in relation to the refugee crisis, leading to the launch, in June 2014, of the UN Commission of Inquiry on Human Rights in Eritrea.[5]

In the following pages, I will look at the informal assemblage of traces and memories that I encountered as the standpoint from which to re-interrogate what is latent both within and behind the discursive and visual constructions of *Eva Nera* in postimperial Italy. In moving from the present to the past, I will consider *Eva Nera* as an "archive in the making." By this term, I do not mean to indicate evidence, archival sources, and new findings that may help fill the gaps in historical knowledge; rather, I wish to point to the transcultural, processual, and conflictual dimensions that allow for the envisioning of the mobility of memory in terms of a "space of appearance."

Scholars such as Nicholas Mirzoeff and Judith Butler have engaged with and reformulated this concept, which was originally put forward by Hannah Arendt with reference to the political space. By focusing on corporeal materiality, subjectivity, and the copresence of bodies, these approaches have shifted the focus from the question of political representation to the process through which subjects are constituted by the ways in which they become visible (Mirzoeff 2017; Butler 2015). The relationship between mobility and archival practices can be read in light of this nexus. In the context of the shifting spatiotemporal intertwining and disjunctions, the assemblage of moving images, pictures, and memories associated with *Eva Nera* emerges as an archive-making process that is closely related to embodiment. What kind of affective, cultural, and historical ties connect *Eva Nera* to living bodies? How is history inscribed on the body? These are salient questions that I seek to address here. Ariella Azoulay's (2015) argument on the challenges that unconventional practices pose to established conceptions of the archive is particularly pertinent for addressing these questions. Drawing on alternative digital and artistic archival practices, Azoulay foregrounds the implicit political and critical relevance of claiming the right to create new archives and to access, unsettle, and rearrange existing ones. This claim is premised on the refusal of the imperial logic that relegates archival material to a foreclosed and completed past and is articulated by practices of sharing, grouping, and reframing images, documents, and traces that are activated by and grounded in forms of copresence and intersubjectivity. It does not simply contest the constituent violence of the archive; rather, it reactivates the potentiality of alternative forms of living together (Azoulay 2015).

This perspective entails envisioning a radically reconfigured notion of the "archive" where the presence of the past does not persist on its own; it only endures in the context of a sustaining set of relations and conflicts. In departing from dualist epistemologies based on the separation of and opposition drawn between social practices and high theory, it allows for a conception of *Eva Nera* as a space of appearance brought into existence by a plurality of subjects in response to the changing contexts and subjectivities concerned with the contemporary reconfiguration of the Mediterranean passage. Accordingly, the mobility of memory addressed in this chapter, and more broadly by the "Bodies Across Borders" research project, engages in a conversation with unconventional archival practices aimed at deepening our understanding of intersubjectivity within a transcultural context. It illuminates the interconnections among memory, movement, and materiality. Remarking on how new archival practices can cross institutional, spatial, and temporal borders, Azoulay makes the following crucial point: "Citizens take part in producing and sharing images, knowing that the images one produces always exceed one's capacity to understand their content and meaning; that the interpretation of images is a task that calls for multiple collaborations; and that each of their images might one day emerge—usually by or through the gaze of others—as 'the missing image'" (2015: 198).

Drawing on Azoulay's insights, I conceive of *Eva Nera*'s "archive in the making" as a collaborative, open-ended project aimed at redefining the relationship between postimperial visuality and sexuality in Italy. I do so not from the standpoint of classifications and borderings that delineate colonialism, decolonization, and postcolonialism as discrete and disconnected periods; rather, I position them within a relational space engendered and operated by the encounter with *Eva Nera*'s traces in the present. In situating myself within this space, I explore the new embodiments to which it directly and indirectly gives shape, affecting "the way one is governed, as well as the ways one shares the world with others" (Azoulay 2015: 199).

After Empire

The construction of *Eva Nera* as an antiracist film within cinematic critical discourse has its point of reference in the debate raised by the censored scenes. The cuts required by the censorship board addressed two issues in particular. The first concerned the details of the interracial relationship between Jamila, a young Bilen girl who flees to Asmara from a small village near Keren, and Giorgio, an Italian businessman. When Giorgio leaves her, Jamila has no choice but to become a prostitute. The second addressed the "ethnographic" scenes and involved reducing images of black women's naked breasts and gory details of the Andinnas trance (Italia Taglia 2008). Two months after the release of *Eva Nera* in November 1954, the journal *Cinema* featured a special insert on the movie, which included script pages for the censored scenes of Jamila and Giorgio's relationship as well as photographs from the set with long and detailed captions. The insert's cover displayed a full-page, black-and-white close-up shot of a naked Kunama dancer that served to introduce a long, polemical article titled "*Realismo d'oltremare e censura imperiale*" ("Overseas Realism and Imperial Censorship"). The then young critic, Callisto Cosulich, described *Eva Nera* as the "first neorealist film shot in the Black Continent." His review focused on the conflict between neorealist aesthetics, according to which "the camera should go overseas not to dream and exalt but only to know." He drew attention to the politically oriented censorship aimed at reproducing a "mythical representation" of Africa that does not allow any other representation "than the rhetoric, colonialist and possibly a little bit nostalgic one to which we have grown accustomed" (Cosulich 1954: 298–99). The issues of "authenticity" and "realism" raised in the review echoed both the statements made by the director and screenwriters of *Eva Nera* and the message conveyed by the advertising campaign—namely, that audiences would have the opportunity to "really get to know the African woman" (Epoca 1954: 82).

Cosulich's critical stance was endorsed a few months later by Guido Aristarco (1955), the influential Marxist critic, founder, and editor-in-chief of the film journal *Cinema Nuovo*. In September 1953, Aristarco was arrested and put on military trial on charges of having published a film treatment about the Italian army's recruitment of Greek prostitutes during the occupation of Greece (Ellena 2006; Clò 2009: 99–103). In this highly politicized conflict marked by Cold War dynamics and internal struggles for cultural hegemony, *Eva Nera*'s use of outdoor filming and the casting of nonprofessional actors and actresses were perceived as a rejection of the country's fascist past, both politically and visually. In such a context, the invitation extended by *Eva Nera* to its audience to "look" at African women became increasingly associated with an antiracist stand and a political break with the recent colonial and imperial past.

The encounter with the digital version of the film prompts a recasting of the relationship between the neorealist approach to Africa and antiracism in light of the narrative framing the movie and its production in the aftermath of the political conclusion of the "colonial question" in postfascist Italy. The docufiction centers on the figure of Domenico Meccoli, a film critic and journalist, who plays himself. On his way back from a reporting trip to Khartoum, he accepts an invitation to spend a few days with a group of Italians traveling across "Africa, the Africa of hunting safaris, the savage-inhabited Africa of childhood readings and Hollywood movies . . . or so I thought." Through Meccoli's voice-over, the narration is positioned from the very beginning to disrupt the conventions of the exotic-colonial travelogue. After showing an elephant hunt and an encounter with the Kunama population, the movie soon shifts gears and turns into an "exploration" of the memories of Meccoli's travel companions. During breaks from the hunt, flashbacks are used to let each male character tell the story of an African woman. Esposito, an agriculturalist who fought in World War II, recalls his encounter with Hassina on an island in the Dahlak Archipelago. Minetti, a landowner, narrates the story of Jamila. Fontana, a medical doctor, describes different attitudes toward sexuality and gender relations among the Sudanese Muslims and the Kunama, commenting on the rituals performed during Takrur dances and the Andinnas trance. The relationship between Meccoli and the other men is conceived as a means of taking Italian audiences through a journey into memory and having them identify with his detached, neutral observer's gaze. The ethnographic gaze on the indigenous peoples is deployed here to establish a spatial and temporal distance between postwar Italy and its recent colonial past. It is indeed the last story—the only one not dealing with the past—that reveals how the narration tying memory to masculinity is aimed at focusing on the troubles and dilemmas faced by Italians in the former colony.

A conversation between Minetti and Colombo, on their way back to Asmara, reveals the drama of a former professor who becomes a truck driver in order to survive under the British administration. Stung by the humiliation induced by his difficult position, he vents his anger on Mariam, the Eritrean woman with whom he has a relationship, and on their two children. In the last scene, after attending a party for the arrival in Asmara of a friend's Italian wife, he changes his mind about wanting to go back to Italy to escape his harsh circumstances.

With the signing of 1952 UN agreements and Eritrea's federation with Ethiopia, all claims to the former colony ended. However, as noted by Valeria Deplano, disengagement from colonial rule opened up new questions in Italy as much as it did in other former colonial empires. Italy needed to reconfigure its relations with its former territories and come to terms with the close relationships and individual bonds forged over the course of sixty years (Deplano 2017: 1–23). Who was to be considered "Italian," both legally and culturally, within and outside of the nation's borders remained a long-debated question (Ballinger 2007; Deplano 2017; Morone 2018). Nevertheless, the movie dwells mainly on the question of how to reposition Italy's relation to the models of heroic and fascist virilities that had framed the Empire as a space of male and national regeneration (Stefani 2007).

The connection between masculinity and the transition years is an issue that was raised by many Italian films in the immediate postwar years. On this question, Ruth Ben-Ghiat (2005), who compared Italian representations with other European cases, has observed how the challenge posed by the role reversal from occupiers to victims of war violence, the surrender to a foreign army, and the loss of agency are often depicted against anxieties raised by female emancipation or by foreign and racialized men. In contrast to these representations, however, here, African women are represented as eager to love Italian men, even if they are enemies, and ready to transform themselves into domesticated Italian wives while black men are almost completely erased from the scene. The way in which the (male) postimperial transition became entwined with the representation of African women is encapsulated in the last frames. The camera shifts from a close-up of Mariam looking at Meccoli and Colombo inside her house to an exterior tracking shot of a jeep leaving. Meccoli's voice-over comments: "Mariam's drama, full of silences, was over. I was thinking about her and the other women I met in those days. True, real women—devoid of false mysteries. I *knew* enough about them to be able to *see* behind each face the same heart, the shared heart of humanity" (italics added).

The speechless image of Mariam is the space where the uncomfortable legacy of colonial violence is simultaneously redeemed and removed. Yet, the question of Italian colonial rule is hardly mentioned in the film, as though there were an implicit pact with the audience able to recognize locations, toponyms, and names. As in other debates of those years, the discussion of the gendered violence perpetrated during military and colonial occupation is subordinated to the political conflict in postwar Italy. The use of the first person and past tense in Meccoli's voice-over reveals how postwar Italy's "will to know" (Foucault 2013) was predicated upon the silence of the former female colonized subject. Acknowledgment of her "universal heart" confirms the antiracist stand of postimperial Italy by simultaneously singling out a pact on the "public silence about the conquests and crimes that had forged Fascism's male communities" (Ben-Ghiat 2005: 338).

The discursive construction of temporal and spatial distance between postwar Italy and East Africa gives rise to both a re-enactment and the concealment of the visual colonial archive. One of the most telling examples is offered by the movie poster in which a black female profile is superimposed on the reproduction of a white Roman Hellenistic statue. The text reads: "For the first time, you'll be able to get to know the African woman—in love, sensuous, vain, devoted and unfaithful. You'll be able to understand and judge her through the story of five women, five personalities, five loves" (Epoca 1954; see figure 6.2). Along with the asymmetry between the aesthetically refined marble embodiment of white beauty and the more realistic black profile, the analogy evoked by this astonishing image suggests that "Eve" is in reality "Venus," the goddess of sensual love. Aimed at countering the "monstrous" representation of African sexuality imposed by antimiscegenation fascist propaganda, these visual representations of black beauty draw from the colonial iconography of the Black Venus. Both in the liberal and in the early fascist period, the hypersexualized images of Abyssinian, Bilen, and Somali women were part of a mechanism through which, as noted by Sandra Ponzanesi, "the black female body became an icon for sexuality in general, and sexuality became a metaphor for domination" (Ponzanesi 2005: 165). Yet the analogy embodies in itself a colonial archive in another sense, too. The image chosen to symbolize white beauty is a reproduction of the Venus of Cyrene, whose story attests to the colonial and postcolonial entanglement of race and gender. The Roman copy of the Aphrodite Anadyomene was accidentally found in 1913 by Italian soldiers during the military occupation of Cyrenaica in Libya. Once restored, the statue was shipped to Italy, where its discovery was widely publicized to celebrate the conquest of Libya as a "return" to the

FIGURE 6.2. *Eva Nera*'s advertising published on the weekly magazine *Epoca*, 1954.

Roman Mediterranean. The Venus of Cyrene was displayed at various colonial art exhibitions in the 1920s and 1930s, and gradually became an icon reproduced on postcards, stamps, and tourist advertisements. Simona Troilo has shown how this process led to a progressive decontextualization through which the statue went from symbolizing a "white Cyrene"—and, by extension, Italian Africa—to embodying a "national self-representation in which the myth of the *stirpe*, of an atemporal Romanity" met the racialized codes of female whiteness. The archetypical Greek-Roman beauty became the ultimate embodiment of the "fascist ideal of femininity: a snow-white body, harmonious forms, and a Mediterranean soul" in opposition to the diseased and corrupting sexuality of the Black Venus threatening the integrity of the Italian race (Troilo 2018: 142; see also Giuliani and Lombardi-Diop 2013).

The shared racial and gender grammar governing the black/white opposition and analogy across imperial and postimperial Italy sheds light on the mechanisms through which "race," systematically foreclosed from postwar public discourse, manifests itself mainly through women (Gribaldo and Zapperi 2012: 40). Within this process, the memory of the past, rather than centering on "absence" or "silence," is shaped by active and historically specific processes of colonial unknowing. These pertain to forms of knowing and seeing whereby both the visual archive and "closure" with the colonial past are constantly re-enacted and at the same time rendered incomprehensible through practices of displacement, disassembly, deletion, and carefully policed reassembly. Thus, it comes as no surprise that the Venus of Cyrene has more recently resurfaced in connection with the management and governance of transmediterranean migration.

Following decades-long negotiations over the artifacts looted during colonial rule, in a highly political and symbolic gesture, the Venus of Cyrene was returned to Libya in 2008. The then prime minister, Silvio Berlusconi, flew to Benghazi on 30 August of that year and handed over the statue to Muammar el-Gaddafi to celebrate the signing of the Trattato di Amicizia, Partenariato e Cooperazione (Treaty of Friendship, Partnership and Cooperation)[6]. The treaty included a $5 billion aid package to be spread over twenty years as reparations for the suffering caused by colonial rule and in exchange for Libya's collaboration with Italy and the EU in preventing illegal immigration and strengthening Europe's external borders. Chiara De Cesari has noted how Italian responsibilities—for colonial cultural and economic dispossession and for the crimes committed during anticolonial repression and in internment camps—found little space both in the treaty and in public debate. The "politics of regret" for past colonial abuses were rather meant "to declare them now settled and resolved," enabling the treaty to serve "as a border device, regulating and filtering population and capital flows across the Mediterranean" (De Cesari 2012: 317, 319). The role played by the Venus of Cyrene in the performance of reparation and in "definitely clos[ing] the painful 'chapter of the past'" (Gazzetta Ufficiale 2009: 5) shows how forms of colonial unknowing explicitly work to reproduce "the carceral archipelago of empire," creating the conditions for exposure to new forms of violence and disenfranchisement (Stoler 2016: 78). Behind these performances lies the dramatic reality of migrant women and men arriving in Libya from Eritrea, Somalia, and Ethiopia, as well as from Nigeria, Mali, Syria, and Sudan who are vulnerable to smugglers and police violence and experience repeated and protracted detention, exploitation, and sexual abuse.

Although driven by different agendas, the connection between black and white women's racialized "beauty" and closure to the colonial question brings to the fore the dematerialization of colonial and postcolonial violence. The way in which postimperial antiracism and postcolonial friendship are predicated upon gendered and racialized representations opens a window on the cultural and historical processes underlying the specificity of Italian colonial aphasia. Here, I apply Ann Laura Stoler's argument regarding the term "aphasia," which refers to disorders of speech, to illuminate the complex dynamics of Italian memory by enabling a shift in focus from amnesia to the power relations that have made the violence of Italian colonialism unintelligible and unspeakable. As Stoler argues, colonial aphasia refers to the convergence of disparate forces that "disassociate resemblances and reject categories that are viable" as well as to the production of "endless replacements of categories with incomprehensible associations that collapse into incommensurability" (Stoler 2016: 167).

This double move is particularly salient to deal with the enduring effects of the unspoken Italian colonial amnesty. It has its roots in the early postwar years, when Italy was grappling with the need to come to terms with wartime violence, foreign occupation, and deep internal divisions. By displacing the relations between actors and their actions, the failure to name and sanction those responsible for enacting racial laws and committing crimes in the colonies during and before World War II made it possible to dissociate colonialism from racism and established the conditions for an understanding of the colonial past framed by the paradigm of "Italiani brava gente."

Thus, for example, while interracial sexuality could be mobilized as an antiracist trope in the former colonial setting, matters of racially grounded sexual violence were deflected to the internal front in relation to crimes committed by Afro-American and colonial troops during the Allied occupation. In this regard, Italy shares commonalities with the Netherlands, despite differences in the durations and ambits of their colonial empires. Both countries have developed national self-representations premised on a conception of "white innocence" derived from intra-European comparisons and narratives of victimization relating to experiences of occupation (Wekker 2016:11–12).

Specifically in the Italian case, the overlap between the war, the defeat of fascism, and the loss of the colonies led to the dislodging of the former colonial subjects from the represented scene. Moreover, it simultaneously fostered a perception that colonial experiences were mainly concerned with geopolitical relations as opposed to constituting a living formation deeply enmeshed in the changing configurations of postwar Italy. What is at stake in the Italian colonial aphasia is the persistent failure to comprehend how the violence of colonialism shaped postimperial relationality. In this regard, Valeria Deplano has demonstrated how the refusal to accept the citizenship claims of former colonial subjects living in Italy after the war, despite their small numbers, is entrenched in deep forms of institutionalized racism that have prompted their construction in Republican Italy as the nation's foreign body (Deplano 2017). This persistent refusal to acknowledge postimperial relationality reveals how the deferred formation of a postcolonial subjectivity is an effect of occluded stories rather than an outcome arising from a delay engendered by Italian exceptionalism.

L'Africa in Casa

In 1968, Joy Nwosu remarked that for Europeans, "Africa means Negro, Negro means Africa," arguing that Europeans deployed "Africa for their racial politics and racism for their colonial politics" (Nwosu 1968: 61). The quotation comes from Nwosu's book, *Cinema e Africa Nera*, which is the first study on visuality written in Italian from an African perspective that has recently become available again thanks to the work of Leonardo De Franceschi (Nwosu 2014).[7] Fleeing war and conflict in Nigeria, Nwosu arrived in Italy in the early 1960s and studied music and cinema at Rome University. The book is a revision of her final degree thesis and offers the first critical assessment of *Eva Nera* in the context of a radical critique uncovering the imbrication of postwar Italian cinema with the Eurocentric and racial codes of imperial visuality. Noting that *Eva Nera* marked Italian cinema's first contact with Africa after 1945, Nwosu points out the title's resonance with *Sentinelle di bronzo* ("Dusky Sentries"), Romolo Marcellini's 1937 movie about the imperial bodies and faithfulness of the Dubat colonial troops, "except that here sex (*l'ammore*) takes center stage" (Nwosu 1968: 56). In her unsparing critique, she positions *Eva Nera* along the lines of other feature films and documentaries set in Africa and released in the 1960s as well as independent productions such as Michelangelo Antonioni's *L'eclisse* (1962). Reading these films in the light of *mal d'Africa*, Nwosu rightly observes how "Italians end up being racist even when they claim to be champions of anti-racism" (1968: 55). The comparison with *Violenza segreta* ("Secret Violence"), directed by

Giorgio Moser in 1963, is especially significant. The movie looks at the Italian community's attitudes toward Somalis in Mogadishu from the perspective of sexual and exploitative relationships. Similar to *Eva Nera*, it was the first movie shot in Somalia by an Italian production company in the postwar period coinciding with the end of the AFIS regime.[8]

In a long footnote, Nwosu quotes a conversation with Guido Manera in which *Eva Nera*'s producer asserts that the movie marked a turning point in cinema's approach to Africa, not only in Italy: "It is a well-known fact that several later films set and shot in Africa, especially the French ones, were built on *Eva Nera*. Jean Rouch himself has publicly acknowledged it." Furthermore, remarking that the film had circulated mainly through specialized networks and events, he adds, "Certainly, what mostly hampered the film's success was its very refusal to indulge in conventional exoticism. On the contrary, that's what made other films successful, even later ones" (Nwosu 1968: 45).

Various sources have endorsed Manera's argument and suggest that the limited distribution of *Eva Nera* and its eventual disappearance from cinema archives was the result of a combination of several factors. Phoenix Film and Ente Nazionale Industrie Cinematografiche (ENIC), the company in charge of its commercial distribution, went bankrupt in the mid-1950s. Combined with the censorship controversy, this event further hindered the distribution of a film that touched on many sensitive issues left unresolved at the end of colonial rule: the status of the *Italiani d'Africa*, the question of citizenship for Afro-Italian children born in the former colonies, and the claims to reparations and subsidies made by former colonial subjects living in Italy (Deplano 2017).

As Manera's statement suggests, however, despite the problems at home, the movie circulated outside Italy during the AFIS period and across networks established in the early stages of decolonization. In 1955, *Eva Nera* was screened and won several prizes at the first Festival Internazionale di Cinematografia Africana, held in Mogadishu between 24 September and 4 October on the occasion of the third Somalia Trade Fair, a biennial event organized by the AFIS.[9]

Although very little is known about the festival, which ran from 1955 to the early 1960s, *Il Corriere della Somalia* reported on the selection process, and the film lineup attests to a network of relations spanning late colonial African and European countries. The films screened in Mogadishu represented fourteen different "nationalities," among which were Nigeria, the Ivory Coast, Libya, Congo, Great Britain, Uganda, Rhodesia, Tanganyika, Kenya, and the Union of South Africa.[10] These transnational circuits were also part of Guido Manera's network in Italy, where he attended several international conferences, events, and debates on the development of educational cinema and the potentialities of new African markets for cinema distribution (Manera 1957).

FIGURE 6.3. First Festival Internazionale della Cinematografia Africana, Mogadishu, 1955. Advertising poster signed by Furlani. Museo Nazionale Collezione Salce, Treviso. Courtesy of MiBACT—Direzione Regionale Musei Veneto.

European and African networks would intersect and become operative, albeit in a different direction, in the late 1950s and 1960s. In a changing context, new possibilities were opened up by Italian Mediterraneanist policies on the one hand, and Independence and Pan-African movements—which would pull down the European imperial edifice by the mid-1960s—on the other hand. In 1959, *Présence Africaine* held its Second Congress of Black Writers and Artists in Rome, while in the same year, Florence hosted the first edition of the Festival dei popoli, a crucial site of circulation and exchange centering on ethnographic cinema, anthropological research, and *cinema-verité*, that was frequently attended by the likes of Edgar Morin and Chris Marker. The festival was closely connected with the Comité International du Film Ethnographique, established by Jean Rouch in Paris (Tasselli 1982; de Heusch 2007). In 1962, Guido Manera directed the documentary *L'Italia vista da un africano* ("Italy as seen by an African") with the Ivory Coast writer, intellectual, and politician Bernard Dadié, while the *Présence Africaine* conference set the stage for the First World Festival of Negro Arts held in Dakar in 1966. Manera was in charge of the festival's technical committee supporting the work of Paulin Vieyra for the cinema section, and Jean Rouch was a member of the scientific committee and of the Cinema's Jury (Quilici 1966; Kala-Lobé 1983).

The close ties existing between trans-European networks of ethnographic visual practices and the debates on the role of cinema in the African decolonization process paved the way for *Eva Nera* to be listed in 1967 in the famous *Premier catalogue international de films ethnographiques sur l'Afrique noire*. The catalogue was the outcome of the decade-long work of the Comité International du Film Ethnographique. Funded and promoted by the United Nations Educational, Scientific and Cultural Organization (UNESCO), it included a detailed description of the film's episodes, followed by the following brief comment: "Film without scientific pretensions. The subject of Europeans' relationships with black women is an issue not sufficiently addressed, even if this was the first attempt of this kind. Very interesting documentation on the life of a prostitute (reconstruction) and on rites of passage (authentic). Beautiful images, editing a little bit slow, insignificant and often useless music, accurate voice-over" (UNESCO 1967: 119).

While *Eva Nera* is somewhat exceptional in the context of Italian cinema in the 1950s, its transnational circulation constitutes a site of encounters across the former colonial space as well as in the new international arena in which Italy was trying to establish itself as an interlocutor with the newly independent African countries in the aftermath of AFIS. These professional and embodied connections were also part of Guido Manera's biography. Born in Murazzano, in South Piedmont, Guido Manera moved to Rome in the late 1940s. After starting out as a documentary maker during the Resistance, he founded Phoenix Film, whose catalog evidenced heterogeneous productions, entailing collaborations and coproductions with Titanus and with Economic Cooperation Administration (ECA)-Italy under the Marshall Plan. However, in the 1950s, Phoenix Film specialized in African documentaries. Besides *Eva*

Nera, it produced other feature films that were presented at the Mogadishu Film Festival. *Africa sotto i mari*, a fiction movie starring Sophia Loren and set in the Dahlak Islands, was screened at the 1955 festival together with documentaries about Eritrean dances and Ethiopian religious and historical sites. More such films were presented at the festival held from 28 September–12 October 1957. Manera's intense professional activity during those years and his interest in African politics, heritage, and history blended together cultural and personal issues. Since his university years, he had spent long periods in Africa, moved by philosophical interests in comparative religion studies. In the late 1940s, he married Caterina Ferrero, the daughter of an Eritrean princess and the Italian director of the Eritrean Salt Plant in Massawa, who repatriated to Italy after the war.[11]

This overlapping of professional and personal itineraries is reflected in Joy Nwosu's book. Nwosu's encounter with Manera was neither casual nor limited to research interests. Not only was she a cinema student at the university she was attending, but she also had personal and professional ties with the film industry in Rome. During her university years, she worked at Cinecittà as an extra in historical costume productions such as *Cleopatra*, but her most significant acting role was in *Il Nero*—a movie directed by Giovanni Vento, with whom she had a close relationship (Nwosu 2014: 111–19). Set in Naples, the movie revolves around the stories of black Italians, the "brown war-babies" born during the Anglo-American occupation. Despite being praised by critics and screened at film festivals, *Il Nero* never achieved wider distribution (Patriarca 2018). Besides Nwosu, its cast featured Silvano Manera the son of Guido Manera and Caterina Ferrero, and a second-generation Afro-Italian.

In the same year that *Cinema e Africa Nera* was published, Vento released a short film titled *Africa in casa* in which he explored the segregation of Afro-Italians in public memory and social space. Rome's colonial street names and the celebrations for the twenty-fifth anniversary of the Italian wars in Africa are contrasted in the movie with the silenced genealogy of black Italians. The movie connects the story of the black general Domenico Mondelli, née Wolde Selassie, who was brought to Italy after the 1896 defeat at Adwa when he was a child, with a conversation with Said Ben Amur, an Ethiopian casting agent specializing in selecting *gente di colore* (people of color) for Cinecittà. As the images from his agency's portfolio of African male and female extras scroll across the screen, the voice-over explains that his services are very much in demand, "especially now that African movies shot in Sabaudia with girls from Ghana, Nigeria, and Somalia have become fashionable, you know, niggers who dance in the nude." The film ends with "Harlem/AOI in casa" (Italy's Harlem/Italian East Africa): the refugee camp in Aversa, near Naples, inhabited by war refugees from the former occupied territories, erstwhile colonial subjects, or the offspring of Italian women and African-American soldiers. Both Harlem and AOI evoke different segregation practices shaped by the color line and reproduced within the Italian territory.

Nwosu's and Vento's works highlight several cross-references and attest to a critical dialog grounded in personal and political ties that were part of wider, politicized circuits of filmmakers and critics in the years before the 1968 revolt.[12] Their voices articulate a positionality on the margins of postwar cinema, revealing how the disassembling of the Italian colonial past was associated with the intertwining of Italian cinema in the 1960s with decolonization. During the period of the anticolonial wars, and the Third-Worldist and tricontinental alliances, they became associated mainly with a "resistance aesthetics" (Srivastava 2018: 211–21) that combined the neorealist legacy and anticolonial solidarity and made Pontecorvo's *La battaglia di Algeri* into an internationally acclaimed manifesto. Nwosu's and Vento's dialogue represents an important antecedent to contemporary postcolonial visual practice and theory. Nwosu's work, in particular, can be considered part of a silenced genealogy that connects the critiques of postwar and present-day women of African descent to colonial visuality.

More generally, these traces urge us to reconsider the larger transnational context that shapes individual as well as cultural and political mobilities. From the late 1950s onward, the mobility of artists and students from Africa to Italy was encouraged through Italian transmediterranean policies and funding. In the 1960s, these processes intersected with African anticolonial insurgency and counterinsurgency shaped by Cold War dynamics—of which the Biafra war in Nigeria is a case in point—resulting in the political radicalization of African artists and students in Italy as in other European contexts. At the same time, resonances and reactions to new forms of racism entangled in the ruins of Italian imperial visuality extended beyond the nation's borders. One of the most significant events was a protest that occurred at the screening of the film *Africa Addio* in Berlin. In 1966, a campaign was launched to demand a ban on the controversial mondo movie directed by Gualtiero Jacopetti and Franco Prosperi. The mobilization around this film was organized by Congolese, Haitian, and West German students and became a pivotal moment in the contribution of African students to the transformation of European activists' visions and forms of action (Slobodian 2012: 135–69). As argued by Pedro Monaville, it was the result of an "act of imagination" operating at both existential and affective levels and "creating a sense of urgency and outrage that rendered the revolutionary outburst of 1968 thinkable" (Monaville 2015: 35).

Assembling Traces, Reactivating Archives

Various movements and displacements produced by the circulation and meaning-making of *Eva Nera* bring to light some of the historical processes that make the entanglement of gender and race one of the dead ends in Italy's postimperial transition. Imperial disengagement, political discontinuity with Fascism, and the ideological conflicts around cultural hegemony in postwar Italy contributed to its codification as an antiracist movie. In that context, interracial sexuality became the loaded figure encapsulating the antiracist instances of Republican Italy, whereby the burden of a disturbing past was purged and neutralized. *Eva Nera*'s poor performance at the box office on one hand and its codification as a neorealist or ethnographic movie on the other hand can be read as signs of the aporia posed by the dissociation between the political postimperial transition and cultural decolonization.

Yet, the paths along which *Eva Nera* and the critical discourses on it circulated are also sites of memory recollection across processes of postimperial transition and decolonization; they generate a circular movement connecting the past to the present. The connections between names, bodies, and histories reveal the unfinished life of postimperial relations. These eclipsed histories travel across geopolitical borders and challenge dominant historical narratives that portray postwar Italy as set apart from late imperial dynamics and reduced to the nation's geographical borders. In addition, they invite us to reconsider the interplay between the transnational and diasporic formations that took shape amid colonial disengagement, decolonization, and postcoloniality.

The problems posed by the connection between contemporary transnational migrations and the diasporic nature of Italian identity formation have been addressed by scholars dealing with the historical specificities and paradoxes raised by the attempt to conceive postcolonial Italy as both a theoretical and analytical frame. Teresa Fiore has foregrounded the relevance of conceptualizing contemporary migrants in terms of an "indirect postcoloniality" rooted in the fact that they come in large numbers from countries that were never Italian colonies, or where Italians were present but not as rulers (Fiore 2012). This approach can be extended to include and read not only forms of indirect rule experienced in contexts such as Tunisia or Latin America (Lombardi-Diop and Romeo 2015: 369) but also Italy's "indirect decolonization." Besides underscoring the highly partial and problematic nature of this phenomenon, such an approach facilitates a rethinking of the ways in which it was historically mediated by third spaces. Although decolonization has mainly been addressed in terms of alliances and solidarity with anticolonial struggles in non-Italian contexts since the late 1950s and early 1960s, it has also intersected with forms of antagonism related to the "internal south," now located on the peripheries of northern cities, and has been mobilized by political struggles centered on categories of class and sexuality.

In her recent study, Neelam Srivastava reassesses the intersection of antifascism and anticolonialism and the enduring influence of Third-Worldism on the creation of Italy's protest movements and political Left (Srivastava 2018). In another contribution, Maud Anne Bracke and James Mark have focused on the impacts of forms of political and cultural transfer on Italian feminist movements, arguing that reinventions, translations, and appropriations were powerful "exactly because" of their mainly imaginary and decontextualized nature and the fact that very often they were not linked to direct contacts (Bracke and Mark 2015: 408). However, the cases of Tiblez Tesfamichael, Guido Manera, Giovanni Vento, and Joy Nwosu, examined here, suggest that these connections extended beyond the realm of texts and discourses as professional, cultural, and anticolonial networks that were deeply intertwined with private and interpersonal ties and affects that anticipated the postcolonial present. The invisibility of these traces is integrally linked to the ways in which translators, extras, screenwriters, and critics of African descent were not credited for their work and to the silencing of their role as agents of memory both in the past and in the present (De Franceschi 2013). The dialogue between Nwosu and Vento points to the interplay between different black diasporas conveyed by forms of resistance shaped by the Italian Empire, the aftermath of World War II occupation, and the mobility of African students and political exiles.

From the perspective of the archive-in-the-making, contemporary Afro-Italian voices and transnational movements across the Mediterranean do not simply convey a hybrid memory; they also point to new assemblages of past relations between differentially situated subjects. At stake in the "space of appearance" underlying contemporary mobile memories is a reframing that, as Stoler suggests, is aimed at re-establishing "connections that are not otherwise readily visible. Such renaming relocates processes dislodged from their specific histories" (Stoler 2016: 361). From this perspective, the "space of appearance" pertains to claims and interventions aimed at reembodying what, in the words of Ariella Azoulay, "continues to exist as present, in the present" (2015: 198). In the case of *Eva Nera*, this embodiment entails material traces and diasporic genealogies as much as individual biographies. Their forms are shaped by and are part of multitemporal and plural processes grounded in the fact that beyond the intention of their authors, each image or document produced always contains "an excess of information concerning others" and it is because of this very excess that they should be understood as "a locus of a potential claim pertaining to this shared world" (Azoulay 2015: 202).

The transformations triggered by the encounter with *Eva Nera*'s afterlife should be read in connection with other practices of archive-making. One such example is Igiaba Scego's *Adua* (2017). In this novel, first published in Italy in 2015, the Italian Somali writer explores the layers of intimacy and violence that define imperial entanglement by focusing on the voice of Adua—a Somali woman who follows an Italian film crew to Rome in the mid-1970s. Adua's dreams, fueled by the images shown at movie theaters built by the Italians during the period of colonial rule, are dashed when she finds herself cast in a soft-porn movie named after Gino Mitrano Sani's 1933 colonial novel: *Femina somala*. A specific event, entailing an unsettling encounter on a bus in present-day Rome, triggers her memory and narrative:

> Yesterday there was this girl on the tram. She was black and had a shaved head and thick legs. We were on the fourteen where it turns toward Porta Maggiore. She'd been staring at me since Termini. I was irritated by her hard gaze. I felt like turning around and saying "Stop," like mixing my mother tongue with Dantean Italian and creating one of those scenes that make public transport in Rome entertaining. I wanted to be vulgar and go overboard. I wanted a big scene, that way I'd stop thinking about Lul, about Labo Dhegax, about the strange peace in Somalia. But the girl got wise. She sauntered over and virtually without warning shot me her question; "You're Adua, right? The actress? I saw your movie." And then, after a pause, as if she'd planned it out, she added: "You really make an impression, you know that?"
> I was completely rattled
> My movie? There was actually someone who still remembered that movie? (Scego 2017: 4–5)

The moment when the two Afro-Italian women encounter each other, mediated by the violently sexualized image, is rife with shame, silence, and conflict and gives shape to a process of memory-making that addresses the wounds left by Italian colonialism and the occupation of East Africa on their lived experience. Adua's voice intersects with that of her father, an interpreter working for the Italians in Rome and Addis Ababa during the Italo-Ethiopian War of 1935–36, and of her young husband, a "made in Lampedusa" Somalian refugee whom she nicknames "Titanic." Their wounded bodies and fractured relationships are the living repositories of a traumatic past that traps the present.

The "historical notes" at the end of the book elucidate how these voices "dance on the architecture" of three historical moments: "Italian colonialism, 1970s Somalia, and our present day, which has seen the Mediterranean transformed into an open grave of migrants." With its reference to bodily movements in space, the verb "to dance" encapsulates the performative work of memory in undoing the architecture of fixed and distinct temporalities and spaces. However, as Igiaba Scego points out, dancing across and over the architecture of time is not aimed at analyzing "these periods" but rather at turning them into "emotions, visions and lived experience."[13]

In light of the perspective sketched out in these pages, Igiaba Scego's *Adua* represents, among other things, the "missing image" allowing us to reread the 1954 and 1976 versions of *Eva Nera* that I introduced at the beginning of this chapter. It rematerializes the different historical articulations of the sex–race political regime in which the expropriated bodies are both the workforce and the merchandise in the production and reproduction of European modernity. Considered in this light, the nexus between Italy and the Netherlands that lies behind the movies' shared title can be seen to be far from casual. Moving away from the pitfalls of comparison, it attests to the convergence of nonlinear trajectories of circulation and transfer that cross different postimperial contexts, shaping the role of visuality in the making and remaking of racialized bodies.

The various connections made visible by *Eva Nera*'s archive also articulate the mobility of memory in nonhierarchical relationships between different subjects, including writers and artists, historians, activists, and their multiple languages. The "archive in the making" envisions a potential dialogue capable of addressing significant historical and cultural differences grounded in the "space of appearance" and shaping different responses to colonial aphasia. In this context, intersubjectivity emerges as a tool for constructing forms of attention and care that seek to learn from social practices, rather than attempting to explain them away. These new ways of knowing and seeing require a decentered approach, the shape of which is continually redrawn in response to the relational entanglements that are encountered. This transformative mode especially challenges colonial and Eurocentric habits embedded in the assumptions that position researchers who are engaged in the field of Mediterranean migrations in the role of experts exploring the plight of others. Within the unexpected encounters that occurred during different stages of my research, these others ceased to appear as former colonial subjects, refugees, or migrants and instead became part of a shared world. This was not just an outcome of reparative work, or of acts of recovery producing more accurate forms of historical knowledge. Rather, these outcomes had to do with the impacts of the interruptions and contestations activated by the occluded stories of actresses, cinema critics, activists, and writers. Alongside the self-contained genealogies of Italian cinema, these stories also interrogated those of the (white) visual and feminist critique that has framed my training and the ways in which I have positioned my work as always being implicated in the relational violence of colonialism.

From this perspective, the "archive in the making" is composed of an assemblage of actions, operations, and dialogues sustained by multiple local and translocal histories of resistance, grounded in the "refusal to look away from what is kept out of sight, off stage" (Mirzoeff 2017: 85). Nevertheless, it is not, strictly speaking, a counter-archive; rather, it is a space where relations and conflicts take precedence over substance, which they constantly alter. Dancing across multiple temporalities, to quote Igiaba Scego, these critical practices call for a situated and embodied engagement with the archive, conceived as "a shared place, a place that enables one to maintain the past incomplete" (Azoulay 2015: 204).

Liliana Ellena was a research associate on the BABE Project at the European University Institute. She was previously a lecturer in women's and gender history at the University of Turin. Her research is situated in the fields of postcolonial, gender, and cultural studies, with a focus on the cultural history of visuality and colonial and postcolonial memory in fascist and postwar Italy. She has edited the new Italian edition of Frantz Fanon's *Les damnés de la terre* (Einaudi, 2001) and, coedited with A. Geppert and L. Passerini, *New Dangerous Liaisons: Discourses on Europe and Love in the Last Century* (Berghahn Books, 2010). Her authored and coauthored articles have appeared in the *Journal of Romance Studies*, *European Review of History*, *Feminist Review*, *Zapruder*, and *Quaderni Storici*.

Notes

The research discussed in this chapter would have been difficult to imagine without the generosity of Silvano Manera and Pia and Giuseppe Sieber in sharing their personal and family memories with me. I wish to thank Daniele Comberiati for letting me read his article on Somali cinema before it was published, and together with the BABE research team I am deeply grateful to Leonardo De Franceschi and Francesco Ventrella for discussing this chapter with me at different stages. Unless otherwise stated in the notes all translations from Italian texts and sources are mine and have benefited from Anna Nadotti's help. A special thanks to Azmera Tesfai for transcribing and translating the dialogues of the ERi-TV clip.

1. *Eva Nera* was Giuliano Tomei's first full-length feature film. Born in Rome in 1918; he directed many short documentaries for Phoenix Film from its early years. In the following decades, he specialized in industrial documentaries and worked for private companies and the Italian state television. However, it should be noted that his only other full-length feature film was *Il paradiso dell'uomo* (1962), also known as *Giappone proibito* and generally regarded as a 1960s mondo movie.

2. For a critical engagement with the notion of 'postimperial' legacies in contemporary Europe see Paul Gilroy (2004). For a reconceptualisation of the historical, political and conceptual relations between post-imperialism and post-colonialism see Dirk Göttsche (2017).
3. The Eritrean People's Liberation Front (EPLF), one of the main fighting formations during the Eritrean War of Independence, was established in 1970 when the Eritrean Liberation Front split into three groups. In 1991, the EPLF managed to defeat the Ethiopian forces in Eritrea and took control of the country (Iyob 1995). In 1994, it was renamed as the People's Front for Democracy and Justice, which is currently the only legal political party in Eritrea.
4. Renato Ferrari posted the pictures on his Facebook page on 28 June 2014, available at https://www.facebook.com/photo.php?fbid=10203249469170613&set=a.107401804 3767&type=3&eid=ARDg6n_D6qr4ScdbyXBQeGs4bAcWsAj9h2duVLFsxOUNKx DRalepwv07uF_8Ra8vwDXIHi73BIuNHRwm (last accessed 1 June 2020).
5. The Commission was established with the 24/26 resolution of 27 June 2014, and its findings were detailed in two final reports in 2015 and 2016, respectively. Information and documents are available at https://www.ohchr.org/commissioninquiryonhrinEritrea EN/HRBODIES/HRC/COIERITREA/Pages/.aspx (UN Human Rights Council). On the interplay between UN sanctions, the diaspora, and the Eritrean political regime, see Hirt (2015).
6. The image of the restitution of the Venus of Cyrene on the same day of the Treaty signature is available at https://i.guim.co.uk/img/static/sys-images/Guardian/Pix/pictures/2012/10/26/1351283556693/Berlusconi-shakes-hands-w-003.jpg?width=880&quality=45&auto=format&fit=max&dpr=2&s=424bd40afd333746e396fb7a7318c34c (last accessed 1 June 2020).
7. I am quoting from the 1968 edition of Nwosu's text; context-related information has been extracted from the 2014 edition.
8. On the movie production in Somalia and its reception in Italy, see Deplano (2014) and Comberiati (2018: 231). It is interesting to note how Nwosu's critique anticipated some of the points more recently articulated and developed by scholars. See, in particular, Ben-Ghiat (2015: 147–66) on Romolo Marcellini's movie and Pinkus (2003) and Giuliani (2018) on the postwar period.
9. The movie was awarded the "Hamar" prize for best Italian film with an African subject and the "Somalia" prize for best director. The Eritrean Letè won the "Città di Mogadiscio" prize for best actress (Corriere della Somalia 1955: 2).
10. From September 6 onward, the newspaper *Il Corriere della Somalia* published an almost daily column about the work of the Selection Committee. For a discussion on cinema partnerships between Italy and Somalia and the birth of Somali cinema after Independence, see Comberiati (2018).
11. Email correspondence with Silvano Manera, whom I would like to thank also for sharing a copy of the Phoenix Film Catalogue. The material on the documentaries shot during the Resistance is housed at the Archivio Nazionale Cinematografico della Resistenza (Turin).
12. On this topic, see Leonardo De Franceschi's interview with the critic Mino Argentieri (Nwosu 2014: 121–28).
13. My own translation from the Italian edition (Scego 2015: 175), given that the reference of the Italian verb "ballano" to dancing gets lost in the English edition.

References

Andall, Jacqueline, and Derek Duncan, eds. 2005. *Italian Colonialism: Legacy and Memory.* Oxford: Peter Lang.
Aristarco, Guido. 1955. "*Eva Nera.*" *Cinema Nuovo* IV, no. 55: 232.
Azoulay, Ariella. 2015. "Archive." In *Dissonant Archives: Contemporary Visual Culture and Contested Narratives in the Middle East,* edited by A. Downey, 194–214. London: IB Tauris.
Ballinger, Pamela. 2007. "Borders of the Nation, Borders of Citizenship: Italian Repatriation and the Redefinition of National Identity after World War II." *Comparative Studies in Society and History* XLIX, no. 3: 713–41.
Ben-Ghiat, Ruth. 2005. "Unmaking the Fascist Man: Masculinity, Film and the Transition from Dictatorship." *Journal of Modern Italian Studies* 10, no. 3: 336–65.
———. 2015. *Italian Fascism's Empire Cinema.* Bloomington: Indiana University Press.
Bracke, Maud Anne, and James Mark. 2015. "Between Decolonization and the Cold War: Transnational Activism and Its Limits in Europe, 1950s–90s." *Journal of Contemporary History* 50, no. 3: 403–17.
Butler, Judith. 2015. *Notes toward a Performative Theory of Assembly.* Cambridge, MA: Harvard University Press.
Clò, Clarissa. 2009. "Mediterraneo Interrupted: Perils and Potentials of Representing Italy's Occupations in Greece and Libya through Films." *Italian Culture* 27, no. 2: 99–115.
Comberiati, Daniele. 2018. "Somali Cinema: A Brief History Relating Italian Colonization, Somali Diaspora, and the Changing Ideas of Nationhood." In *Cine-Ethiopia: The History and Politics of Film in the Horn of Africa,* edited by M. W. Thomas, A. Jedlowski, and A. Ashagrie, 227–48. East Lansing: Michigan State University Press.
Corriere della Somalia. 1955. "Concluso il I Festival della Cinematografia: Consegnati ai vincitori i premi 'Africa,' 'Hamar,' 'Somalia' e 'Città di Modagiscio.'" *Il Corriere della Somalia* 236 (6 October): 2.
Cosulich, Callisto. 1954. "Realismo d'oltremare e censura imperiale." *Cinema* III, no. 46: 298–302.
De Cesari, Chiara. 2012. "The Paradoxes of Colonial Reparation: Foreclosing Memory and the 2008 Italy-Libya Friendship Treaty." *Memory Studies* 5, no. 3: 316–26.
De Franceschi, Leonardo, ed. 2013. *L'Africa in Italia: Per una controstoria postcoloniale del cinema italiano.* Rome: Aracne.
de Heusch, Luc. 2007. "Jean Rouch and the Birth of Visual Anthropology: A Brief History of the 'Comité international du film ethnographique.'" *Visual Anthropology* 20, no. 5: 365–86.
Deplano, Valeria. 2014. "'Settimana nera' e 'Violenza segreta': Denuncia e rimozione dell'eredità coloniale negli anni Sessanta." In *Subalternità italiane: Percorsi di ricerca tra letteratura e storia,* edited by V. Deplano, L. Mari, and G. Proglio, 121–38. Rome: Aracne.
———. 2017. *La madrepatria è una terra straniera: Libici, eritrei e somali nell'Italia del dopoguerra (1945–1960).* Milan: Mondadori-Le Monnier.
Ellena, Liliana. 2006. "Guerre fasciste e memoria pubblica nel cinema del dopoguerra." In *Crimini di guerra,* edited by L. Borgomaneri, 183–213. Milan: Guerini e Associati.
———. 2015. "Geografie della razza nel cinema italiano del primo dopoguerra 1945–1955." In *Il colore della nazione,* edited by G. Giuliani, 17–31. Milan: Le Monnier-Mondadori.
Epoca. 1954. "*Eva Nera* Advertising." *Epoca* V, no. 204: 82.
ERi-Tv. 2014. *ERi-TV Tiblez Tesfamichael Eritrean Actress from the 1940s – Italian Movie* Eva Nera. Accessed 7 April 2015. http://eastafro.com/2014/12/13/video-eri-tv-tiblez-tesfamichael-eritrean-actress-from-the-1940s-italian-movie-eva-nera2/.

Fiore, Teresa. 2012. "The Emigrant Post-'Colonia' in Contemporary Immigrant Italy." In *Postcolonial Italy: Challenging National Homogeneity*, edited by C. Lombardi-Diop and C. Romeo, 71–82. New York: Palgrave.
Foucault, Michel. 2013. *Lectures on the Will to Know*, edited by A. I. Davidson. London: Palgrave-Macmillan.
Gazzetta Ufficiale. 2009. "Ratifica ed esecuzione del Trattato di amicizia, partenariato e cooperazione tra la Repubblica italiana e la Grande Giamahiria araba libica popolare socialista, fatto a Bengasi il 30 agosto 2008." *Gazzetta Ufficiale della Repubblica Italiana* 40 (18 February): 1–13.
Gilroy, Paul. 2004. *After Empire: Melancholia or Convivial Culture?* London: Routledge.
Giuliani, Gaia. 2018. *Race, Nation and Gender in Modern Italy: Intersectional Representations in Visual Culture*. London: Palgrave Macmillan.
Giuliani, Gaia, and Cristina Lombardi-Diop. 2013. *Bianco e nero: Storia dell'identità razziale degli italiani*. Milan: Le Monnier-Mondadori.
Göttsche, Dirk. 2017. "Post-Imperialism, Postcolonialism and Beyond: Towards a Periodization of Cultural Discourse about Colonial Legacies." *Journal of European Studies* 47, no. 2: 111–128.
Gribaldo, Alessandra, and Giovanna Zapperi. 2012. *Lo schermo del potere: Femminismo e regime della visibilità*. Verona: Ombre Corte.
Hirt, Nicole. 2015. "The Eritrean Diaspora and Its Impact on Regime Stability: Responses to UN Sanctions." *African Affairs* 114, no. 454: 115–35.
Italia Taglia. 2008. *Eva Nera*. In *Banca Dati della Revisione Cinematografica: 1944–2000*. Rome: Ministero per I Beni e le Attività Culturali. Direzione Generale per il Cinema. Accessed 9 July 2018. http://www.italiataglia.it/search/1944_2000.
Iyob, Ruth. 1995. *The Eritrean Struggle for Independence: Domination, Resistance, Nationalism, 1941–93*. Cambridge: Cambridge University Press.
Kala-Lobé, Iwiyé. 1983. "Alioune Diop et le cinema africain." *Présence Africaine* 125: 329–50.
Lombardi-Diop, Cristina, and Caterina Romeo. 2015. "Italy's Postcolonial 'Question': Views from the Southern Frontier of Europe." *Postcolonial Studies* 18, no. 4: 367–83.
Lugones, Maria. 2010. "Toward a Decolonial Feminism." *Hypathia* 25, no. 4: 744–59.
Manera, Guido. 1957. "Il cinema in Africa nei suoi riflessi economici." *Africa: Rivista trimestrale di studi e documentazione dell'Istituto italiano per l'Africa e l'Oriente* 12, no. 1–4: 72–74.
Mirzoeff, Nicholas. 2011. *The Right to Look: A Counter History of Visuality*. Durham, NC: Duke University Press.
———. 2017. *The Appearance of Black Lives Matter* (2017). Accessed 9 July 2018. namepublications.org/item/2017/the-appearance-of-black-lives-matter.
Mitrano Sani, Gino. 1933. *Femina somala: Romanzo coloniale del Benadir*. Naples: Detken & Rocholl.
Monaville, Pedro. 2015. "Congo Street." In *Personne et les autres*, edited by K. Gregos and V. Meessen, 29–37. Brussels: Mousse Publishing.
Morone, Antonio M. 2018. "Gli italo-somali e l'eredità del colonialismo." *Contemporanea* 2: 195–222.
Nwosu, Joy. 1968. *Cinema e Africa Nera*. Rome: Tindalo.
———. 2014. *Cinema e Africa: L'immagine dei neri nel cinema bianco e il primo cinema africano visti nel 1968*, edited by L. De Franceschi. Rome: Aracne.
Patriarca, Silvana. 2018. "The Invisibility of Racism: On the Reception of Giovanni Vento's *Il Nero* and Antonio Campobasso's *Nero di Puglia*, 1967–1982." *Modern Italy* 23, no. 4: 445–59.

Pinkus, Karen. 2003. "Empty Spaces: Decolonization in Italy." In *A Place in the Sun: Africa in Italian Colonial Culture from Post-Unification to the Present*, edited by P. Palumbo, 299–319. Berkeley: California University Press.
Ponzanesi, Sandra. 2005. "Beyond the Black Venus: Colonial Sexual Politics and Contemporary Visual Practices." In *Italian Colonialism: Legacies and Memories*, edited by J. Andall and D. Duncan, 165–89. Oxford: Peter Lang.
Quilici, Folco. 1967. *Malimba la nuova Africa al Festival di Dakar*. Bari: De Donato.
Sanogo, Aboubakar. 2011. "Colonialism, Visuality and the Cinema: Revisiting the Bantu Educational Kinema Experiment." In *Empire and Film*, edited by L. Grieveson and C. McCabe, 227–45. London: Palgrave McMillan.
Scego, Igiaba. 2015. *Adua*. Florence: Giunti.
———. 2017. *Adua: A Novel*. Translated by Jamie Richards. New York: New Vessel Press.
Sieber, Pia. 2017. Interview collected in Lamone (Switzerland). 20 January.
Slobodian, Quinn. 2012. *Foreign Front: Third World Politics in Sixties West Germany*. Durham, NC: Duke University Press.
Srivastava, Neelam. 2018. *Italian Colonialism and Resistance to Empire 1930–1970*. London: Palgrave Macmillan.
Stefani, Giulietta. 2007. *Colonia per maschi. Italiani in Africa Orientale: una storia di genere*. Verona: Ombre Corte.
Stoler, Ann Laura. 2016. *Duress: Imperial Durabilities in Our Times*. Durham, NC: Duke University Press.
Tasselli, Maria Pia. 1982. *Il cinema dell'uomo: Festival dei Popoli 1959–1981*. Rome: Bulzoni.
Troilo, Simona. 2018. "'Casta e bianca': La Venere di Cirene tra Italia e Libia (1913–2008)." *Memoria e Ricerca* 1, no. 57: 133–56.
UNESCO [United Nations Educational, Scientific and Cultural Organization]. 1967. *Premier catalogue sélectif international de films ethnographiques sur l'Afrique Noire*. Bruges: UNESCO.
Wekker, Gloria. 2016. *White Innocence: Paradoxes of Colonialism and Race*. Durham, NC: Duke University Press.

Filmography

Africa addio [*Farewell Africa*]. 1966. Gualtiero Jacopetti and Franco Prosperi. Italy: Rizzoli Film.
Africa in casa. 1968. Giovanni Vento. Italy: Corona Cinematografica.
Africa sotto i mari. 1953. Giovanni Roccardi. Italy: Phoenix Film.
Eva Nera. 1954. Giuliano Tomei. Italy: Phoenix Film.
Eva Nera [*Black Cobra*]. 1976. Joe D'Amato. Italy: Matra Cinematografica.
Il Nero. 1967. Giovanni Vento. Italy: Armando Bertuccioli.
Il paradiso dell'uomo. 1963. Giuliano Tomei and Susumu Huni. Italy: Rotor Film.
La battaglia di Algeri [*The Battle of Algiers*]. 1966. Gillo Pontecorvo. Italy: Igor Film and Algeria: Casbah Film.
L'eclisse. 1962. Michelangelo Antonioni. Italy: Cineriz-Interopa Film.
L'Italia vista da un africano. 1962. Guido Manera. Italy: Corona Cinematografica.
Sentinelle di bronzo [*Dusky Sentries*]. 1937. Romolo Marcellini. Italy: Generalcine-Fono Roma.
Violenza segreta. 1963. Giorgio Moser. Italy: Globe Film.

Part IV

VISUALIZING MEMORY AND RESISTANCE

Chapter 7

COUNTER-IMAGES OF MIGRATION

(Visual) Memories of Refugee Migration
That Resist an Anti-Immigrant Discourse

Iris van Huis

Border crossings are imbued with corporeal experiences, images, and texts that are seen, heard, made, and displayed, en route and on arrival. They include memories of home and expectations of the future, besides of the journey itself. However, images of migration differ for those who have not themselves experienced such trajectories. Lacking direct experience, people (including myself) mainly encounter (refugee) migration via the media or the presence of refugee centers and newcomers within their neighborhoods, viewed either from a distance or through closer interactions. Yet, outsiders' perceptions of migration can affect the experiences of migrants themselves. Superficial, unidimensional understandings of migration experiences can feed into an anti-immigrant discourse that impacts on daily interactions and on policies that constrain rather than facilitate (refugee) migrants. Conceived in this way, the experience of migration entails interdependencies between newcomers and the receiving population, often unfolding in visual and embodied ways (e.g., van Reekum and Schinkel 2017).

While interviewing recently arrived migrants in the Netherlands for my research on memories of migration, I observed that individuals with refugee trajectories are not simply passive recipients of superficial images, texts, and constraining policies. Some actively counter them with alternative images channeled through social media and art, including drama, installation art, photography, designs, and paintings, conveying their personal experiences.

In this chapter, I discuss these counter-images found in social media and obtained through interviews. During interviews, mainly with people from the Middle East, I encouraged respondents to draw maps or use other means to visualize their trajectories. I then explored the memories represented in all of these images, the messages conveyed, and how they engaged with feelings and experiences of (non)belonging to their countries of origin, the Netherlands, Europe, and beyond. I examined how such representations constituted forms of resistance or components of normalizing processes, which, as I discovered, were not rigidly opposed. I also examined how such representations were related to experiences of (non)belonging. The underlying premise of my research is that visual representations of migration produced by those with migrant or refugee backgrounds can offer counternarratives to constraining governmentality (Foucault 1991) and to dominant discourses entailing superficial, stereotypical, and stigmatizing images of migrants. More complex, individualized, and humanizing images and narratives conveying agency can deepen understanding of migration trajectories.

Migrating Subjects, Anti-Immigrant Discourse, Resistances, and Belonging

Macro studies on migration have investigated how political economies, the global market, and interstate relationships have shaped migration and how "receiving" states attempt to shape migrants' bodies and actions through laws and policies regulating migration and through language that legitimizes these policies (Castles, de Haas, and Miller 2013: 26). Although elucidation of these processes and forms of power is important, subjects' agency is often obscured within narratives about shaping and controlling policies, resulting in the reduction of migrants into a homogenous mass of bodies that lack subjectivity or individual identities (for critiques, see Boyd 1989; Castles, de Haas, and Miller 2013: 37; Freemantle and Misago 2014; Lindley 2010: 3; Lubkemann 2008: 5; Monsutti 2005; Passerini 2014). A homogenizing perspective on migration reinforces antimigrant discourses in which migrating subjects are portrayed as masses that cause or themselves represent a "crisis" and are metaphorically equated with examples of natural "crises," such as floods or tsunamis (Freemantle and Misago 2014: 143). Therefore it is important to emphasize subjects and their agency, including their resistance to anti-immigrant discourses.

Anti-immigrant discourses assume many forms and languages, entailing more or less extreme "othering," constraining, and dehumanizing effects. They are expressed in repetitive language and behavioral repertoires (Hall

2001), articulated by politicians, conveyed in the media, inscribed in policies and in cross-national agreements that physically restrict migrants, or privately expressed. They are grounded in an understanding and a framing of the sociopolitical situation that reflects fear of change, and/or attempts to gain votes by tapping into potential xenophobia. Moreover, these discourses resonate with ethnonationalist discourses and desires to belong to social entities that foster a sense of primordial unity (Jones 2012; Smith 2013). These discourses are rooted in a colonial, historical context entailing rigid, hierarchical lines demarcating races, ethnic groups, and continents and determining who belongs and who does not to Europe, and who is and is not entitled to a safe haven when in danger (Gikandi 2011; Said 2016). While current forms of hierarchy do not exist in exactly the same shape as their historical antecedents, the latter nevertheless constitute a cultural archive that continues to influence ways of framing inclusion and exclusion within European nation–states (Goldberg 2006: 352; Wekker 2016), producing images, sentiments, behaviors, and policies that disparage and hamper those in search of refuge and a new home. This cultural archive and prevailing anti-immigrant discourses produce "others" within and outside of national and regional (European) borders by falsely portraying Europe, "the West," and white Europeans as free and just, with the rest of the world and their descendants in Europe conceived as oppressed (mainly women) and oppressors (mainly men) (Khan 2005; Roggeband and Verloo 2007; Scharff 2011: 120). Distinctive stereotypes of men and women from Middle Eastern Muslim majority countries are evident: women are conceived as passive victims of male oppression and men as aggressive patriarchs, and more recently as terrorists (Roggeband and Verloo 2007; Scheibelhofer 2012). Discourses rooted in colonial history are further reinforced by prevailing fears of terrorist attacks. Besides the gendered angle, such stereotypes include expectations that refugee migrants will be poor, low skilled, and of little value for receiving European countries. Thus, the racial, gendered, and class-based stereotypes of colonially rooted anti-immigrant discourses are reinforced by neoliberal discourses that argue for keeping borders closed.

Foucault (1991) offers an important methodology for uncovering power relations that otherwise remain hidden. While he addresses both subjugating power and resistance to subjectification processes, the latter are less empirically grounded in his work. Therefore, there is a need for studies that demonstrate how governmentality and dominant discourses are resisted, offering perspectives for change in the direction of more equal and just societies (Fraser 1981). Accordingly, encounters with governmentality should be viewed as unequal and bidirectional (or multidirectional) processes, leading not only to normalization but also entailing resistance (van Huis 2018: 14). In their encounters with governmentality, the varied responses of migrants/refugees to normalizing and constraining structures, which include conforming and resisting forms of subjectivity, require investigation.

Resistance to anti-immigrant discourses, conveyed not only in words but also in images, reveals agency and offers insights into how such discourses are and can be resisted. By resistance, I mean a wide spectrum of protests entailing diverse forms and effects that occur in micro settings (including the interview context) or in collective organized forms. Unlike other scholars, I do not distinguish between resistance, revolution, rebellion, and revolt, and I do not explore transitions (e.g., Buikema 2014; Kristeva 2000) and outcomes of resistance. Even though all acts of resistance are changes in the social and physical world, their reception or precise effects, and how they travel, are beyond the scope of this study.

In contemporary "visual culture" (Mirzoeff 1999; Rogoff 2006: 28), acts of resistance are inevitably not only verbally or textually conveyed but also visually through photography, videos, and forms of art that are disseminated through social media. These images offer insights into the complexity of migration and related acts of resistance.

Because resistance and subjugation are not strictly opposed, individuals may choose forms of normalization that may or may not be in their own interest. Goffman (2009), who famously wrote about responses to stigma, or "spoiled identity," envisaged the possibility of adhering to existing stereotypes ("minstrelization"), or minimizing differences in relation to "normal" or dominant groups ("normification"). He further identified "militant chauvinism" as the perception of being outside of and better than the dominant group. Moreover, these responses are performed in overlapping and combined ways. I will take such responses into account in my exploration of how subjects who have migrated respond to antimigrant discourses.

Besides identifying resistance in encounters with governmentality and other responses to (stigmatizing) anti-immigrant discourses, explicit reflection on how such practices relate to (non)belonging is necessary to better understand the effects of these discourses and of responses to them. Yuval-Davis (2011) argues that belonging is multifaceted, referring to (1) social locations (practices, possibilities, and constraints that depend on and construct intersectional positioning in relation to dimensions of inequality, such as class, race/ethnicity, and gender); (2) identities and emotions (related cognitive and emotional processes of belonging); and (3) social norms (values and/or norms accompanying these intersectional positionings). Here, I focus mainly on the second dimension of belonging centering on identities and emotions. In line with this approach, I examined how visual and oral memories of migration could be acts of resistance and of normalization/normification and how these are related to intersectional processes of belonging.

Research Methods: Gathering Visual and Oral Memories

I conducted interviews over the period of 2015–17. Thirteen of my respondents[1] had refugee backgrounds. Most were from Syria (seven), two were from Iran, one from Iraq, and one from Eritrea. Three were earlier migrants: one migrated from the former Yugoslavia in the 1990s and one from Chile in the 1970s. Apart from three respondents (including the latter two and one who arrived from Iran), all of the interviewees had arrived recently in the Netherlands (within three years of being interviewed). Earlier migrants helped to situate current experiences and policies that they compared with their own experiences within an embodied historical perspective. I found respondents through personal connections, social media, and by volunteering at a music studio located near a refugee center that offered guitar lessons. I found the images through these contacts either by asking them to produce drawings or provide other visual material that represented their journey.

The process of data collection entailed asking interviewees to produce drawings, which Yanow (2014) describes as "generated images,"[2] and collecting respondents' previously created images (Yanow's "found images") stored on their phones, posted on social media sites, or displayed in galleries prior to interviews. I included "found images" because they demonstrated agency more actively than drawings made on request. I obtained the permission of the creators of these visual memories to reproduce these images in this text. I also found it helpful to consider some narratives as images, thus including "evoked images" (van Huis and van der Haar 2015). These are images that arise during the narration of vivid stories that are evoked mentally but are difficult to express visually.

"Found images" in this research include theatrical performances as well as (visual) commentaries on migration trajectories posted online. The theatrical productions I included in my study are "Home?," a production of the Light and Shadow theater group; "In Between Time," directed by Titia Bouwmeester; and "Zohre," produced by Marjolijn van Heemstra. In each of these productions, the subjects narrate and act out their migrant experiences. My analysis also includes a video performance by Razan Hassan as well as paintings and installations by Yara Said and a collage by Hala Namer.

I applied an iterative process, analyzing and comparing different types of oral and visual memories that included drawings, videos, paintings, photographs, theater performances, and verbal narratives by artists and nonartists who chose to visualize their experiences publicly, and images generated by respondents on request. This process entailed considering the origins of and intentions behind the images as well as what they "do" to the viewer to examine how they shape "identity constitution and identity fragmentation" (Rogoff 2006: 10), conceptualized here as processes of belonging (Yuval-Davis 2011).

In the following section, I show how memories of migration become (visual) acts of resistance and/or normalization, or what lies between or outside of such classifications. I present my findings for three stages of the migration trajectory: home/departure, the journey, and arrival that are not as linear, or easy to distinguish, as they might appear to be.

Memories of Home: Contrasts between "Normal" Life and War

Many stories of departure narrated by refugees from conflict zones begin with descriptions of families, houses, villages, and cities, often conveying a form of "normality" or even a "happy" start: everyday life, followed by, or interwoven with, narratives about war. These stories reveal that it is not just war that people leave behind but also their families and homes. Evidently, there is not just one story of home, and these narratives are not just about harmony. Every family has its troubles and complexities—some more than others—and longer experiences of coping with and resisting oppression are also evident.

During an interview, twenty-six-year-old Laila showed me pictures that she "stole" from the family album just before leaving her hometown, Latakia, a Syrian city bordering the Mediterranean. The pictures she took, depicting smiling faces, are somewhat faded and yellowed. She pointed to herself in a group photo as a little girl sitting on a couch, dressed in pajamas. Laila explained that she recalled this scene whenever she thought of home: her house and her family members. Her reasons for leaving were the proximity of bombings to her home and the looming threat of the approach of ISIS. As a young divorced woman who worked in bars, colored her hair in vivid hues, and sported tattoos, she feared—besides the physical threat of war—the compulsion to live in an alien, undesirable way. Her family supported her decision to leave, and along with a friend, she crossed the border into Lebanon in a taxi and bought an airplane ticket to Turkey. That was how her journey started.

The migration stories narrated by actors with refugee backgrounds in "Home?" (which I viewed at the Bijlmerpark Theater on 2 February 2018) evoke similar but simplified and truncated images of home: first uncomplicated and peaceful and then the bombings. Background images of the historical city of Aleppo are displayed, followed by familiar news pictures of bombings and ruins. The sound of an explosion suddenly erupts and an actress falls to the ground, her motionless body picked up by an actor. One of the actors explains that his decision to leave hinged on his refusal to join the army and add to the violence. Although the stories of home, family, and war of four men and one woman are compressed into the play's duration of an hour and a half, they succeed in drawing in the audience, aware that these are lived experiences of the actors.

In "In Between Time" (which I watched on 4 November 2017), refugee migrants and nonmigrants share memories of home and youth. Paired refugees and nonrefugees act out their stories and converse with each other, sometimes compassionately and at other times arguing or joking with each other. This arrangement not only presents the story of the "other" to an audience, most members of which probably lack refugee experiences, but it also stages and complicates the personal trajectories of white Dutch individuals in an interactive, researching, and intersubjective manner (Passerini 2014: 3) that in no way diminishes the gravity of the refugee experience. This play also depicts representations of home that combine everyday experiences of home and work, more complicated subjectivities, as well as narratives of war. Some of the actors disrupt the image of the Middle East as (only) a restrictive place. In addition to governments' restrictions, it also portrays liberal or modern aspects of Middle Eastern (Syrian) cities. For example, a young Syrian man acts out driving to a dance party, feeling wild and free (music by the Doors is playing), with his white Dutch counterpart sitting with him in his (cardboard) car, thus disrupting temporal linearity. The actors are involved in each other's memories, sharing similar experiences of freedom and youth.

Sometimes memories of "home" are not grounded in lived experience but extend further back in time. "Zohre" enacts the shared history of a young female refugee (Zohre) in the Netherlands and Marjolijn van Heemstra, the play's producer, writer, and a participating actress. A similar "pairing" of a migrant and nonmigrant occurs, entailing considerable contemplation about helping and receiving help. In this play, Zohre's memories of a "normal" or "happy" past are conveyed in video images of Afghanistan in the 1960s, in which women are unveiled and attired in "modern" dresses. In her early twenties and too young to have witnessed such images herself, Zohre reflects that "sometimes the future is in the past," nostalgically evoking a romanticized past and a wish for a future in a more liberal Afghanistan.

A performance by Razan Hassan, a Syrian, posted on YouTube[3] also highlights the contrast between everyday life with family and friends and war, depicted on three large encircling screens. She sits in between these screens, reading "One Art," a poem by Elizabeth Bishop and reciting phrases from it: "The art of losing isn't hard to master; so many things seem filled with the intent; to be lost that their loss is no disaster," and: "I lost two cities, lovely ones. And, vaster; some realms I owned, two rivers, a continent; I miss them, but it wasn't a disaster." The images on the screens alternate between beautiful landscapes and happy scenes of her smiling mother and her enjoying life, sunbathing, or riding in a car, and images of war and fleeing people. Her own presence as a beautiful young woman with hair dyed green, dressed in a black spaghetti-strap dress, within this artwork produced in the Netherlands disrupts and resists the image of a refugee victim and the stereotypical images of traditional and oppressed Middle Eastern women. Positioned between images of the past, she contemplates, reciting a poem that clearly resonates with her own "losing" of cities and people close to her, and affirming, through the poem, her ability to cope ("it wasn't a disaster"), perhaps more to demonstrate her strength and desire to be strong than to convey her actual feelings.

These examples reveal how "normal" and complex life is disrupted by war, compelling departure. "Normality" here is evidently an ambiguous concept, because norms are spatially and contextually dependent. Nevertheless, the audiences receiving these images and narratives may evoke the familiar and in that way the "normal" for them, thus forging connections with the actors/characters. These are not acts of normification in the sense of Goffman's "passing" acts (Goffman 2009) because the actors are representing their former embodied lives rather than putting on acts to appear "normal." At the same time, the scenes of everyday life that they depict, offering possibilities for interconnectedness or intersubjectivity (Passerini 2014), reflect a performance of "normal" life, which in this case constitutes a form of resistance against "othering."

In addition to displaying this "normality" and more complex images of "home" juxtaposed with armed conflict, memories of more long-term oppression were also evident, which were countered by a longing for a more liberated existence and resistance in the place of departure. Twenty-five-year-old Yara Said, a young Syrian-born artist, had just graduated from the art academy in Damascus when she decided to leave because of threats of violence and to improve her ability to work as an artist. Many of her friends had already left. Yara's father was an artist and an activist, and she grew up living with her mother and grandmother, both working women. Besides leaving her mother and grandmother, she also left behind many of her paintings. Despite the war, one of her paintings (figure 7.1) was exhibited in a Damascus café after her departure. It portrayed the violence and her way of dealing with it.

The painting shows a missile, which is a reoccurring motif in Yara's work. Often, as in this painting, the missiles take the shape of fish, signifying her working class background, "because working class people eat more fish because meat is more expensive." At the same time, she renders the bombs less harmful through this transformation and controls their effect and violence.

The bomb-fish in the painting penetrates a red-painted circle that seems to have dribbled upward (a technique she often uses). At art school, she was criticized for the sexual connotations of her art, indicating the lack of freedom she experienced while living in Syria and her acts of resistance against these forms of oppression.

While Yara Said, and also Laila and some of the men I interviewed, had to leave, they all share a desire to be in a country where they could have more freedom. Several respondents explained that despite the beauty of the

FIGURE 7.1. A painting by Yara Said (untitled). Published with permission.

country where they grew up, and their love for their families, there were also reasons for not feeling "at home" in these places, which either they tried to resist or else they envisioned themselves living elsewhere. Through "new" media, they perceived other possibilities, the freedom to express themselves, democracy, and more liberated forms of education, art-worlds, and popular cultures. At the same time, their perceptions of Europe were not necessarily uncritical, as Western countries were also held at least partly responsible for the chaos and violence in the Middle East, either in recent or colonial history. It was the pull of freedom, departures of friends and family members, but above all the violence, the bombs and threats of bombing, and the physical tension accompanying this threat that pushed them to leave.

The narratives and the images I have described were attempts to show "normality" through family or liberal city life as a means of creating a connection with the audience or countering possible stereotypes of the Middle East prevailing in the Dutch or European context. War images provide a rationale for their presence and belonging in the Netherlands. While the women's narratives reveal their experiences of patriarchal oppression, these experiences were not accepted passively and were resisted even before departure. Moreover, there was a hypothetical sense of belonging to a freer world, whether in their places of origin in the future, in the past (illustrated in "Zohre"), or elsewhere in Europe. This sometimes coincided with a critical view of the roles of

Europe (and the United States) in creating chaos in the Middle East, which disrupts the geographical dichotomy between the Middle East as a place of oppression and Europe as a place of freedom (Khan 2005; Scharff 2011). Altogether, the images and verbal narratives reveal a complex understanding of home, including forms of resistance in the countries of departure as well as departure as a form of resistance.

The Journey: Bodies across Borders

Maps drawn during the interviews depict long and complicated journeys, connecting many place names, with some connections being made more straightforward due to booking a flight.

Marahi, a thirty-seven-year-old technician from Deir Ezzor in Syria, listed the names of the places he passed through, revealing the importance of nation–states as referential places before arriving in the Netherlands. He sometimes mentioned the means of transportation (a "big ship," "bus," and "walking"), or the duration of travel between two places. In the Netherlands, the names signified the locations of refugee centers or "camps." Because so many names were mentioned, the "map" meandered beyond the page. Marahi first fled within Syria, then left for Turkey and crossed the Mediterranean to Chios, continuing in a big ship, on buses, and on foot through Macedonia, Serbia, Croatia, Hungary, Austria, and Germany to the Netherlands. But the journey did not end there. Figure 7.2 reveals that Marahi made ten more stops after Amsterdam, each lasting from a couple of days to several months. At the time of the interview (and also six months later), he was still in a refugee center. So when does the journey end and when does "arrival" actually take place?

The images in figure 7.3 depict Marahi's narrated memories of waiting in queues, buses, temporary beds, food offered in a camp, and luggage containing all that is physically brought by the traveler from a past life. They depict not only in-between places, or a "long tunnel" between departure and arrival (Salter 2006), conveying situations of waiting, of being (temporarily) stuck, but also personal objects and those that are necessary, such as clothes, accompanying bodies passing across borders.

Just as Laila "stole" photographs from her mother's album and took them with her in her bag, Yara also carried some personal items with her, revealing that not only images but also objects are significant in these situations. She brought two rings with her; one that her father gave her and the other that, for her, represents "Damascus." She also brought a toy that her mother gave her. In 2017, she created an art installation representing her journey. The most startling feature is the shoes she wore when crossing nine countries,

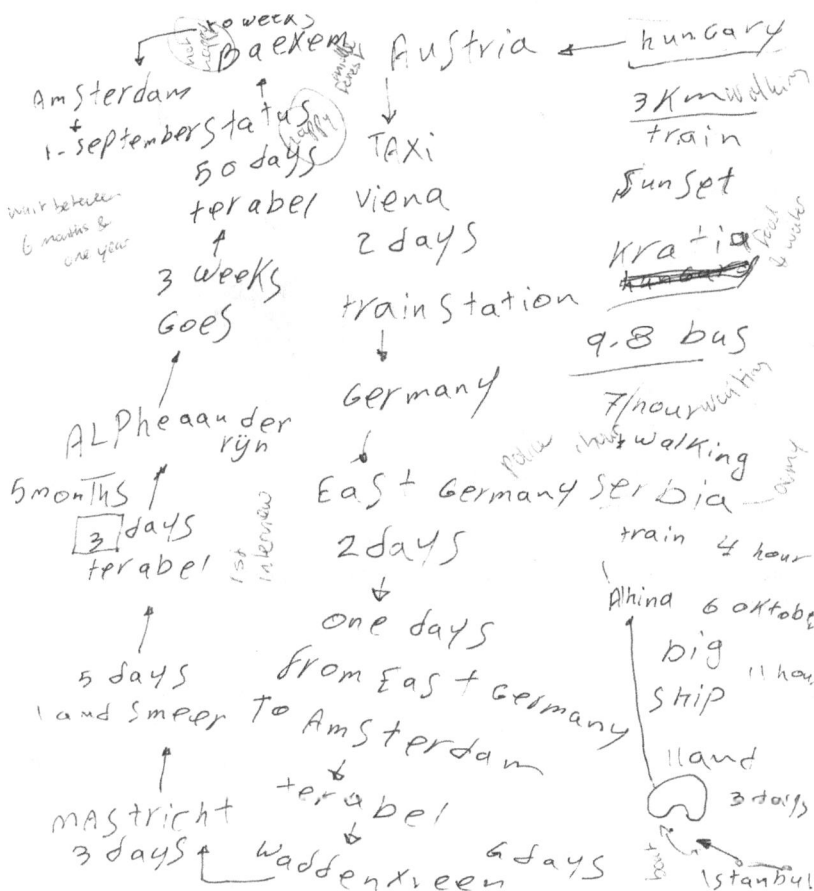

FIGURE 7.2. Marahi's drawing produced during his interview. Published with permission.

placed on the ground in front of a large map depicting her journey. The map includes her drawings of her grandmother, mother, and pet dog, representing the memories of home she carried with her. The few items she brought with her are also positioned on or below the wall: the rings, the toy, a lipstick, blush, an extra phone battery, her diploma, and her passport. On the wall are the words "forbidden" in nine languages, signifying her protest against the restrictions she encountered en route. The personal items displayed in this work bring the viewer close to her experience. They include unexpected items that disrupt ideas on what someone takes when fleeing a place; how personalized and individual such choices are, and how items from home—in her case, items that convey her femininity as well as the possibility to communicate, namely a phone battery—can help preserve human dignity during

FIGURE 7.3. Photographs by Marahi, taken during the journey. Published with permission.

the most difficult times. Thus, the physical objects that accompanied her on the journey and contributed to her sense of belonging, individuality, and human dignity are revealed and shared upon arrival. This sharing deepens understanding of migration and arrival, thereby resisting superficial, homogenizing, nonindividual, anti-immigrant discourses.

The play "Home?" portrays images similar to those in figure 7.3. In the background, there is a photograph of the same ferry line in Greece. There are also photographs of the camps, including beds, and the actors appear on stage holding plastic plates, indicating the temporary situation they were in. In their performances, the actors convey tensions in the camps between people waiting in lines, but they also portray friendships forged by acting out dancing together and taking selfies with their smartphones.

As migration is strongly associated with mobility, the phenomenon of waiting in relation to migration requires further reflection. Periods of waiting were common during the journey. A critical point to note is that waiting is not only a "particular experience of time" but also an act of bureaucracy (Khosravi 2014: 66) or governmentality (Foucault 1991); a way of experiencing the effects of power (Bourdieu 2000: 228). Part of the process of formal decision making on admission or denial—but also affecting emotions, identification, and health—waiting crucially impacts processes of belonging. Waiting presumes passivity: "expecting something coming from others"; but individuals can also deploy it as a strategy for improving their situations (Khosravi 2014: 67). As represented on stage and described in interviews, periods of waiting were experienced as stressful, affecting the mental and physical health of the concerned people. At one point in "Zohre," the protagonist reveals bald patches on her head, attributing them to the stress induced by bureaucratic processes. Accounts of suicides in proximity to interviewees were also part of narratives of waiting for life-changing decisions made by others. At the same time, by enduring these hardships, respondents reached destinations where they could feel safe and continue progressing toward their futures.

Strongly contrasting with the hardships experienced by respondents were the selfies and group photos they had taken with people they met on the journey, conveying smiling faces and a sense of closeness. Yara showed me a selfie of her posing and smiling with a group of friends on the small boat on which she crossed the Mediterranean from Turkey to Greece. She explained that these images are important because they disrupt expectations: "You can have a good time, or look hot, and be a refugee crossing the Mediterranean at the same time. It is not that black and white; we are not just victims but humans with many experiences and ways of expressing ourselves. The experience was scary but these moments took place as well."

She told me this in response to the commotion on social media raised by images of refugees traveling with smartphones, with questions being raised on whether these people were poor "victims," deserving of help and refuge (O'Malley 2015).

As photographs often depict smiling people, representations of journeys bring to mind fun trips or tourist adventures. Consequently, they convey a somewhat illusory image of safety and lightness associated with the journey. To contextualize this, Yara recalled her experiences in Damascus and the physical dangers entailed in crossing the Mediterranean:

> Physically something has changed. I used to be fearless. I used to do sports like rock climbing, but now [when] I tried it, [I] was too scared. I felt it in my body. This is the trauma, I think. It was from the crossing, from the real fear of losing your life. . . . But I also still feel the time in Damascus—I was so tense during that time, I still carry that with me.

The combination of the smiling photo and the intense physicality of the fear experienced during the war and the journey disrupts media images of migration that obscure the migrating subjects' individuality, depicting them as a threatening mass. For many respondents, the Mediterranean crossing was the part of the journey that left the strongest impression on them, not only because of the dangers at sea but also because of their treatment by the smugglers organizing the operations. Others, for example, thirty-one-year-old

Yonas from Asmara in Eritrea, highlighted the desert crossing and eluding armed groups.

Zahir, a thirty-seven-year-old Syrian from Damascus, only told me about his Mediterranean crossing, which had a strong impact on him, after getting to know me. Speaking about it, he emphasized that he did not want to be seen as part of the masses. "In Between Time" similarly conveys a reluctance to speak about the crossing. In the last scene of the play, Yazan Hakim, a Syrian actor, says to another character with whom he has exchanged memories of youth: "Alright, now I will tell it to you, but this is the last time I will talk about it. I'm tired of telling this story over and over. The more I tell it, the more I become it," and he starts to talk about the crossing. Clearly, talking about this part of his migration experience is not easy and interferes with the way he self-identifies with the person he chooses to be. Sharing memories of the crossing is problematic for him, perhaps because he has been asked about it too often, because it was traumatic and therefore hard to talk about in casual conversation, or because, like Zahir, he wants to present himself as an individual distinct from the sensationalist media images of mass migration.

Yara noted that blunt representations of the suffering of people during war or when seeking refuge are dehumanizing. Through the transformation achieved through art, this becomes bearable. In a student magazine, she was quoted: "It's better to show art than a picture of a dead child. Photographs of war are an intrusion in people's privacy. It's rude. Did photographers get permission before they put images on social media? . . . It is like they are selling our sorrow" (Bernhard and Visbeen 2017).

The journeys continued after the crossing. The greatest distances were covered traveling on buses, trains, and cars (and sometimes airplanes), but there were also lengthy distances covered on foot. Yara and her friend traveled a long distance with a Syrian family. They helped carry a child and at other times some of the family's luggage. At the camps, she translated for others, because she spoke English well. Sometimes she was mistaken for a European volunteer because of her translating skills and because she had dyed her hair blond. She and her friend did this intentionally to avoid being identified as refugees when crossing borders, which turned out to be helpful. At one point, when people were taken off the train by the police, she and her friend were skipped, indicating the use of racial profiling. Thus, Yara and her friend strategically and successfully anticipated the racism of European governments. Their ploy of "passing" as Europeans can be viewed as a form of resisting—a strategic individual action that exposes the conditions on which racist governmentality is founded.

To summarize, memories of the journey—of moving across a landscape as well as waiting—were partly about the means of transportation and the places passed through, revealing how long the journey remains after arrival in

Europe or in the Netherlands. Respondents also recalled receiving help and helping others and remembering loved ones at home through the items they took with them. Their narratives of encounters en route reveal governments' attempts to shift the burden to the next country and to manage refugees' bodies in camps by grouping them together and transporting them to places that were perceived as less burdensome, or where they wanted to go themselves. Help was also offered along the way through encounters with "smugglers" or what they called "mafia," indicating how governments were present by their absence, allowing refugees to cross to the next country, perhaps benefitting via corruption. There were encounters with potential dangers at sea, which can also be seen as the violent presence by absence of governments, who were not doing enough to prevent people from drowning. These memories, including images and personal items, reveal the subjectivity and individuality of border crossings, and how these are articulated and shown to audiences, and to the interviewer, and sometimes avoided to resist the spectacle (Huysmans 2000: 762) and the media's homogenizing images of migration.

"Arrival": Resisting a Constant State of Arrival

When does arrival take place? For forty-five-year-old Karim, an English teacher from Aleppo, an important moment of arrival occurred in Austria. After crossing the Mediterranean with his brother, walking long distances, undergoing many bus rides, and staying in camps, he felt relief on crossing the border into Austria. Here, he willingly would have his fingerprints taken—he showed this with a movement, pressing his thumb down on the table. "Why? This was a free country that would allow my family to come over, and allow us to prepare for a new life." However, he moved on, taking two more trains to the Netherlands because he heard that the procedure for getting the family over would be shorter there. This did not turn out to be the case, as he had to wait two more years for his family to join him, which was especially difficult for him because his children could not attend school while waiting in Turkey. They worked in factories for low wages to survive. Karim felt restless and incomplete as long as he was apart from his family. Similarly, "Home?" portrays the arrival of family members at Schiphol Airport a year and a half after departure as the conclusion of the story of one of the actors. These crucial memories of arrival in Europe—or in European countries perceived as more welcoming, offering a safe environment and professional opportunities—did not necessarily signal the end to the story of arrival.

Photographs taken with mobile phones of refugee centers (see figure 7.4), and especially the precarious situations described by many respondents, evi-

FIGURE 7.4. Images of refugee centers in the Netherlands. Published with permission.

dently do not offer a clear experience of "arrival." Instead, they convey a situation entailing constant waiting.

My use of scare quotes around "arrival" is intended to show that arrival is never really completed—how there is a "constant state of arrival" (Gerard 2014: 200) even when arriving in a country that is expected to be safe and to offer a new home because of the struggles to belong in formal and informal ways. Despite anti-immigrant discourses and forms of governmentality, the visual and oral/textual material collected for this research provides examples of subjects with refugee backgrounds who did not passively undergo categorizing and subjugating acts but instead resisted them. Their narratives and images of their places of departure and journeys convey resistance to anti-immigrant discourses. Next, I discuss five types of resistance on "arrival" that I found in my research material. As will become clear, they are not completely mutually exclusive and I do not expect them to be collectively exhaustive.

Resistances to Constraining Images and Narratives

First, individuals resist simplifying images and narratives of countries or regions of origin and of the "journey" through their own renderings of their stories of home and migration, including those they tell without prompting, as in the examples above. The complex lives of people with migratory backgrounds, and their deviance from and resistance to governmental and patriarchal oppression in their countries of origin, were revealed in their interviews and art as resistance to superficial, uncomplicated images of migrants. They represented themselves not merely as victims but as active agents upon their departures and during their journeys.

Resistance to Categorization and Labeling

Closely related to the above is resistance to categorization and labeling. A collage by Hala Namer, a Syrian artist, (figure 7.5, top-left image) shows a female soldier asking a young woman where she is from. A line forms a border separating them. It is not clear whether the question "Where are you from?" consolidates the line or creates an opportunity to cross or erase it. The soldier, in her military attire, represents the violence embedded in the question.

The first question people are usually asked upon arrival is where they are from. The question is experienced in informal encounters and embodied in the demand to see a passport. It conveys a process of categorization whereby states police their borders and determine access or exclusion. In informal situations, people may ask questions about someone's background as a matter of curiosity, or a desire to know more about the person's identity and past experiences. However, it may also be experienced as an act of "othering" and being boxed in categories associated with stereotypical characteristics. Therefore, this collage constitutes an act of resistance against labeling and categorization.

More explicit opposition to labeling is evident in the self-representations of Yara Said and Razan Hassan on the "I am not a refugee" website (http://

FIGURE 7.5. Resistance in art. Top-left: a collage by Hala Namer; top-right: Refugee Nation Flag by Yara Said; bottom-left: the Refugee Company logo with "Refugee" crossed out; bottom right: paintings by Yara Said (untitled). All published with permission.

iamnotarefugee.com). These self-representations, along with many others there, disrupt involuntary categorizations and labels, highlighting aspects of identity distinct from a refugee background. The website depicts portraits as well as quotes that reveal the professions or personal statements of the individuals portrayed. This initiative seeks to connect them to a wider network that enables them to pursue their professions or passions and "lose their label" (These words were used in an online conversation with one of the initiators of the website, Frédérique Buck.) Individuals with refugee backgrounds who self-represent as nonrefugees disrupt an ascribed and imposed refugee victim identity. By highlighting self-chosen identities, often related to desired or past professions, the individuals profiled on the website demonstrate their own agency with "rehumanizing" effects. Arguably, these attempts partly constitute acts of normification (Goffman 2009), entailing forceful behavior according to a norm of being a "good working citizen" as a response to stigma. However, in this case, they are aimed at opposing a subjugating, imposed label.

Creating Solidarity and a Strong Refugee Identity

A third form of resistance against anti-immigrant discourses opposes victimhood by choosing and creating solidarity and a strong refugee identity, which at first glance appears to contrast with the above-described form of resistance. Yara Said designed a flag representing the "refugee nation" (see figure 7.5). This flag was displayed at the 2015 Olympics, fostering unity of refugee contestants who could not represent their nationalities because they had fled their countries. The design is based on the life vests used by many refugees when crossing the Mediterranean. Thus, the colors and design are those of a physical object used to reach the European border that has been reappropriated as a symbol of unity. It symbolizes one of the most notable and recognizable stages of the journey to Europe, representing danger, trauma, survival, and also the death of those for whom a life jacket was insufficient to guarantee their survival. The deployment of a flag and the "refugee nation" label mimics a discourse of nationality. However, Yara Said argues that this is comparable to the rainbow flag for the LGBTQ community, viewed as a sign of solidarity rather than an attempt to create a nation.

It is noteworthy that an individual can choose to resist categorization and stereotypes, while also deploying the refugee label. Thus, the refugee label is a complicated one, particularly for people struggling to attain official refugee status, but not necessarily wanting a refugee identity. In line with Zetter's (1991) observations regarding ambiguous experiences associated with the refugee identity, the facilitating aspects of the label are conjoined with its stigmatizing effects, which are resisted, as illustrated by the above examples.

Exposing Inefficient and Harmful Forms of Bureaucracy

A fourth type of resistance against the dominant discourse and governmentality entails exposing inefficient and harmful forms of bureaucracy. On her YouTube channel, Zohre Norouzi exposes the alienating complexity of what refugees have to undergo to be included in Dutch society. She does this (often in a humorous way) by questioning many of the diverse people concerned: fellow migrants, professionals implementing policies, as well as people on the street. She reflects on what she sees as typically Dutch, offering a critical commentary on Dutch society and on the bureaucratic procedures that constrain her. My interviewees experienced many of the issues she exposes. The slow pace of bureaucratic processes can be extremely demoralizing, inducing stress, depression, and physical issues. In the play titled with her name, Zohre enacts similar issues. The play not only represents Zohre's struggle, but also that of Marjolijn as she reflects on her own values and on the power positioning between Zohre and herself when she (often unsuccessfully) attempts to guide Zohre through her bureaucratic struggles.

It is noteworthy that the critiques of bureaucracy and governmentality offered by Zohre Norouzi (and Marjolijn van Heemstra) have had some impact on local policies. Their initiatives have been perpetuated in several local public debates with politicians, and Zohre is engaged in conversations aimed at finding new ways of organizing citizenship courses for new immigrants.

Resistances beyond the Country of Residence

A final example of resistance against dominant discourses and policies that I observed extended beyond the country of residence. Besides her refugee-nation flag that was featured in the Olympics, Yara Said has also created politically engaged work that protests against governments beyond Dutch borders. Figure 7.5 shows three paintings by Yara Said that provide commentaries on the foreign policies of the EU, United States, and Russia. As she states: "These show the countries that fucked up my country. I thought it was funny to show it like this." In these paintings, she demonstrates her newly found freedom, expressing herself in ways denied to her in her art school in Syria. At the same time, her use of this freedom, including the use of sexuality in her metaphorical depiction of power, demonstrates resistance. Some of my interviewees became or have remained politically engaged with their former home countries or with international political issues. They publicly comment on the ways in which refugees are portrayed or treated internationally or on the political situations in other countries. Fifty-five-year-old Pablo migrated from Chile with his parents in the 1970s because left-wing political activists like his mother were persecuted. As he grew up, he became politically active and participated in several organizations and journalistic venues focusing on the political situation in South America and Africa. Currently, he is involved with migrant organizations in the Netherlands. Comparing current policies on refugees with those in the 1970s, he perceived harshness in contemporary Dutch society that negatively impacts integration or processes of belonging in the Netherlands. Furthermore, his international work enables him to see how Europe's colonial history continues to be reflected in perceptions of South America and Africa within Europe. However, a division of the world into "blocks" such as "Europe" and "the Third World" was, he felt, too simplistic, as "there are just as many colonialists" in Europe as in Latin America. Thus, he focuses his critique on corrupt politicians and complicit relations of governments in Latin America and Africa with multinationals that exploit people and resources. These examples show how feelings of solidarity combined with personal histories of activism and political awareness (for Yara and Pablo, this was intergenerational) promote ongoing international or transnational political activism and the development of transnational identities for the actors themselves. In some cases, these identities may also be fostered or strengthened in others.

In sum, a (constant) state of arrival means finally feeling safe and free, while also encountering new constraints, being relocated, and entering a new state of waiting. On arrival, subjects are subjected to categorization and labeling, which some resist actively in interview situations, during public events, and through the creation of art or video blogs. The refugee label can function as a self-chosen but still complicated label through solidarity forged with other refugees. On their arrival, some individuals critique the bureaucracy, which can be demoralizing. Ultimately, political commentary and involvement is not limited to the nation–state but crosses borders through continuing engagements with the countries of origin and beyond.

Conclusion

Using images and interview fragments, I have shown oral and visual memories of migration and of bodies crossing borders that reveal the resistance and agency of migrants during several stages of migration: departure from home, journeys en route, and the place of "arrival" where struggles continue. Interviewees and artists/actors with migratory experiences commonly present these stages in ambiguous and nonlinear ways as experiences of arrival/home/belonging that were taken away, lost, retrieved, and (re)constituted in differing ways, depending on their circumstances and their agency/subjectivity. The images and narratives not only offer insights into the complex reasons for migration—and how these can be acts of resistance—they also show how migration is embedded in and has consequences for belonging, and how the journey constitutes an embodied act as well as something inscribed on the body. Expression of this embodied experience in a self-chosen way provides an opportunity for others—audiences that include researchers who have not experienced forced migration—to approach this experience, not through perceptions of victimhood but in a manner that contributes to building or preserving dignity, subjectivity, and humanity.

The visuals and oral narratives reveal how subjects who migrate, seeking refuge, encounter governmental violence and policies that restrict them (in addition to the violence of conflict, smugglers, and natural threats), which some also resist. Subjects were compelled to leave not only because of violent conflict but also because of their resisting acts, including resistance to participation in the war through their departures. During the journey, these subjects encountered more violence and restrictions imposed by governments, or through their absence, which they overcame through endurance and by actively seeking ways to circumvent them, while also helping others. On arrival, the journey was not always concluded, with the continuation of "camp" status, a "long tunnel," or "in between time," which some actively countered through various forms of resistance against constraining images and narratives, categorization and labeling, and victimhood. They did so by expressing symbolic unity and resisting governmentality and governments' foreign policies, exposing harmful bureaucracy and engaging in (artistic) protests, thereby creating resisting (inter-/transnational) identities.

The images and interviews also reveal that resisting acts are not just the acts of "refugees" who oppose oppressive governments and dominant discourses but entail more complex struggles. This complexity relates, firstly, to attempts to forge new ways of belonging through combinations of resistance and normification/normalization, respectively, entailing behavior that accords with and conforms to dominant norms. Second, my research revealed that refugee migrants' initiatives demonstrate forms of cooperation between people with refugee experiences and nonmigrants/Dutch people—as allies, facilitators, fellow actors, or paid professionals. This also encompasses government policies aimed at "integrating" migrants. Complicated power relationships unfold in the receiving or availing of help offered, and in helping others, whereby some aspects of the dominant discourses are reproduced while others are opposed. These issues complicate processes of belonging for subjects who may benefit from help and sanctuary, but who may be constrained too when policies simultaneously stigmatize or hamper them.

The fact that women enacted many of the above forms of resistance, and that some of their forms of protest were gendered, is noteworthy. The freedom of expression applied in critical representations reproduces freedom of expression, including forms of sexual liberation. Forms of self-expression and activism debunk stereotypical images of women from the Middle East or from Muslim-majority countries. For some of the men, the threat of coerced participation in a war in which a "just" side cannot be perceived, or of being perceived as potential terrorists, whether at "home," during the journey, or on "arrival," is also gendered. This is because it has specific negative consequences for how Muslim men are perceived and scrutinized and for how they oppose those images through self-representations as "normal," "kind" people who can be related to as family members and potential workers that can also, however, constitute forms of "normification." The interviews and observations have shown how "normality" can be deployed as a form of protest against perceived essentialist otherness and that its use as a strategy against opposition or a form of subjugation depends on the specific situation. Thus, resistance and normalization are not rigidly opposed; there are spaces in between. A final reflection concerns the research methods used. The combination of found, generated, and evoked images selected in this study helped reveal forms of agency and the complexity of the migration experience in which encounters with governmentality include forms of subjugation and resistance and forms of subjectivity that are hard to place in either slot.

Iris van Huis is a lecturer in the Department of Interdisciplinary Social Science at the University of Amsterdam. She earned her PhD at Nijmegen School of Management, Department of Political Science, Radboud University Nijmegen. Her research and teaching experience is in migration, gender studies (with a focus on masculinities), visual studies, social interventions, and urban sociology. Her PhD research explored the multifaceted nature of inequality in social locations, identities, and social norms through an inquiry into the impact of social interventions for disadvantaged men on intersectional gender-, ethnicity-, and class-based inequalities. As a research associate on the BABE Project at the European University Institute, she carried out an empirical study of practices of resistance to anti-immigrant and colonial discourses among migrants with refugee and postcolonial backgrounds.

Notes

1. As part of the broader BABE research project on migration to the Netherlands, I interviewed twenty-seven people in total. However, here I focus only on interviews relating to refugee migration.
2. "Generated" images (Yanow 2014) resemble but are not exactly the same as "induced reception" (Passerini 2018). Images can be generated by the researcher or by the research subject. In the latter case, they are generated based on the researcher's request, encourage-

ment, or influence. Induced reception more specifically refers to the method of letting research subjects respond orally or visually to images shown to them by the researcher. Induced reception images are therefore generated images, but the reverse is not necessarily true.
3. Razan Hassan, "The Art of Losing," YouTube, accessed 7 February 2018, https://www.youtube.com/watch?v=SEW9Og6gZUs.

References

Bernhard, Alrun, and Kim Visbeen. 2017. "Een vlag als steun." *Babel: Maandblad voor de faculteit Geesteswetenschappen UvA* 25, no. 8: 8–10.
Bourdieu, Pierre. 2000. *Pascalian Meditations*. Stanford: Stanford University Press.
Boyd, Monica. 1989. "Family and Personal Networks in International Migration: Recent Developments and New Agendas." *International Migration Review* 23, no. 3: 638–70.
Buikema, Rosemarie. 2014. "Political Transitions and the Arts." In *Gender, Globalization, and Violence: Postcolonial Conflict Zones*, edited by S. Ponzanezi, 196–213. New York: Routledge.
Castles, Stephen, Hein de Haas, and Mark J. Miller. 2013. *The Age of Migration: International Population Movements in the Modern World*. London: Palgrave Macmillan.
Foucault, Michel. 1991 [1975]. *Discipline and Punish: The Birth of the Prison*. London: Penguin Books.
Fraser, Nancy. 1981. "Foucault on Modern Power: Empirical Insights and Normative Confusions." *Praxis International* 1, no. 3: 272–87.
Freemantle, Iriann, and Jean Pierre Misago. 2014. "The Social Construction of (Non-)Crises and Its Effects: Government Discourse on Xenophobia, Immigration and Social Cohesion in South Africa." In *Crisis and Migration: Critical Perspectives*, edited by A. Lindley, 136–57. New York: Routledge.
Gerard, Alison. 2014. *The Securitization of Migration and Refugee Women*. New York: Routledge.
Gikandi, Simon. 2011. *Slavery and the Culture of Taste*. Princeton: Princeton University Press.
Goffman, Erving. 2009 [1963]. *Stigma: Notes on the Management of Spoiled Identity*. New York: Simon and Schuster.
Goldberg, Theo D. 2006. "Racial Europeanization." *Ethnic and Racial Studies* 29, no. 2: 331–64.
Hall, Stuart. 2001 [1997]. "Foucault: Power, Knowledge and Discourse. In *Discourse Theory and Practice: A Reader*, edited by M. Wetherwell, S. Taylor, and S. J. Yates, 72–81. London: Sage Publications Ltd.
Huysmans, Jef. 2000. "The European Union and the Securitization of Migration." *Journal of Common Market Studies* 38, no. 5: 751–77.
Jones, Guno. 2012. "Slavery Is (Not) Our History: On the Public Debate and Divergent Meanings of the NTR Television Series Slavery." *BMGN—Low Countries Historical Review* 127, no. 4: 57–82.
Khan, Shahnaz. 2005. "Reconfiguring the Native Informant: Positionality in the Global Age." *Signs: Journal of Women in Culture and Society* 30, no. 4: 2017–35.
Khosravi, Shahram. 2014. "Waiting." In *Migration: The COMPAS Anthology*, edited by B. Anderson and M. Keith, 66–67. Oxford: Centre on Migration, Policy and Society.

Kristeva, Julia. 2000. *The Sense and Non-Sense of Revolt*. Vol. 1. New York: Columbia University Press.
Lindley, Anna. 2010. *The Early Morning Phone Call: Somali Refugees' Remittances*. Vol. 28 of *Studies in Forced Migration*. New York: Berghahn Books.
Lubkemann, Stephen. C. 2008. "Involuntary Immobility: On a Theoretical Invisibility in Forced Migration Studies." *Journal of Refugee Studies* 21, no. 4: 454–75.
Mirzoeff, Nicholas. 1999. *An Introduction to Visual Culture*. London: Psychology Press.
Monsutti, Alessandro. 2005. *War and Migration: Social Networks and Economic Strategies of the Hazaras of Afghanistan*. New York: Routledge.
O'Malley, James. 2015. "Surprised That Syrian Refugees Have Smartphones? Sorry to Break This to You, but You're an Idiot." *Independent*. 7 September.
Passerini, Luisa. 2018. "Bodies across Borders: Oral and Visual Memory in Europe and Beyond.", Fact Sheet, Grant Agreement No 295854, European Research Council. https://cordis.europa.eu/project/id/295854. Accessed 29 May 2020.
———. 2014 [2007]. *Memory and Utopia: The Primacy of Inter-Subjectivity*. New York: Routledge.
Rogoff, Irit. 2006 [2000]. *Terra Infirma: Geography's Visual Culture*. New York: Routledge.
Roggeband, Conny, and Mieke Verloo. 2007. "Dutch Women Are Liberated, Migrant Women Are a Problem: The Evolution of Policy Frames on Gender and Migration in the Netherlands, 1995–2005." *Social Policy & Administration* 41, no. 3: 271–88.
Said, Edward W. 2016 [1995]. *Orientalism: Western Conceptions of the Orient*. Hammondsworth: Penguin.
Salter, Mark B. 2006. "The Global Visa Regime and the Political Technologies of the International Self: Borders, Bodies, Biopolitics." *Alternatives* 31, no. 2: 167–89.
Scharff, Christina. 2011. "Disarticulating Feminism: Individualization, Neoliberalism and the Othering of 'Muslim Women.'" *European Journal of Women's Studies* 18, no. 2: 119–34.
Scheibelhofer, Paul. 2012. "From Health Check to Muslim Test: The Shifting Politics of Governing Migrant Masculinity." *Journal of Intercultural Studies* 33, no. 3: 319–32.
Smith, Anthony. D. 2013 [1994]. *Nationalism: Theory, Ideology, History*. Hoboken: John Wiley & Sons.
van Huis, Iris. 2018. "Engaging Men in Gender Equality: How Social Interventions for Disadvantaged Men in the Netherlands Impact on Gender+ Equality." PhD dissertation, Nijmegen, Radboud University.
van Huis, Iris, and Marleen van der Haar. 2015. "Coffee, Cookies and Cards: The Use of Visuals and Materiality to Reproduce and Transform Masculinity in Dutch Social Work Interventions." *Gender Rovné Příležitosti Výzkum* 16, no. 1: 57–66.
van Reekum, Rogier, and Willem Schinkel. 2017. "Drawing Lines, Enacting Migration: Visual Prostheses of Bordering Europe." *Public Culture* 29, no. 1 (81): 27–51.
Wekker, Gloria. 2016. *White Innocence: Paradoxes of Colonialism and Race*. Durham, NC: Duke University Press.
Yanow, Dvora. 2014. "Methodological Ways of Seeing and Knowing." In *The Routledge Companion to Visual Organization*, edited by E. Bell, S. Warren, and J. Schroeder, 165–89. New York: Routledge.
Yuval-Davis, Nira. 2011. *The Politics of Belonging: Intersectional Contestations*. London: SAGE Publications Ltd.
Zetter, Roger. 1991. "Labelling Refugees: Forming and Transforming a Bureaucratic Identity." *Journal of Refugee Studies* 4, no. 1: 39–62.

Chapter 8

VISUALIZING VIOLENCE

Political Imaginations from the
Syrian Diaspora in the Netherlands

Sara Verderi

> In every person there is a male part and a female part. We are killing our female part every day. The violence in Syria has frozen our female part.
> —Fadwa Souleimane, personal communication, November 2016

The task of tracing the contours of the Syrian uprising is not an easy one, given the existence of opposing accounts regarding whether or not the "revolution" actually happened. In the Global North, many intellectuals—on the Left and the Right—journalists, and policy makers have expressed skepticism and are reluctant to acknowledge that a movement promoting civil rights and political and religious pluralism has even occurred (Al-Haj Saleh 2017).[1] The question of whether the first Syrian uprising should be considered a legitimate political project that was triggered by earlier uprisings in Tunisia, Egypt, and Yemen in 2011, or whether it should be viewed as a "civil war," features centrally in informal discussions among scholars from the Global South who have migrated to Europe (Al-Haj Saleh 2017; Verderi 2016; Yassin-Kassab and Al-Shami 2016).[2]

Some of the activists whom I name in this chapter still insist that the Syrian uprising must be categorized as a revolution advocating civil rights and pluralism, whereas other intellectuals argue that the revolution lasted for only a year and a half before turning into a conflict. Whatever the answer might be, the question of violence—and its gendered dimension in particular—that is implicated in the uprising as well as in the subsequent war and displacement has remained a constant preoccupation of Syrian artist-activists. This point was powerfully articulated by Fadwa Souleimane, one of the leading proponents of the Syrian nonviolence movement, when I interviewed her in Paris, where she lives in exile. For Souleimane, the "killing of the female part" and the consequent masculinization of "the person" in society occurred in parallel with the militarization of the Syrian uprising that she experienced in her homeland. Although the uprising began as a *thawra selmiyyeh* (peaceful revolution) for *dawla medeniyyeh*[3] (a civil state), national unity, and justice, it was soon transformed by the ruling regime, and by international forces, into an armed conflict. Artists and activists who supported a peaceful uprising were the first pushed to leave the country because of the increasing violence, religious radicalization, and hardship.

The question of how to engage nonviolently with violence, and with processes of justice and accountability, is a central one in feminist theory (Braidotti 2007; Butler 2009) and one of critical relevance in the current context of an increasingly militarized and violent world. Drawing on this strand of feminist theory, my aim is to explore the continued commitment of Syrians in Europe—and specifically in the Netherlands—to use art for political and ethical purposes, and especially for representing the Syrian uprising and the violence that followed from the perspective of Syrian artist-activists. Within Europe, these representations have been largely forgotten and obscured by hegemonic narratives—especially by the representational categories of "refugee" and "conflict" that are deeply rooted within a masculine, hegemonic conceptualization of justice informed by the human rights discourse (Slaughter 2007). To do justice to the origins of the Syrian uprising and its consequences for narratives concerning the Syrian presence in Europe, I examine the ways in which violence is interpreted, resisted, and remembered in critical and affirmative ways by subjects of the Syrian diaspora. I use the term "artist-activists" to highlight the historical entanglement between art and politics in the Syrian context and its continuation within the diaspora (Cooke 2017). By examining contemporary visual artifacts and memories that activist-artists within the Syrian diaspora bring to the Dutch cultural market and public space, I aim to demonstrate how Syrians in the Netherlands continue to connect art with politics and ethics through different forms of culture, art, and visuality, revealing how their visions of political transition are informed by a feminist stance of nonviolence. Thus, a key question that I address in this chapter is: How do Syrians live, remember, and interpret violence through visual materials, and how do they position themselves in relation to hegemonic representations of Syria within the human rights discourse and in the media?

My reading of the nonviolent responses to violence and militarism of Syrian artist-activists within the diaspora is informed by various feminist theories. Feminist theory posits an ethics of nonviolence in response to violence, favoring a collective pursuit of justice over individual acts of vengeance or state repression. The nonviolent ethics of feminism stand in contrast with the glorification of violence that pervades the mainstream media, with its representations of fighters of all kinds and genders (Braidotti 2007). Although subjects are generally constituted within and through violence, feminists assert and assume the responsibility of not repeating the violence through which the subject is formed (Butler 2009). Following this ethics, feminist theory has shown commonalities with, as well as critiques of, the concept of human rights. Posthumanists, in particular, have argued that claims to universal justice and egalitarianism are fictional, because the example they take as their illustrative model is a very specific, white, male, middle-class subject, thus marginalizing groups such as women and minorities (Slaughter 2007). The actual exclusion of certain subjects in favor of others is determined by the nature of the perpetrator of violence. If the perpetrator is a national state, the subject falls outside the framework of recognition as a national subject, and ultimately ceases to be regarded as a "grievable life" at all (Butler 2009). Reproduction of these asymmetries vis-à-vis violence is also perpetuated through specific representational tropes such as children's faces that prompt paternalistic "affective transactions" among consumers concerned about human rights (Zarzycka 2016). Feminist theory has also highlighted advantages and disadvantages of the conceptualization and design of international law, which informs organizations that support human rights, such as the UN (Kannout 2016). The peace negotiations and conflict resolution principles as well as the actors who conduct such negotiations are overwhelmingly male-oriented (Bell and O'Rurke 2007).

I would like to argue that in the specific case of the Syrian diaspora, these insights as articulated in feminist theory are echoed, and worked through, in the work of Syrian artists and activists in three particular directions: The first entails their formulation of a critique of the exclusionary character of human rights and media imaginaries, entailing a binary opposition between bodies that are "grievable" and those that are not. The second relates to their aestheticization of violence. In other words, they enact practices of aestheticizing violence with the aim of interrogating the representation of Syria as merely a place of conflict by intertwining images of violence with the beauty of children, life, and art. The third dimension entails the articulation of mourning and ghost haunting as dynamic practices (Gordon 2008). In this chapter, I examine how these three dynamics unfold through the lens of gender and art theory, focusing specifically on the historical relation between art and political dissent in Syria (Cooke 2007; Ziter 2015), and the continuation of this relation during the 2011 uprising (Halasa, Omareen, and Mahfoud 2014; Yassin-Kassab and Al-Shami 2016) and within the subsequent diaspora. In doing so, I conceptualize the use of art as a form of resistance and memorialization of violence and trauma (Cooke 2017). I follow the trajectory of this historical intertwinement from its origins in Ba'athist Syria to a contemporary European context.

In order to illustrate how subjects from the diaspora live through and interpret violence via visual material in relation to hegemonic representations of Syria in the human rights discourse, and in the media, I will focus on the narratives and practices of Syrian artists and activists whom I met in the Netherlands. Drawing on a set of empirical data gathered through my fieldwork in the Netherlands from May 2016 to May 2017, I have chosen to focus on what the interviewees *do*—that is, art and activism—using the term "artist-activists" to emphasize the connection between art and politics in Syria; a connection that persists in the wider context of the Syrian diaspora. Art is also understood as a practice of resistance against violence and the most effective form of memorialization of the uprising, unlike other forms of visual representation such as ephemeral documentaries (Cooke 2017).[4] Given the importance of artifacts, which were used as a channel in the Syrian uprising and as a narrative tool for conveying the violence that followed, the main methods that I applied in this study were curation and interviews. I have relied on interviews conducted with artist-activists because they integrate and give context to the meanings conveyed in the artifacts, allowing me to explore the ways in which subjects inhabit the present after undergoing traumatic events (Das 2007). As a method, curation allows for a resignification of the presence of the Syrian diaspora in Europe in a way that affirms political subjectivities, creating new meanings beyond the category of the "refugee" and the humanitarian discourse and emphasizing, instead, the importance of memory and visuality in creating constructive dialogues (Acord 2010; Levitt 2007). Moreover, I have drawn on my own experience of the uprising while living in Damascus in 2011, as well as on my experiences as a migrant—first, moving from southern Europe (i.e., Italy, which is the country of my birth) to Egypt, where I spent two years as a student (2013–15), and later moving from Egypt to northern Europe (the Netherlands and the UK) to pursue my doctoral studies. These experiences influenced my curatorial choices as well as my analysis of artifacts and events, as presented in this chapter. Specifically, the stories of Syrian artist-activists coincide with my own experiences in Syria and Egypt as a scholar and a witness of the uprisings. Although my own experiences of ghost haunting are more difficult to articulate as a logical argument, I believe that they were influenced by my specific location in the European context.

Among such commissioned intellectuals, some were committed to producing dissident forms of art, mocking the Asad cult, despite imprisonment. [...] artistic and cultural productions were compliant to the regime's hegemony, [while] otherwise prohibited topics, such as [...] the regime's commissioned intellectuals, [...] artists. One of the leading figures in the area [...] Sa'dallah Wannous whose "theater of politicization" (*masraḥa al-tasyīs*) aimed. This genre of theater is aimed at lending artistic shape to politics. As stated by Wannous: "[A]ll [...] historical theater, should engage the present in such a way [as to produce] a 'new utterance' (*qawl*) that truly reflects the concerns of its time. And when this utterance comes into being we must find [the] form that will accommodate and reveal it" (cited in Cooke 2007:

In two of his most well-known plays, *The Elephant, oh King of Times!* (1969) and *The King is the King* (1977), Wannous deploys satirical and allegorical techniques associated with the theater of politicization to point out the inadequacy of the leader and of the political opposition. Wannous's theatrical genre strongly influenced other activist-artists during the 1990s (Cooke 2007) as well as artistic productions during the 2011 uprising. A study of political theater in Syria provides insights into the strategies employed, because theater tropes featured in performances were used by cyber activists during the uprising (Ziter 2015: 3). The impacts of the uprising and the war on the Syrian diaspora have manifested as profoundly different and divided political imaginations. One of these divisions, which has been evident since 2011, separates those who still see Syria as Al-Asad's Syria, those who envision a shift to a *dawla madaniyya* (civil state), and those who do not take sides. In Western Europe, for example, groups supporting the Asad regime, such as European Solidarity Front for Syria, have forged connections with various nationalist organizations in Italy, the Netherlands, and other European countries. The ideological commonalities of Ba'athism, which is the founding ideology of the Syrian government (Strickland 2018), and fascist political elements in Europe, connect these two political cultures. In the case of diasporic organizations or individuals, who contrastingly envision a political transition and a post-Assad state, the connection takes place through artistic and cultural channels and in the human rights sector, maintaining continuity with the practices of dissident artists and activists in Syria. Dissident art is performed in Europe as a form of activism. Two examples of such productions are *Le Passage*, a monologue presented by Fadwa Souleimane (2013) in which she elaborates on her experience of her passage from Syria to Paris, and *Message to . . .* (2017), a dance theater performance by the same artist in collaboration with Rami Hassoun that thematizes the violence perpetuated by the Syrian regime against its people, and appeals to Europe for justice. From the activist perspective, the work of Razzan Zaitouneh, a lawyer and civil society activist and a founding member of the Violations Documentation Center in Syria, remains one of the guiding lights for artist-activists such as Samar Yazbek, a novelist and member of Women Now, an NGO founded in Paris in 2012.

One of the aims of diaspora studies is to examine how the political imagination of the diaspora articulates with the specific political culture of the host country (Baeza and Pinto 2016). The role of the arts in the Dutch political culture (Klamer 1996) has so far provided Syrian artist-activists with a fertile space for expressing their imaginations, provided that they remain within the ambit of "art and culture." In fact, from 2014, the proliferation of events focusing on "the Syrian culture" organized both by first and second diasporic generations and by "native" Dutch, has occurred in tandem with the expansion of the Syrian diaspora. It goes with the territory that many of the events more or less openly conveyed the organizers' political imaginations, which were frequently imbued with their experiences of the 2011 uprising or "revolution," which is the term used by artist-activists. Whereas some of these events have been tolerated, local and national governments have also restricted them, perceiving them as reflective of Syrians' unwillingness to integrate into the Dutch culture. These developments should be seen in light of current shifts in national policies from diversity to assimilative forms of integration that in recent years have strongly influenced national-level policy making relating to immigration (Hoekstra 2015) and the rise of nationalist and populist discourses across Europe.

The 2011 civil uprising signified a cultural revolution (Yassin-Kassab and Al-Shami 2016). During this uprising, Syrians deployed a range of vibrant cultural productions, ranging from visual arts to comics, songs, music, graffiti, and documentaries to contest the prevailing dictatorship. Until the time when increasing militarization of the uprising began in 2012, dissident art in Syria had become the most important channel available to press for change. In her recent book about Syrian diasporic artists, Cooke (2017) argues that the inextricable entwinement of art and activism is characteristic of the ways in which Syrians have enacted the revolution during the last seven years (2011–17). Central to her study is the subject of the artist-activist, which is characteristic of Syrian diasporic artists whose works, which focus especially on political violence, combine aesthetics and politics. This combination of politics and art can be traced back to the theater of politicization introduced by Sadallah Wannous. The works of diasporic artists and activists share commonalities with the canon of art established by Wannous that can be used for political purposes, as demonstrated by the initiatives described in the following section.

Visualizing Violence: Grievability, Aestheticization, and Mourning

In the following analysis, building on the historical investment in art and politics outlined in the previous section, I engage in a close examination of three initiatives that are rooted in the Syrian diaspora. The banners of the Het Syrische Comité (HSC), the "Women for Freedom" (WFF) exhibition, and the work of the renowned artist Amer Al-Wahibi focus on different political concerns of the Syrian diaspora in Europe, expressed through visual forms. Through their respective emphases on grievability, aestheticization of violence, and mourning, these artistic productions demonstrate how violence is lived, critiqued, and remembered in ways that do justice to the feminist political imagination that imbued the civil uprising in Syria. Through an analysis of these three initiatives, I show how a commitment to visuality, as a means of asserting such political claims, persists in contemporary Europe and specifically in the Netherlands.

HSC is an independent, self-funded organization that promotes the Syrian revolution in the Netherlands. HSC organizes sit-ins using banners, street performances, and songs to engage with and be rendered visible to Amsterdam's residents and the Dutch media. Although in some cases songs and slogans are created specifically for the Dutch public, the majority of the banners and images are recycled from existing material circulating on social media that are produced by other artist-activists located in Syria, Lebanon, and elsewhere.[8] Even though HSC's visual artifacts are influenced by the transnational work of Syria-based artist-activists, their work is more orientated toward the national context of the Netherlands, and is exhibited in Dutch public squares. This was confirmed to me in an interview I conducted with Mostafa, an HSC member who produces the banners. During my meeting with Mostafa, I asked him about the role of art in conveying HSC's message to people in the Netherlands. His response was as follows:

> I am not an artist; I am not a cartoonist. When I arrived in the Netherlands, I did not know the language, not even English, so I used the cartoons to convey our messages to the Dutch people—not to the Dutch government, which already knows everything, but to the people. I tried all possible artistic forms and came to the conclusion that caricatures are the best artistic form [to fit that purpose]. There are people that get disappointed with us because we organize sit-ins in the weekends. Dutch people—and they are right in doing so—use the weekend to rest. They sit in cafes with their friends and families. They have worked all week, so they use those days to rest. They are surprised to see us showing banners about Syrian people dying and so on. This thing upsets me. It is not that I came here and they can tell me, "Okay, Mostafa, shut up, stay at home, learn Dutch, and work." Sometimes I feel that I have lost everything

I had in my life. What keeps me still breathing is [the desire] to state my freedom and [the] freedom of my people. (Mostafa, personal communication, Sassenheim, 6 August 2016)

As observed by Butler (2011) in her reflections on the 2011 sit-in conducted in Tahrir Square in Cairo, Egypt, the practice of assembling bodies in the square to talk (and to perform) also shapes the articulated message. As Mostafa explains, the desire of refugees to state their freedom is of equal importance to obtaining access to housing and acquiring language skills—that is, to their duty to integrate. In my interpretation, Mostafa's statement that "it is not only about working, learning Dutch, and staying home" reveals his thinking on how the presence of Syrian migrants is perceived in the Netherlands and further illustrates that he does not want to be reduced to the representational trope of the "refugee." Through their banners and performances, members of HSC lay claim to the grievability of the Syrian people—a claim that is made through a critique of both the human rights discourse and mainstream media representations. On the one hand, such critiques center on the affirmation of the equal value of human life in the human rights discourse, and on the other hand, they emphasize the de facto inequalities that are enacted when the lives of Syrian civilians are not protected as a result of the perpetration of war crimes. The enabling fiction of human rights is based on the paradox that exists between what is known and what should be known—that is, between the prescriptive teleological narrative of egalitarianism and universal rights on the one hand, and material inequalities based on gender, race, and class on the other (Slaughter 2007). It also relates to Butler's (2009) concept of grievability, according to which the lives of non-European war victims are not considered to be as grievable as European lives. Introducing the notion of "frames of recognition" that determine a given subject's degree of grievability, Butler focuses on the inclusion in, and exclusion of certain subjects from, the cultural manifestation of the Global North, introducing the idea of "frames of recognition" that determine a given subject's grievability. Such frames determine the ontological nature of the subject—that is, who is subject and who is not, who is life and who is not, who is grievable and who is not. Life that falls outside these frames is ungrievable. For Butler, war is dividing populations into those who can be mourned, and are hence counted as "lives," and those who were never counted as lives and are thus unmourned.

The scene depicted in a banner titled *Human Rights*, shown in Figure 8.1, is set in an anonymous Syrian city that is under shellfire. The planes dropping the bombs bear the flags of the Russian and Syrian regimes, emphasizing the responsibility of these states for the bombing. In the center of the painting, a female figure and a child lie covered in blood, barefooted. A male figure, also

216 • Sara Verderi

FIGURE 8.1. *Human Rights*. Photograph taken by the author on 9 August 2016. Published with permission.

barefoot, is kicking the book of *ḥuquq al-insan* (human rights) in a gesture of his rage. This banner was displayed in The Hague's central square, close to the headquarters of the International Criminal Court (ICC). The banner powerfully conveys a critique of the prevailing system of human rights and particularly the failure of the Security Council to file the Syrian case at the ICC. The activists who produced this banner depict a recurring theme in the work of transnational Syrian activists, namely the incapacity of the international community to "practice what they preach." As the banner demonstrates, the inequality lies in the discrepancies between what is promised in the "books," namely the protection of civilians—and what is happening on the ground, which is the UN's de facto compliance with the regime's violence perpetrated against civilians.

According to Slaughter, human rights are extensions of the Enlightenment project to "modernize, normalize and civilize" (2007: 5). The universalizing tendency of the human rights discourse is also a characteristic inherited from this tradition: "Contemporary human rights incorporation is a figurative process of naturalization . . . that enfranchise[s] the individual as world citizen" (Slaughter 2007: 21). Yet, as Brown states, they are expressed as "promises of futurity" (2005: 15). The human rights imperative envisions a future

FIGURE 8.2. *Je Mag Je Gelukkig Prijzen Aylan!!* Photograph taken by the author on 9 August 2016. Published with permission.

in which all human beings will be considered *as* humans. Through the images depicted in this banner, Syrian activists unmask the fictional character of this egalitarian claim made by the human rights discourse, reconnecting it to material conditions that are currently being experienced by Syrian civilians—particularly the most vulnerable subjects, notably women and children.

The banner titled *Je Mag Je Gelukkig Prijzen Aylan!!* ("You Must Consider Yourself Lucky, Aylan!!") refers to the famous photograph that made global headlines in September 2015. The photograph portrayed the body of a dead child named Aylan Kurdi lying on Greek shores as the dramatic outcome of his family's attempt to escape Syria and reach Europe. The banner shows Aylan on the right (from the viewer's perspective), standing on a cloud in an angelic pose and listening to other (Syrian) children who are also floating on a cloud in Paradise. One of the children says to him: "You must consider yourself lucky, Aylan!! We are all victims of the same war, but nobody represents our deaths at the Public Persecution Service." The language is a mixture of English—the use of words such as "our"—and Dutch abbreviations, such as "OM," which stands for *Openbaar Ministerie* [Public Persecution Service]. This banner critiques the sensationalist nature of the news and the way in which Aylan's death was portrayed while disregarding other innocent victims. The banner thus suggests that unequal value is given to life in Syria, which is considered less important and less "grievable" than life in Europe.

Butler (2009) argues that the regime of representation in the United States wields certain frames of recognition that determine whose lives are considered important and whose are not, and, accordingly, who is grievable and who is not. Specifically, she points out that victims caused by forms of state violence, such as war, are considered acceptable or justified, whereas the violence perpetrated by non-state actors is seen as unjustifiable. Recognizing and acknowledging the "grievability" of victims of violence perpetrated by the Syrian state, and its ally Russia, is therefore an act of radical egalitarianism. The banner also reflects upon the hegemonic representation of war and conflict—a representation that is deeply entrenched in the aestheticization of violence. Specifically, the figure of the child is highly exploited in this kind of representation (Zarzycka 2016). Here, activists "play" with this perverse logic, questioning the exceptionality of Aylan's figure when juxtaposed by a whole ensemble of anonymous Syrian children whose deaths were not represented in the media. In doing so, they make these children grievable by appealing to the same representational trope of the child as the ultimate victim of conflict.

A third banner, titled *Zo Is het Begonnen* ("This Is How It Started"), depicted in Figure 8.3, is a simplified representation of the "Dara'a graffiti," which triggered the uprising in Syria. In March 2011, in the Syrian agricultural city of Dara'a, situated close to the Jordanian border, spray painted slogans of "freedom," "Down with Bashar," and "Doctor, your time has come" appeared on public walls, evidently denouncing the Syrian president, Bashar Al-Assad. A group of youths claimed responsibility for the graffiti, and were subsequently jailed and tortured. Protests gained momentum after the public outcry following the murder of thirteen-year-old Hamza Khateeb—one of the children responsible for the graffiti. These protests were fueled by the successful revolts in Tunisia and Egypt, leading to the respective overthrowals of presidents Ben Ali and Hosni Mubarak. Despite the far-reaching geopolitical consequences, Syrian activists continued to refer to the conflict as the "17 March 2011 Revolution," as this was the day on which the Dara'a graffiti appeared. The banner shows the children of Dara'a writing the word "freedom," their expressions suggesting happiness and amusement. Then, on the right side, a soldier is pointing his gun at them. The soldier belongs to the army of the regime (evidenced by the flag on his uniform). His facial expression is one of anger, and he is screaming at the children. The banner appears to hold the Syrian army responsible for the violence inflicted against the children who created the graffiti, and to commemorate how the uprising began. The banner renders visible the activists' mourning for the peaceful uprising that began in 2011.

FIGURE 8.3. *Zo Is het Begonnen*. Photograph taken by the author on 9 August 2016. Published with permission.

This sense of mourning for a political project that could have been informed by peaceful transition and signaled the end of dictatorship, but instead was erased by the militarization of the conflict, is close to what Eva Ziarek (2014) calls feminist aesthetics. Feminist aesthetics are characterized by a sense of mourning relating to the lost object, and signifies the possibility of simultaneously articulating the present and the future in a manner that resonates with the banner's aim of mourning the loss of the children of Dara'a, who symbolize, metaphorically, the loss of nonviolence that characterized the initial uprising. However, the banner draws attention to the fact that the project has not been erased in the course of history—it is displayed at public demonstrations as a reminder of its peaceful origins. The act of mourning itself testifies and recalls the memories of the Syrian diaspora in Europe, thus representing an act of resistance against historical and memorial erasure, and the Syrian presence in Europe. In this case, mourning conveys a sense of possibility; the possibility that the radical project of the "revolution"—that is, the defeat of the nation–state, the international world order, and the capitalist war machine—might still be accomplished.

By critiquing the enabling fiction of human rights as well as asymmetries in the distribution of grievability to war victims, and the sensationalistic use of children in the media, HSC aims to critique both the human rights discourse and media imaginaries. In their place, it seeks to demonstrate how the subjects of the Syrian diaspora are conceptualizing violence from a different perspective. The way in which this critique is articulated, both visually and conceptually, entails deconstruction of the established language of human rights and media. Activists deploy images that are familiar to the Dutch public—such as Aylan—and make them "strange" by adding other characters, or placing them in unfamiliar contexts. In addition, the practice of mourning is realized through the process of commemorating the children of Dara'a. By establishing a metonymic relation with the civil uprising, the artistic practices of HSC perpetuate a sense of continuity as the children of Dara'a were also producing dissident artistic graffiti for political purposes.

Another initiative in which violence has been interpreted, resisted, and remembered by subjects of the Syrian diaspora is the "Women for Freedom" (WFF) exhibition. The physical exhibition took place in a cultural center situated in Rotterdam in the spring of 2016. I met one of the exhibition organizers for an interview in Amsterdam in 2016, and again in Amsterdam for the exhibition opening.

While perusing the WFF exhibition, I observed that several of the exhibited artistic works commemorate the uprising's protagonists and condemn violence. For example, a short film commemorates the figure of Basel Shahada, a well-known filmmaker who was killed in Homs in 2011 while filming the uprising. Artworks such as this reflect the historical continuity in the deployment of art to serve the political project of the peaceful uprising. I further observed that the approach to violence taken in the WFF exhibition is characterized by the aestheticization of violence, entailing images of destruction juxtaposed with images of beauty and life. Aestheticization of violence in this case is apparent in the figure of the child. Children were portrayed as subjects in the works of ten out of the thirty-one visual artists, fifteen out of the twenty-eight photographers, and one out of the seven filmmakers featured in the WFF exhibition. In these works, they represent beauty. Aestheticizing violence is a common practice in the artistic-activist productions of the diaspora. For example, Tammam Azzam, who is one of the most internationally acclaimed Syrian artists, applies this practice by superimposing digital images of European masterpieces on images of shelled buildings in Syria. His most famous work depicts Gustav Klimt's *Kiss* over the bullet-ridden walls of a building in a Syrian city.

Syria has featured prominently in war photography that reproduces mainstream media representations of Syria as a place of violence and radicalism—representations that are critically targeted by the WFF exhibition. Aestheticizing violence is one of the ways in which the artists of the diaspora interpret and resist these mainstream media representations of violence. They do so in an affirmative way by creating "beauty within ugliness," as well as in a critical way by subverting the media's vision. However, the aestheticization evident in the WFF exhibition differs from the approaches adopted by HTC and Souleimane, both of which explicitly demonstrate the intertwinement of art and politics and a clearly articulated moral and ethical approach toward violence. In my opinion, the reason for this difference lies in the fact that WFF does not directly engage with the claim for justice (in the sense of making it explicit) directed at Europe. Moreover, this initiative does not engage in a critique of war (at least, in my view). The figure of the child is problematic because of the asymmetrical distribution of power that it entails and its embeddedness within the humanitarian discourse (Slaughter 2007; Zarzycka 2016), while remaining central to the imagining of beauty in this context. At any rate, aestheticizing violence—as a way of interpreting violence in relation to hegemonic representations of Syria as a humanitarian tragedy—has been one of the red threads in the works of artist-activists from the beginning of the uprising in 2011 up to the present diasporic experience.[9]

A fine arts graduate from the University of Damascus, Amer Al-Wahibi currently lives in the Northern Dutch city of Groningen. He was kind enough to meet with me in this city to discuss and show me his work. Amer is the son of another Syrian artist, Mohammed Al-Wahibi. His work adds a more nuanced dimension to the interpretation of violence in comparison with the previously discussed banners and exhibition. I refer to this dimension as mourning and ghost haunting. In her analysis of the relation between ghost haunting and the sociological imagination, Gordon (2008) argues that although the experience of ghost haunting produces knowledge, this kind of knowledge is considered marginal and is disqualified in the social sciences. Gordon thus incorporates the ghostly visions experienced during her research as concurring to the formulation of her analysis.

Al-Wahibi's exhibit at the WWF was a portrait of a (potentially female) figure (see figure 8.5). The figure is dressed in black—a symbol of mourning—with the only touch of color provided by a bunch of flowers depicted on the left side of canvas, possibly symbolizing the Left as an ideological formation. Her expression seems to suggest feelings of nostalgia, and she is portrayed looking into what appears to be a crystal ball, the contents of which remain unknown to the spectator. The ball is surrounded by an orange and yellow background, which could suggest flames. Behind the figure is a green section, while some white, abstract shapes are depicted at the bottom of the painting.

Al-Wahibi's works portray violence in a surrealistic and oneiric manner. This is well illustrated by the painting in figure 8.5, which the artist showed me during our interview in Groningen. The image portrays faces and flames, suggesting a world populated by ghosts.

222 • Sara Verderi

FIGURE 8.4. Amer Al-Wahibi, acrylic and gold leaf painting on canvas, courtesy of the author.

These ghosts could belong to the artist's memories of violence experienced in Syria, representing his visions that are now manifesting in the Netherlands. The ghostly faces depicted in the painting are deformed and insidious. Spectral figures emerge from the flames, some screaming in pain or fear. At the center of the painting, we see a face with closed eyes—possibly the artist himself—in the act of sleeping or meditating. I read Al-Wahibi's artwork in relation to Gordon's (2008) argument that ghost haunting always registers

FIGURE 8.5. Amer Al-Wahibi, direct etching on metal, courtesy of the author.

the loss sustained through social violence in the past or the present. The loss sustained can be related to individual circumstances or to the unfolding of historical events. In both cases, ghosts manifest themselves, seeking a convivial memory and out of a concern for justice (Gordon 2008: xvi). Thus, social violence in Syria manifests itself like a ghostly haunting in Europe as a reminder of the responsibility that falls on the latter to offer memory and to address the question of justice. In sum, Al-Wahibi's intimate portrayals render mourning and ghost haunting as dynamic practices that take on new forms and shapes in the lives of artist-activists who have lived through and fled from the situation in Syria. In doing so, he establishes a connection between ghosts, past and present.

As I have shown in this section, the visual materials of HSC, WFF, and Al-Wahibi exemplify the ways in which feminist political and ethical imaginations that characterize Syrian dissident art in the homeland continue to live on through memory, interpretation, and resistance to violence, persisting in the works of artists and activists within the Syrian diaspora in Europe. The three sets of work presented and analyzed here reveal different nuances in their approaches to the issue of violence. Thus, HSC's approach, which is critical of the power of nation–states and the international community, and of war and peacemaking efforts, responds to the political demands of the committee. Accordingly, its banners (for example, *Zo Is het Begonnen*) not only communicate the memory of the uprising as it initially began in 2011 but the use of visual artifacts themselves; and their direct, illustrative shapes also serve as a legacy of the creative resistance that has informed the uprising from the time of its inception in Syria. HSC activists emphasize the fact that the lives of Syrian civilians fall outside the framework of recognition and hence are not considered lives at all, pointing to the unequal distribution of grievability. The second set of artwork displayed at the WFF exhibition reflects a preoccupation with interpretation and genuine research or inquiry into truth and the real nature of things and is less concerned with politics. The exhibited artists have adopted the tradition of aestheticizing violence, aimed at subverting the mainstream media's representation of Syria as merely a place of conflict by intertwining images of violence with those of the beauty of children, life, and art. Last, Amer Al-Whaibi's works thematize a mourning community, establishing an oneiric, visionary relation between the violence of the present and that of the past, materialized through images of the ghosts that are haunting the artist's imagination. Thus, the artifacts discussed in this section question static categories of "refugee" and "conflict," fostering alternative representations of the situation in Syria that are historicized and politicized, as well as deeply personal and connective.

Conclusion

This chapter started with the affirmation that the war in Syria began as a nonviolent uprising and was later subjected to a process of simultaneous militarization and masculinization. Focusing on the specific context of artist-activists from the Syrian diaspora engaged in the European cultural scene, and specifically in the Dutch context, I have demonstrated how visual artifacts and narratives of artist-activists raise political and ethical concerns related to violence that are echoed in feminist theory. In doing so, they show a historical continuity through the intertwinement of art and politics that is characteristic of the homeland. At the same time, I have demonstrated how violence is re-thematized, lived, and remembered from the specific location of Europe along three different axes: grievability, aestheticization, and mourning. Concluding, I have demonstrated how these axes challenge the hegemonic narratives of the "refugee" and "conflict," which lie at the core of the hegemonic, masculine imaginary that informs prevailing transitional processes (i.e., institutional politics), modes of representation, and experiences of migration.

However, it is also important to point out the limitations of artistic and activist engagements in light of the contingent situation of war and displacement in Europe and elsewhere. A deep awareness that art and activism are performative acts is associated with the understanding that they do not change the material inequalities of the violence taking place in Syria; nor do they lessen its implications in Europe for war economies and peace negotiations, at least not in the short run. However, this contribution is first and foremost an attempt to do justice to the initial spirit of the revolution ideals of a peaceful, political, and just transition—ideals that continue to animate many Syrian artist-activists in the Netherlands today. It is also an attempt to do justice to an uprising that was overshadowed by the regime's war waged against its own citizens and subsequently by myriad geopolitical interests seeking to gain control of the region.[10]

Sara Verderi is a PhD candidate in Gender and Postcolonial Studies at Utrecht University and research assistant on the EU Marie Sklodowska-Curie ITN project GRACE (Gender and Cultures of Equality in Europe). She graduated in Gender and Women Studies from the American University in Cairo and received her BA in Arabic and English Languages from the University of Bologna. She was an exchange fellow at Damascus University, the University of Manchester, Jawaharlal Nehru University, and Central European University. Her interests include memory, migration, diaspora, postcolonial studies, gender theory, political economy, linguistics, Arabic literature, and Islamic philosophy.

Notes

1. From the inception of the uprising, and following my departure from Syria in late 2012, "Razzaniyat," the blog of Razzan Ghazzawy, a Syrian feminist anarcho-activist, has served as my reference point, enabling me to follow events and debates. After Ghazzawy moved to the UK, her blog was restructured and renamed "Exiled Razzaniyat" (https://razan ghazzawi.org/). While I recall her attack on European left-wing activists for dismissing the uprising, I have been unable to retrieve the specific blog post in which she did so. As I recall, this post served to introduce me to this debate, which later resonated substantively in the work of others, for instance, Yassin al-Haj Saleh.
2. I witnessed an example of this informal debate at a conference held in Padua in 2017. Among the many themes that participants at the conference touched upon was the problematic nature of opposing conceptualizations of the 2011 uprising as a grassroots movement or civil war. I am grateful to Lama Kannout, a feminist activist and writer, for clarifying this point further for me after the conference and in an email exchange.
3. This term has been used specifically in the context of the uprising to express the demands to end the state of emergency and hold regular elections. In addition, it has been used to oppose the concept of *dawla ta'ifiyya* (a sectarian state).
4. This affirmation is paraphrased from Cooke's (2017) interview with Khaled Akil, an art photographer from Damascus, who was living in Istanbul at the time of the interview. Akil argues that the 2011 uprisings were obsessively recorded but that most of the recorded images will disappear in time, and that in fact, many have disappeared already. Conversely, art is something that endures.
5. 5. The real name of this exhibition has been anonymized due to the wishes expressed to the author by organizers.
6. During my stay in Damascus in 2011, a recurrent chant that I heard during such parades was "*mnḥabbak*" [we love you]. A song with the same title, featuring this chant, was often broadcast on public television and radio.
7. In the context of this study, commissioned critics are those connected to the structure of the ruling Ba'ath Party and to Asad's kinship network.
8. The prominent role of social media in influencing and disseminating artistic productions relating to the Syrian uprising was evident from the outset. Social media functioned as an alternative space for communication and organization among activists and intellectuals because of the particularly harsh means of controlling the public space adopted by the Syrian security services. Al-Zubeydi (2012) was one of the first scholars to point this out. In the material examined in this section, it is still possible to see the similarities in terms of style between artist-activists' works distributed via the Internet. For example, HSC banners are drawn in a relatively simple, nonprofessional manner (not typical of a designer or artist), yet evidence a clear style that evokes the works of the artist-activist group, Liberated Kafernabel, broadcast on social media. Liberated Kafernabel is a group of artist-activists based in the Syrian province of Idlib. The group's satirical banners, targeting the regime, have become one of the key visual symbols of the uprising for the international community. The aspiration of artist-activist groups such as Liberated Kafernabel has been to convey images of the uprising beyond its representation in the mainstream media of the Global North as well as that of the regime.
9. Another example of this aestheticization can be seen in the series of graffiti art in Saraqeb (a city located in northeastern Syria), which went viral on the Web in the period between 2011 and 2013 (see Alwan 2016), and remained so during the war (see Syria Untold).

10. The dynamics of geopolitical interests as well as military and economic interventions in Syria and in the wider region are extremely complex, and a discussion of them is clearly beyond the scope of this study. For insight into these issues, see Hinnebusch (2012) and Hinnebusch and Zintl (2015).

References

Acord, Sophia K. 2010. "Beyond the Head: The Practical Work of Curating Contemporary Art." *Qualitative Sociology* 33, no. 4: 447–67.
Al-Haj Saleh, Yassin. 2017. "Suriyyawa wa al-yasar al-gharbi al-anti-imberialiy" ["Syria and the Western Anti-Imperialist Left"]. Accessed 19 February 2018. https://www.aljumhuriya .net/ar/content/.
Alwan, F. M. 2016. "Ashkal al-watan: Shukran Saraqeeb" ["Shapes of a Homeland: Thank you Saraqeeb"]. Accessed 19 February 2018. http://alwan.fm/news_veiw?id=8291&cat=27.
Al-Zubeydi, Layla. 2012. "Syria's Creative Resistance." Accessed 10 November 2017. http:// www.jadaliyya.com/pages/index/5920/syrias-creative-resistance.
Baeza, Cecilia, and Paulo Pinto. 2016. "Building Support for the Asad Regime: The Syrian Diaspora in Argentina and Brazil and the Syrian Uprising." *Journal of Immigrant & Refugee Studies* 14, no. 3: 334–52.
Bell, Christine, and Catherine O'Rurke. 2007. "Does Feminism Need a Theory for Transitional Justice?" *The International Journal of Transitional Justice* 1, no. 1: 23–44.
Braidotti, Rosi. 2007. "Dympna and the Figuration of the Woman Warrior." In *Doing Gender in Media, Art and Culture*, edited by Rosemarie Buikema and Iris van der Tuin, 241–60. London: Routledge.
Brown, Wendy. 2005. *Edgework Critical Essays on Knowledge and Politics*. Princeton: Princeton University Press.
Butler, Judith. 2009. *Frames of War: When Is Life Grievable?* London: Verso Books.
———. 2011. "Bodies in Alliance and the Politics of the Street." *European Institute for Progressive Cultural Politics*. Accessed 29 November 2017. http://eipcp.net/transversal/1011/ butler/en.
Cooke, Miriam. 2007. *Dissident Syria: Making Oppositional Art Official*. Durham, NC: Duke University Press.
———. 2017. *Dancing in Damascus: Creativity, Resilience and the Syrian Revolution*. London: Routledge.
Das, Veena. 2007. *Life and Words: Violence and the Descent into the Ordinary*. Oakland: University of California Press.
Gordon, Avery, F. 2008. *Ghostly Matters: Haunting and the Sociological Imagination*. Minneapolis: University of Minnesota Press.
Halasa, Malu, Zaher Omareen, and Nawara Mahfoud, eds. 2014. *Syria Speaks: Art and Culture from the Frontline*. London: Saqi Books.
Hassoun, Rami, and Fadwa Soulimane. 2017. "A Message to . . ." YouTube. https://www .youtube.com/watch?v=N_5-gnl8Oqc&t=115s.
Hinnebush, Raymond. 2012. "Authoritarian Upgrading and the Arab Spring: Syria in Comparative Perspective." *The British Society for Middle Eastern Studies Conference*, London, March 2012. London: The British Society for Middle Eastern Studies.

Hinnebush, Raymond, and Tina Zintl. 2015. "Introduction." In *Syria From Reform to Revolt.* Vol 1: *Political Economy and International Relations*, edited by Raymond Hinnebush and Tina Zintl. Syracuse: Syracuse University Press.

Hoekstra, Myrte. 2015. "Diverse Cities and Good Citizenship: How Local Governments in the Netherlands Recast National Integration Discourse." *Ethnic and Racial Studies* 30, no. 10: 1798–814.

Kannout, Lama. 2016. "Resolution 1325, Pros and Cons." Paper presented at the International Conference *Rethinking the Transition Process in Syria: Constitution Participation and Gender Equality.* 3 October. University of Padua.

Klamer, Arjo. 1996. "The Value of Art." In *The Value of Culture: On the Relationship between Economics and Art*, edited by Arjo Klamer, 13–28. Amsterdam: Amsterdam University Press.

Levitt, Peggy. 2007. "Critical Spatial Practice: Curating, Editing, Writing." In *Issues in Curating Contemporary Art and Performance*, edited by Judith Rugg and Michèle Sedgwick, 59–77. Bristol: Intellect Books.

Souleimane, Fadwa. 2013. *Le Passage.* Translated by Rania Samara. Manage, Belgium: Lansman Editeur.

Slaughter, Joseph R. 2007. *Human Rights, Inc: The World Novel, Narrative Form, and International Law.* New York: Fordham University Press.

Strickland, Patrick. 2018. "Why Do Italian Fascists Adore Syria's Bashar al-Assad?" Al Jazeera. 13 February. https://www.aljazeera.com/news/2018/01/italian-fascists-adore-syria-bashar-al-assad-180125115153121.html.

Syria Untold. 2015. "Walls of Saraqeb: The Vitality of Colors in War-weary Syria." Syria Untold. 28 February. http://www.syriauntold.com/en/creative/walls-saraqeb-vitality-colors-war-weary-syria/.

Verderi, Sara. 2016. "The Glue of a Mosaic: State, Citizenship and Feminist Political Imaginations in Syria (2011–2012)." *Deportate, Esuli, Profughe* 30: 76–84.

Wedeen, Lisa. 1993. *Ambiguities of Domination: Politics, Rhetoric, and Symbols in Contemporary Syria.* Chicago: University of Chicago Press.

Yassin-Kassab, Robin, and Leila Al-Shami. 2016. *Burning Country: Syrians in Revolution and War.* London: Pluto Press.

Zarzycka, Marta. 2016. "Save the Child: Photographed Faces and Affective Transactions in NGO Child Sponsoring Programs." *European Journal of Women's Studies* 23, no. 1: 28–42.

Ziarek, Ewa P. 2014. "Feminist Aesthetics: Transformative Practice, Neoliberalism, and the Violence of Formalism." *Differences* 25, no. 2: 101–15.

Ziter, Edward. 2015. *Political Performance in Syria: From the Six-Day War to the Syrian Uprising.* Basingstoke: Palgrave Macmillan.

Epilogue

Bodies Crossing Borders

Rosemarie Buikema

The Mobility of Memory deals with key issues in both Migration Studies and Critical Memory Studies. As one of the outcomes of the *Bodies Across Borders in Europe: Oral and Visual Memory in Europe* (BABE) Project, this rich compilation of essays emerges from the tensions between roots and routes, history and memory, minds and bodies, macrostructures and micro stories, control and resistance, the discursive and the visual. In productively shifting the boundaries between these concepts *The Mobility of Memory* implements the configuration of intersubjectivity as a means by which to investigate the dynamics of identity formation as an ongoing and dialogical process of adaptation and change. Taken as a unified whole, by deploying this configuration of intersubjectivity as a technology of the self—as Foucault would say—the chapters become an innovative and epistemologically important gesture. Intersubjectivity epitomizes the way in which bodies crossing borders necessarily entail the mobilization of signs; a process in which language and affect intra-act to such an extent that we start to realize how borders also cross bodies.

Bodies crossing borders and borders crossing bodies make imperative the need to open up historically and geopolitically delineated boundaries of time and place and thus of cultural canons, vocabularies, iconographies, and even disciplines. In a time when bodies are frequently forced to cross borders, the very idea of beginning and ending is constantly disrupted. As Awam Ampka (2017) aptly suggests, instead of assuming a linear or circular form, time might best be described as a spiral, perceived differently by different people. It is impossible to survive the escape of violence, poverty, exclusion, and/

or repression if one sticks to the unity of time and place. Rather, one must assume the plurality of times and places, not to say a plurality of modernities, between which bodies and borders commute in order to evoke multiple existences. Only if we agree to accept intersubjectivity as a process of simultaneously belonging to different times and places might we be able to conceptualize displacement not as alienating, but as part of what it means to be a citizen in the world of today—notwithstanding the concomitant and inevitable experiences of loss and suffering. This is exactly where Migration Studies and Critical Memory Studies meet in their efforts to constitute an archive of the concepts of movement, memory, time, and place based on a dialogical response to oral histories and artworks in times of migration and mass displacement.

Critical Memory Studies consider politically engaged or trauma-related artifacts as history seen through affect. In this context, affect is understood as a residue of an event reactivated through the reiteration of that event by something equivalent to it—for example, by means of art. The historical event is thus studied in connection to the medium that gives access to the experience of the event. Affect, in this sense, is therefore related to cathexis: the power to relate. As historian Jay Winter suggests: "History is memory seen through and criticized with the aid of documents of many kinds—written, aural, visual. Memory is history seen through affect. Therefore, it is difficult to examine the claims of memory in the same way as we examine the claims of history" (2010: 12). History is thus a discipline of which we learn and teach the rules and methods. Memory is a faculty: the faculty to be affected. It is a claim of Critical Memory Studies that contemporary artifacts dealing with traumatic events should not be studied only for their representation of history or reality, but also for the part they play in the production of affects and deep thought. As such, in order to open up new worlds, and to connect the personal and the political, Critical Memory Studies scholars consider artifacts as a form of thinking. Critical memory discourses link micro stories to macrostructures and thus, Critical Memory Studies scholars are interested in the ways in which artifacts, as critical memory discourses, counteract the threat of socially produced amnesia and/or the engineering of hegemonic concepts of citizenship, subjectivity, time, and place. They concentrate on the analysis of both oral histories and artifacts as inventions of techniques for transmitting and storing information, deemed vital for the constitution or continuation of a specific group or a specific constellation of groups (Assmann 2010; Huyssen 2003; Rothberg 2009).

As elegantly demonstrated again and again in the essays of *The Mobility of Memory*, bodies that have crossed borders need to insert their potentially disruptive presence by producing something new, something that is not yet there. Bodies crossing borders inevitably have to intervene in existing iconographies and vocabularies. In the appreciation of both oral histories and artifacts as vehicles of new beginnings, as well as instruments to evoke the articulation and visualization of multiple existences, this publication contributes to new conceptualizations of citizenship, subjectivity, time, and place. As such, *The Mobility of Memory* is an invaluable contribution to the work of Critical Memory Studies and Migration Studies. Together these fields will continue to produce knowledge through the study of the visual arts, literature, dance, and performance, and to theorize about different conceptions of the disunity of time and place as a process of endless renewal and beginning.

Rosemarie Buikema is professor of Art, Culture and Diversity at Utrecht University. She chairs UU's Graduate Gender Studies Programme, is the scientific director of the Netherlands Research School of Gender Studies (NOG), and is the project leader of the Museum of Equality and Difference (https://MOED.online). Her most recent publications include the monograph *Revolts in Cultural Critique* (Rowman&Littlefield International, 2020) and the coedited volume *Cultures, Citizenship an Human Rights* (Routledge 2019).

References

Ampka, Awan. 2017. *ReSignification: European Blackamoors, Africana Readings*. Rome: Postcart.
Assman, Aleida. 2010. "Re-Framing Memory: Between Individual and Collective Forms of Constructing the Past." In *Performing the Past: Memory, History and Identity in Modern Europe*, edited by Karin Tilmans, Frank van Vree, and Jay Winter, 35–50. Amsterdam: Amsterdam University Press.
Huyssen, Andreas. 2003. *Present Pasts: Urban Palimpsests and the Politics of Memory*. Stanford: Stanford University Press.
Rothberg, M. 2009. *Multidirectional Memory: Remembering the Holocaust in the Age of Decolonization*. Stanford: Stanford University Press.
Winter, Jay. 2010. "The Performance of the Past: Memory, History, Identity." In *Performing the Past: Memory, History and Identity in Modern Europe*, edited by Karin Tilmans, Frank van Vree, and Jay Winter, 11–35. Amsterdam: Amsterdam University Press.

Index

9/11, 10, 37, 44

academic development and identity affirmation, 119
acceptance or rejection of request for asylum, 108
acquisition of languages, 64, 110, 115, 117
activist, 190, 208, 209, 210, 212, 213, 214, 216, 218, 220, 221, 224, 225
affect, 56, 57, 73, 209, 230
Africa, 13, 14, 24, 96, 97, 131, 138, 139, 140, 143, 141, 146, 147, 150, 152, 153, 154, 155, 156, 158, 159, 160, 161, 163, 165, 166, 167, 168, 169, 170, 172, 173, 202
Afro-Italians, 166, 169, 173
agency, 2, 32, 33, 41, 121, 134, 160, 184, 186, 187, 200, 202, 204
Ahmed, Sara, 33, 36
aide-mémoire, 85
Al Haj Saleh, Yassin, 226
Al-Wahibi, Amer, 211, 214, 221, 222, 223, 224
Al-Zubeydi, Layla, 226
allochtoon, 33, 46
ambescià, 143
Ammaniti, Massimo, 4
amnesia, 6, 154, 164, 230
Ampka, Awam, 229
anfez, 141, 142, 143, 145, 146, 147, 149
anti-immigrant discourse, 183, 184, 185, 186, 194, 198, 200, 204
aphasia, 6, 18, 91, 102, 136, 164, 165
Applebee, Arthur, 69
archive, 6, 132, 135, 145, 146, 147, 149, 153, 154, 157, 163, 166, 174, 173, 175, 230

archival assemblages, 145, 155, 156, 157, 172
archival practices, 6, 157
audiovisual, ix, 1, 6
colonial, 16, 20, 23, 145, 149, 161
cultural, 6, 185
in the making, 156, 157, 158, 172, 174, 175
living archives, 6
Aristarco, Guido, 159
art
artifact(s), 163, 208, 210, 211, 224, 230
artworks, 3, 6, 220, 230
installation art, 183, 187, 193
paintings, 42, 43, 187, 190, 191, 201, 215, 222
production, 86, 95, 101, 187, 212, 213, 214, 220, 226
theater, 187, 212, 213
video art, 3, 86, 186
video performance, 187, 189
Asmara, 137, 140, 142, 146, 155, 156, 158, 160, 196
Assmann, Jan, 84
asylum seeker(s), 16, 29, 30, 34, 40, 42, 44, 49, 135, 156
awareness, 4, 38, 84, 90, 100, 106, 202
Azoulay, Ariella, 157, 158, 172

Baauw, Sergio, 23, 123
Balibar, Étienne, 11
Barthes, Roland, 52
beliefs and ideologies, 118, 121
belonging, 22, 33, 34, 36, 39, 45, 46, 59, 60, 91, 94, 100, 101, 132, 135, 184, 186, 187, 191, 194, 202, 203
Ben-Ghiat, Ruth, 160

Benghazi, 163
Berlusconi, Silvio, 163
Bhambra, Gurminder K., 18
Biemann, Ursula, 98, 101
biographies, 69, 81, 83, 115
Black Venus, 161, 163
blackness, 139, 146, 148, 152, 153
blood, 19, 60, 141, 215
bodies, 3, 11, 16, 17, 33, 36, 57, 82, 84, 85, 88, 90, 95, 97, 135, 143, 146, 147, 149, 153, 157, 173, 174, 184, 209, 215, 229, 230
body, 30, 54, 56, 57, 66, 80, 84, 86, 87, 88, 89, 95, 97, 98, 99, 141, 146, 157, 161, 163, 188, 195, 203, 217
Bologna, 136, 141, 142, 147
Bonansea, Graziella, ix
border(s)
  apparatus, 44
  border crossers, 106
  border crossing, 16, 84, 104, 146, 183, 196, 197, 229
  border-making processes, 14
  bordering, 7, 14, 154, 158, 188
  system, 10, 15
Bosma, Ulbe, 40
Braidotti, Rosi, 42
Brown, Wendy, 216
Buikema, Rosemarie, ix, 6
bureaucracy, 201, 194, 202, 203
Butler, Judith, 157, 215, 218

Caracas, 53
cartography, 10, 19, 73, 123
Casablanca, 53, 69
categories and categorization processes, 17, 36, 42, 106, 123, 199, 202, 203
cathexis, 230
Cemulini, Gino, 155, 156
changing school practices, 115
children, 72, 80, 81, 84, 85, 86, 96, 99, 101, 105, 106, 107, 108, 113, 116, 119, 122, 140, 160, 166, 197, 209, 217, 218, 219, 220, 224
children's experiences, 86, 105, 113, 217
citizenship, 6, 15, 16, 30, 33, 34, 39, 68, 69, 85, 100, 133, 138, 140, 165, 166, 201, 230, 231
Cole, Debbie ix, 23, 123

colonial
  aphasia, 6, 18, 102, 164, 165
  colonialism, 13, 14, 15, 20, 41, 81, 83, 102, 131, 132, 135, 137, 140, 141, 142, 143, 144, 145, 147, 148, 149, 153, 154, 164, 165, 173, 174
  coloniality, 18, 19, 144, 153
  durabilities, 18
  legacies, 10, 12, 18, 20, 142
  masculinity, 160
  neocolonial, 19, 41, 81
  practices, 12, 14, 16, 20, 149, 163, 170
  and postcolonial violence, 20, 142, 161, 164
  sexuality, 154, 158, 161, 163, 164
Comité International du Film Ethnographique, 168
Common European Framework of Reference for Languages, 109, 110, 111
communication, 5, 50, 52, 54, 56, 57, 59, 62, 63, 70, 73, 91, 92, 94, 117, 226
complex social and linguistic landscapes, 115
complicated migration laws, 107
"constant state of arrival," 197, 198, 202
constraints, 18, 22, 32, 34, 39, 186, 202
  institutional, 33, 42
  societal, 33
Conversations on Visual Memory, 7
corporeality, 1
cosmopolitan, 39, 41, 42, 44, 72
  cosmopolitanism, 41
  cosmopolitanization, 41, 45
Cosulich, Callisto, 158, 159
counter-images, 184
counter-narratives, 184
Critical Border Studies, 14, 15
Critical Memory Studies, 229, 230, 231
crossing the Mediterranean, 146, 192, 195, 196, 197, 200
cultural
  archive, 185
  canon, 229
  heritage, 5, 10, 81, 85
  identity, 131, 132, 140, 147
  memory, 19, 23, 59, 84, 100, 101, 105
culture
  pluricultural, 22, 72
  curriculum, 23, 117, 118

D'Amato, Joe (alias Aristide Massaccesi), 153
Dadié, Bernard, 168
Dainotto, Roberto, 9
dance, 4, 70, 86, 88, 159, 169, 173, 174, 189, 212, 231
De Cesari, Chiara, 163
De Franceschi, Leonardo, 176
de Leeuw, Marc, 39, 41
dehumanization, 30, 133, 196
deficit approach, 112
Dekker, Suzanne, ix, 23, 123
Deplano, Valeria, 160, 165, 176
Derrida, Jacques, 11, 44, 47, 150
  différance, 132, 134, 136, 150
desires, 43, 68, 79, 100, 121, 185
dialogical, 4, 5, 6, 229, 230
dialogue, 12, 20, 30, 70, 72, 86, 95, 131, 137, 149, 170, 172, 174, 175, 210
diasporic
  cultural narratives, 17, 132, 135
  identity, 171
  memory, 23, 131, 133, 134, 135, 136, 146, 147, 148, 149
  networks, 17, 20
didactic, 5, 90, 99
didactic practices, 22, 105
disciplines, 2, 3, 7, 50, 81, 104, 229
discourse
  discursive, 9, 10, 11, 14, 21, 29, 31, 35, 39, 41, 42, 44, 104, 154, 156, 161, 229
  dominant, 18, 31, 33, 201, 184, 185, 203
  political, 11, 24, 31, 34, 35, 46, 155
  popular, 11, 24, 45, 46
  public, 45, 155, 163
  social, 35
displacement
  mass, 230
displacements, 32, 55, 171
disruptive presence, 230
Dissident Syria, 211, 212, 213, 224
diversity talk, 104
division between sedentary and mobile, 3
documentary, xi, 4, 168
dominant language, 109
Dutch
  Dutchness, 36, 38, 39, 46
  response, 13, 30, 33
  situation, 33, 38

Echterhoff, Gerald, 60
educational, 21, 31, 50, 72, 73, 80, 81, 82, 84, 99, 101, 105, 112, 114, 116, 119, 121, 122, 124, 166
el-Gaddafi, Muammar, 163
Ellena, Liliana, x, xi, 23, 175
emotion(s), 4, 23, 33, 54, 55, 56, 57, 58, 60, 61, 63, 64, 65, 70, 71, 72, 80, 83, 84, 91, 95, 99, 136, 147, 148, 174, 186, 194
empathy, 94, 131
empire(s), 81, 105, 143, 154, 160, 164, 172
epistemology, 23, 144, 157, 229
era of globalization, 104
Eritrea
  Eritrean diaspora, 23, 136, 141, 143, 155
Essed, Philomena, 37
Ethiopia, 134, 140, 143, 160, 169, 173
ethnography, 11, 21, 23, 24, 160, 168, 171
Europe
  European Union, ix, x, xi, 6, 41
  Europeanness, 9, 17, 36, 39
  Fortress Europe, 12, 15, 17, 131, 149
Eva Nera, 6, 23, 152, 153, 154, 155, 156, 157, 158, 159, 162, 165, 166, 168, 169, 171, 172, 173, 174, 175
exclusion, 14, 33, 36, 86, 87, 88, 92, 117, 118, 135, 138, 185, 199, 209, 215, 229
exhibition(s), ix, xi, 87, 163, 211, 214, 220, 221, 224
existences
  multiple, 231
expat, 34, 35
expectations, 35, 36, 79, 96, 97, 100, 112, 133, 183, 185, 195

family, 34, 55, 56, 58, 59, 61, 65, 68, 71, 84, 92, 94, 137, 138, 139, 142, 152, 188, 189, 191, 196, 197, 204, 217
Fanon, Frantz, 132, 175
Fascism, 7, 100, 140, 153, 161, 171
fears, 100, 185
feelings, 29, 52, 57, 62, 63, 65, 71, 80, 83, 84, 94, 99, 100, 136, 146, 148, 184, 190, 202, 221
femininity, 163, 193
Ferrero, Caterina, 169

Festival Internazionale di Cinematografia Africana, 166, 167
Florence, ix, x, xi, 6, 49, 100, 168
Foucault, Michel, 57, 185, 229
freedom, 10, 50, 65, 134, 138, 189, 190, 191, 192, 201, 203, 211, 214, 215, 218, 220
Frontex, 15

gaze(s), 20, 57, 82, 86, 87, 93, 99, 146, 147, 158, 160, 173
gendered, 2, 81, 153, 161, 164, 185, 203, 204, 208
generations, 2, 53, 58, 80, 92, 99, 100, 131, 133, 142, 213
geographies, 20, 21, 79, 135, 146
Gemser, Laura, 152
gestures, 56, 57, 81
Ghorashi, Halleh, 37, 38
ghost(s), 141, 148, 209, 210, 221, 222, 224
Gilroy, Paul, 11, 19, 175
Giuliani, Gaia, 152, 176
Giustetto, Giada, x, 22, 83
Global South, 131, 144, 145, 207
globalization talk, 104, 105
Goffman, Erving, 186, 190
Goldberg, David Theo, 13
Gordon, Avery, 221, 222
Grigorjeva, Olga, 43, 44, 47
grieveability, 214, 215, 218, 219, 224, 225

Habtemariam, Asmerom, 154
Hall, Stuart, 131
Hassoun, Rami, 212
hegemonic
and assimilative ideologies, 119
heritage(s), 5, 10, 12, 20, 81, 85, 91, 100, 144, 147, 150, 169
Hernández Nova, Leslie N., x, 4, 8
Hirsch, Marianne, 58, 74
history
representation of history, 230
homeland, 94, 97, 136, 208, 224, 225
Horn of Africa, the, x, 24, 131, 139, 143, 150, 156
Hovil, Lucy, 45
human languages
as context-bound, 115
as fragmented, 115
as individual, 115
as multiple, 115
as partial, 115
as shifting, 115
human migration, 104
hybridity, 104

iconographies, 229, 231
identity, identities
cosmopolitan, 72
cultural, 82, 131, 132, 133, 147
formation, 59, 153, 171, 229
marker(s), 39
spoiled, 185
transnational, 85, 101, 202, 203
identity-related activity, 119
ideology
ideological, 10, 19, 30, 34, 42, 44, 46, 113, 118, 171, 212, 221
images
evoked images, 137, 146, 187, 204
found images, 187, 204
generated images, 187, 204, 205
imagery, 47, 90, 99
imaginary, 10, 11, 12, 16, 17, 18, 91, 100, 132, 134, 140, 141, 172, 225
imagination(s), 5, 87, 91, 102, 170, 212, 213, 214, 221, 224
immigrant(s)
immigration, 13, 16, 45, 59, 68, 213
imperialism(s), 10, 14, 41, 175
In Between Time, 187, 189, 196, 203
inclusion
and exclusion, 14, 33, 36, 86, 117, 135, 185, 215
differential, 10, 14, 133, 135
individual agency, 115
inescapability of categorization processes, 106
institutional momentum of processes, 106
integration, 13, 16, 33, 39, 40, 72, 108, 110, 111, 113, 117, 123, 202, 213
interactions, 3, 72, 81, 83, 85, 117, 145, 148, 183
interpellation, 33, 46
interracial sexuality, 164, 171
intersubjectivity
indirect, 3
mediated, 3

primacy of, 2, 7
visual, 3
interview
   interviewee(s), ix, x, 32, 3, 149, 187, 195, 201, 202, 210
   interviewer(s), 2, 3, 197
   interviewing, 3, 4, 46, 183
Intra-Act, 229
Italian colonial aphasia, 164, 165
Italian decolonization, 153
Italian East Africa (AOI), 152, 169, 170
Italian Trusteeship Administration of Somalia (AFIS), 153, 166, 168
itinerary, itineraries, 50, 56, 58, 71, 73, 80, 85, 96, 97, 100, 118, 169

journey, journeys, 12, 17, 31, 49, 58, 61, 63, 66, 71, 73, 96, 131, 159, 183, 187, 188, 192, 193, 194, 195, 196, 198, 200, 202, 203, 204

Kaasik-Krogerus, Sigrid, xi, 5
Keim, Jean, 52
Kristof, Agota, 65

label
   labeled, 31, 32, 34, 38, 41, 44, 60, 106
   labeling, 34
Lacan, Jacques, 51
LaCapra, Dominick, 70
Lähdesmäki, Tuuli, xi, 5
Lamberti, Elena, 59
language
   biographies, 105, 115, 121, 123
   body language, 56
   bridging language, 62
   nonverbal language, 56, 57
   planning, 117, 118, 121, 122
   policy development, 118
   proficiency and early literacy, 116
   repertoire of students second language, 116
   vehicular language, 50, 64, 72, 73
Le Pichon-Vorstman, Emmanuelle, 23, 123
lens of language, 104
Libya, 13, 81, 137, 139, 143, 161, 163, 164, 166
linguistic anthropologist, 104
Lloyd, Genevieve, 42
logical, 22, 44, 46, 56, 210
Lombardi-Diop, Cristina, 153
loneliness, 84, 86, 100
Luhman, Meghan, 45

macrolevel language planning, 117
Magnusson, Nicola, 29
Manera, Guido, 166, 168, 169, 172
Manera, Silvano, 176
map(s)
   mapping(s), 9, 13, 21, 50, 105, 134, 137
Marghera, 49
marginalization, 87
marker(s), 29, 38, 39, 42, 123, 136
masculinity, 160
Mbembe, Achille, 145
Meccoli, Domenico, 159, 160, 161
Mediterranean
   area, 15
   migration(s), 153, 163, 174
   sea, 15, 137, 146
memory
   collective, 10, 18, 59, 64
   counter memories, 70
   cultural, 19, 59, 84, 100, 101, 105
   multidirectional, 19, 185
   plurimedia constellations, 19
   postmemory, 58
   practice, 18, 19, 133
   visual, ix, x, 1, 3, 5, 6, 7, 9, 24, 29, 45, 56, 61, 63, 71, 138, 229
Mestre, 49, 53
metaphor, 14, 17, 90, 99, 144, 145, 146, 148, 161
microlevel language planning, 118
Mignolo, Walter, 144
migration
   crisis, 10, 13, 18, 19, 30, 33, 37, 45, 184
   migratory, 17, 20, 29, 30, 34, 45, 53, 61, 62, 71, 107, 136, 137, 143, 198, 202
   trajectory, trajectories, 20, 29, 30, 36, 37, 83, 107, 183, 184, 187, 188
Migration Studies, 229, 230, 231
Milan, 136, 138, 139, 147
mirror neurons, 4
Mirzoeff, Nicholas, 60, 157
mobile, 1, 2, 3, 19, 21, 29, 42, 99, 172, 197
mobility, ix, x, 1, 3, 4, 5, 7, 9, 10, 12, 14, 15, 16, 17, 18, 19, 20, 21, 22, 23, 35,

42, 50, 51, 71, 72, 100, 104, 108, 109, 119, 147, 157, 170, 172, 174, 194, 229, 231
mobility of memory, ix, x, 1, 3, 4, 21, 22, 104 147, 157, 174, 229, 231
modernities
  plurality of modernities, 230
modernity, 144, 146, 152, 174
Mogadishu, 96, 166, 167, 169
monolingual ideologies, 118
monolingual lens, 114
monolithic approaches, 114
Montale, Eugenio, 87
Morocco, 16, 53, 60, 68, 81, 97
Moschitz, Ed, 85, 86
multidimensional and heterogeneous memories of languages and learning, 105
multiperspectival, 14, 17
multiple, situated, evolving memory as the norm, 113

Nader, Laura, 21
narrative patterns, 92
nation
  nationalism, 41
  nationhood, 33
national policy, 108, 213
negotiate
  negotiation, 19, 44, 113, 163, 209
neorealist cinema, 158, 159, 170
network(s), 17, 20, 64, 83, 84, 85, 93, 118, 123, 154, 155, 156, 166, 167, 168, 172
neuroscience, 2
normalization, 185, 186, 188, 203, 204
normification, 186, 190, 200, 203, 204
nostalgia, 42, 65, 71, 84, 221
Nwosu, Joy, 165, 166, 169, 170, 172

occluded stories, 165
opposition, 20, 93, 149, 163, 199, 204, 209, 212
oral
  oral history, histories, x, 2, 7, 83, 230, 231
  orality, 92
  orally, 53, 56, 58, 69, 71, 145, 205
Other
  cultural Other(s), 11, 13, 16, 37, 46
  Muslim Other, 37
  ungrateful Other, 37
Other, the, 11, 16, 30, 38, 39, 45

Paci, Adrian, 85, 95
Padua, 136, 139, 226
Paradis, Michel, 64
Parma school, 4
Pascoli, Giovanni, 88
passage(s), 84, 85, 90, 92, 98, 136, 169, 212
Passerini, Luisa, xi, 6, 49, 70, 100, 145, 175
pedagogy, 80, 82, 101
performance(s), 4, 57, 116, 164, 171, 187, 189, 194, 214, 215, 231
Phoenix Film, 152, 166, 168, 175, 176
pillarization, 38
place
  plurality of time and place, 230
  unity of time and place, 230
politically controversial pedagogies, 121
politics
  anxiety-ridden, 10
  right-wing, 10, 45
Ponzanesi, Sandra, 11, 30
populism(s), 16
postcolonial
  Europe, 7, 10, 18, 20
  literature, 12
  turn, 12
postimperial
  cinema, 153
  Italy, 156, 161, 163
prejudices, 84, 92, 100
Présence Africaine, 168
Prins, Boukje, 37
proficiency in school languages, 105, 108, 109, 116
Proglio, Gabriele, x, xi, 23, 24

Quijano, Anibal, 144

race
  racial denial, 18
  racial disavowal, 18
  racial laws, 153
  racialization, 10, 19
  racialized, 13, 19, 36, 38, 39, 46, 148, 153, 154, 160, 163, 164, 174
  racism, 12, 13, 17, 34, 37, 38, 147, 149, 164, 165, 170, 196

new realism, 37, 38
reception
  induced, 3, 101, 204, 205
redefining the interpretative categories, 115
refugee
  center(s), 108, 187, 192, 197, 198
  label, 22, 29, 30, 31, 32, 33, 34, 35, 36, 39, 40, 41, 44, 45, 200, 202
  migration, 183, 204
  studies, 32
  trajectories, 183
rejection, 35, 39, 44, 84, 87, 88, 108, 114, 159
relationships, 2, 3, 5, 12, 32, 64, 73, 79, 84, 85, 90, 92, 93, 118, 160, 166, 168, 173, 174, 184
Renan, Ernest, 59
representations, 11, 14, 16, 20, 51, 55, 71, 80, 83, 84, 91, 98, 99, 101, 117, 118, 120, 149, 160, 161, 164, 184, 189, 195, 196, 199, 200, 203, 204, 208, 209, 210, 211, 215, 220, 221, 224
research-based professionalization material, 112
resistance
  to categorization and labeling, 203
  to constraining images and narratives, 203
  beyond the country of residence, 201
  exposing inefficient and harmful forms of bureaucracy, 201
  to plurilitihic models, 114
  creating solidarity and a strong refugee identity, 200
respondent(s), 29, 30, 31, 32, 33, 34, 35, 36, 37, 38, 39, 40, 41, 42, 43, 44, 45, 46, 131, 145, 148, 184, 187, 190, 195, 197
rethinking movements of memories across borders, 115
revolution, 65, 186, 207, 208, 213, 214, 218, 225
Ricoeur, Paul, 136
Romeo, Caterina, 153
roots, 11, 59, 68, 73, 100, 131, 135, 153, 164, 229
Rothberg, Michael, 19
Rouch, Jean, 166, 168
routes, 15, 49, 50, 137, 143, 229
Rumford, Chris, 14

Said, Yara, 187, 190, 191, 192, 195, 196, 199, 200, 201, 202
Sassen, Saskia, 68
Scego, Igiaba, 173, 174, 175
school assessments, 116
school language proficiency, 108, 109, 105, 115, 116
Settat, 53
shadow(s), 86, 87, 88, 98, 99, 187
shareable narratives, 2
Sieber, Giuseppe, 155
Sieber, Pia, 156
signs, 33, 38, 171, 229
silences, 56, 84, 91, 94, 131, 149, 160
Single Memory Culture Schooling Practices, 105, 108
skin color, 16, 38, 138, 142, 147
slave, 143, 144
social space, 80, 86, 95, 98, 169
social status of languages, 117
Socially Oriented Theories of Language and Identity, 117
sociolinguistic theory, 106
Somalia, Somalian, 86, 96, 97, 139, 153, 154, 164, 166, 169, 173, 176
Souleimane, Fadwa, 207, 208, 212, 221
spiral, 134, 229
Spivak, Chakravorty Gayatri, 132
Steffens, Marie, ix, 23, 123
stereotype(s), 84, 91, 92, 93, 94, 95, 100, 121, 185, 191, 200
Stewart, Kathleen, 57
sticky sign, 33
Stoler, Ann Laura, 18, 102, 164, 172
strategic-relational approach, 33
structure(s), 5, 10, 22, 32, 33, 35, 41, 42, 52, 64, 92, 111, 186
student, 6, 29, 39, 40, 49, 59, 66, 85, 88, 94, 98, 105, 169, 196, 210
Students' first languages, 121
students' linguistic repertoires and cultural experience, 107, 119
students' migration memories, 105
studying down, 21, 29
studying sideways, 22, 31
studying up, 21, 29
subjectivity, 1, 2, 3, 16, 22, 24, 42, 43, 45, 46, 80, 84, 94, 97, 100, 101, 132, 133, 134, 136, 140, 145, 147, 148, 149,

150, 157, 165, 184, 186, 197, 202, 203, 204, 230, 231
Sudan, 143, 164
super-diversity talk, 104
symbolic, 4, 9, 12, 14, 17, 23, 31, 35, 41, 50, 51, 53, 63, 66, 90, 95, 96, 97, 98, 99, 163, 203
Syria
　Syrian, 23, 36, 188, 189, 190, 196, 199, 207, 208, 209, 210, 211, 212, 213, 214, 215, 216, 217, 218, 219, 220, 221, 224, 225, 226
Szczepaniková, Alice, 32

teacher training, 112, 117, 121
teachers' professional identities, 118
teaching and assessing linguistic competences, 110
technology of the self, 229
tensions, 87, 90, 147, 194, 229
Tesfamichael, Tiblez, 155, 172
time
　plurality of time and place, 230
　unity of time and place, 230
Tolia-Kelly, Divya, 66
Tomei, Giuliano, 152, 175
trajectories, ix, 20, 23, 24, 29, 30, 45, 53, 83, 107, 113, 119, 121, 154, 174, 183, 184, 187, 189
Trakilović, Milica, xi, 24, 45
transcultural memories and new literacies, 119
transition(s), 36, 42, 61, 85, 99, 107, 108, 153, 154, 160, 171, 186, 208, 211, 212, 219
transits, 85
translanguaging, 106, 116, 121, 122
translingual, 105, 121
transmediterranean, 153, 154, 163, 170
transmission, 49, 50, 51, 54, 55, 57, 82, 91, 99, 102
transnational, 22, 85, 96, 100, 101, 112, 121, 134, 146, 149, 156, 166, 168, 170, 171, 172, 202, 203, 216
travel
　travelers, 66, 69, 71
Troilo, Simona, 163
Turin, x, xi, 24, 49, 53, 60, 66, 69, 83, 85, 86, 88, 96, 100, 102, 136, 150, 175, 176

unbalanced competences, 113
Ungaretti, Giuseppe, 94
uprising, 207, 208, 210, 211, 212, 213, 214, 218, 219, 220, 221, 224, 225, 226

van Huis, Iris, x, xi, 23, 204
van Wichelen, Sonja, 39, 41
variable and varying facts of language, 114
Venezuela, Venezuelan, 53, 55, 56, 58, 59, 71
Venice, 49, 58, 59, 62
Vento, Giovanni, 169, 170, 172
Venus of Cyrene, 161, 163, 164, 176
Verderi, Sara, ix, 23, 225
Vieyra, Paul, 168
visual
　culture, 66, 186
　visual language(s), 51, 53, 71, 86, 100
visuality, 1, 2, 3, 85, 100, 153, 154, 158, 165, 170, 174, 208, 214
vocabularies, 229, 231
Vuoristo, Kaisa, 45

waiting, 192, 194, 195, 196, 197, 198, 202
walls, 15, 90, 219, 220
Wedeen, Lisa, 211
Wekker, Gloria, 38, 39
West, the, 10, 30, 35, 170, 185
Western, 11, 30, 38, 39, 41, 191, 212
white
　whiteness, 20, 38, 135, 141, 147, 163
Whitley, Leila, 15
Winter, Jay, 230
Wittgenstein, Ludwig, 63
word, 34, 35, 39, 43, 44, 50, 51, 52, 53, 55, 59, 62, 63, 64, 65, 69, 73, 92, 122, 137, 138, 140, 141, 142, 143, 144, 145, 146, 147, 148, 218
working conditions, 93
World War II, 15, 152, 153, 154, 159, 164
written, ix, 5, 7, 49, 50, 51, 52, 53, 54, 55, 56, 60, 62, 63, 69, 71, 72, 86, 88, 90, 91, 119, 135, 165, 230

Yanow, Dvora, 187
youth universe, 92
Yuval-Davis, Nira, 186

Zetter, Roger, 34, 35, 200
Zohre, 187, 190, 191, 195, 201

www.ingramcontent.com/pod-product-compliance
Lightning Source LLC
Chambersburg PA
CBHW051536020426
42333CB00016B/1957